By the Same Author

Smart Simple Design

VISUAL SYSTEMS

VISUAL SYSTEMS

Harnessing the Power of the Visual Workplace

Gwendolyn D. Galsworth

amacom

American Management Association

New York • Atlanta • Boston • Chicago • Kansas City • San Francisco • Washington, D.C.
Brussels • Mexico City • Tokyo • Toronto

Library of Congress Cataloging-in-Publication Data

Galsworth, G. D. (Gwendolyn D.)
    Visual systems : harnessing the power of the visual workplace / Gwendolyn D. Galsworth.
        p.   cm.
    Includes bibliographical references and index.
    ISBN 0-8144-0320-4 (hc)
    1. Factory management. 2. Office management. I. Title.
    TS155.G193   1997
    670.42—dc21   96-46034
                                                          CIP

Printing number

10 9 8 7

To the millions of associates working in companies around the world who want to do work that makes sense

To **John Croft** of Packard Electric, in gratitude for and in recognition of his own commitment to work that makes sense, an early and important inspiration for this book

And to my dear brother, **Gary L. Galsworth**

Our deepest fear is not that we are inadequate.
Our deepest fear
is that we are powerful beyond measure.
It is our light, not our darkness,
that most frightens us.
We ask ourselves, who am I
to be brilliant, gorgeous,
talented and fabulous?
Actually who are you not *to be?*
You are a child of God.
Your playing small doesn't serve the world.
There is nothing enlightened about shrinking
so that other people
won't feel insecure around you.
We were born to make manifest
the glory of God within us.
It is not just in some of us; it's in everyone.
And, as we let our own light shine,
we unconsciously give other people
permission to do the same.
As we are liberated from our own fear,
our presence automatically liberates others.

—Marianne Williamson

Table of Contents

List of Illustrations

Chapter 10   People: What to Expect

Chapter 11   +1: Building and Sustaining the 5S Habit

Chapter 12   +1: Leading by Example

A Foreword From Industry

An Aesop's fable from my childhood comes to mind as I walk through our factory at United Electric:

> A farmer complains about his cramped living quarters to a sage adviser. The adviser proposes a cure. Over a period of weeks, the farmer is instructed to bring each of his barnyard animals into his house to live. First come the chickens, then two pigs, a goat, and finally the cow. With each new occupant, the farmer becomes more miserable but is consoled by the sage that a solution to his original problem will shortly be at hand.
>
> Finally, when all his animals are inside, the farmer is instructed to boil pots of spaghetti—enough to fill all remaining spaces in his dwelling—and dump it there. Desperate and discouraged, the farmer visits the sage once more for advice. His final instructions are to return each farm animal to the yard and remove all the spaghetti from the house. Suddenly, the farmer's previously inadequate living space seems spacious.

I think Aesop intended the moral to be something like this: "In order to appreciate what you have, you must lose it." The only problem with this moral as it relates to business is that our factories and offices have been filled with spaghetti for so long that we have forgotten that we put it there. In fact, it has been there for so long, we no longer notice it. We don't see it. And instead of removing it, we try to organize around it.

Like the farmer, we complain about the lack of space and our inability to move freely. Yet, unlike Aesop's farmer, we remedy our problem by adding *more* space. Then we fill that with spaghetti too. This is sometimes referred to as a capital expansion.

Indeed, if managers could see all the spaghetti around them, they would surely remove it—and they would save millions of dollars. The key is in the seeing. This is why visual order is so valuable. It enables the factory to tell us what is needed and what is not (the spaghetti).

At United Electric, visual order (the first step in implementing visual systems) has contributed to a 60 percent reduction in floor space, companywide. Departments are closer together, physical barriers to communication have been removed. You can "see" what's going on in each department and work cell. Our investment to achieve this has been very small—and the payback has been enormous.

I first learned about the power of visual order in 1990 during a site visit from a team of examiners for the Shingo Prize. The lead examiner left behind a large banner proclaiming "5S." It referred to five Japanese words which were roughly translated as follows:

seiri: Throw out things you don't use.
seiton: Organize the things you have left, and set standards.
seiso: Clean everything spotless.
seiketsu: Keep everything clean and orderly.
shitsuke: Follow standards religiously.

At first, we were skeptical of the value of this advice, but at the urging of the examiners, we embarked upon a project to tackle the first *S*. To our amazement, we quickly identified truckloads of tools, tables, bookcases (and things on bookcases, like outdated directories), machines, fixtures, and inventory that were not needed. These had accumulated over many years, and we had expanded our factory and office space to accommodate them. In our engineering departments, for example, over half of the floor space was dedicated to redundant or outdated information.

We were so satisfied with the outcome of this risk-free improvement after doing just the first step that we thought we were done. For several years thereafter, spot attempts were made under the heading of "visual systems": color coding containers, visual mistake-proofing (*poka-yoke* devices), and similar stand-alone improvements. Though we did not realize it at the time, the full benefit of visual order continued to elude us. We had removed much of the spaghetti but had not thought about organizing the remainder in a way that would prevent its return.

Enter Gwendolyn Galsworth. Our work with Dr. Galsworth in another area (Smart Simple Design: The Variety Effectiveness Process®) had given us an opportunity to become familiar with the body of knowledge she had developed on the visual workplace. A commitment in 1993 to employ her approach and methods led to measurable improvements in quality and manufacturing lead time and to remarkable levels of employee participation. Within several months of working with her, we had developed the basis for a true *system* of visual information sharing at United Electric—starting with 5S + 1, visual order.

At the outset of implementation, employees learned about four kinds of visual devices: indicators, signals, controls, and guarantees. Then they learned to identify significant amounts of "spaghetti." This was followed immediately by a series of hands-on techniques for finding "homes" and "addresses" for all needed material, documentation, tools, and equipment. Dr. Galsworth's ability to translate everyday life into factory-specific examples created rapid understanding of these concepts. Production employees intuitively grasped the importance of locating oft-needed tools for easy retrieval. Areas of production were redefined, as clusters of visual devices called minisystems were linked together and the entire process was clarified.

Soon the workplace began to "speak." Out-of-place items could be instantly spotted. Opportunities for improvement to material and information flow became apparent. Employees, focusing on "what I need to know and what I need to share," began communicating in work areas where little communication had previously existed.

The system developed by Dr. Galsworth added another dimension previously lacking in UE efforts: a mechanism for building and sustaining the gain, the + 1 tools. With the establishment of an employee steering team, 5S standards became factorywide standards. Locally, within departments, 5S patrols used checklists to encourage people to maintain current levels of improvement and to suggest additional opportunities. In all, UE had a true system of visual order in place.

Dr. Galsworth's knowledge as a consultant and skill as a teacher in visual order and visual information sharing are captured and contained within this volume, the best how-to book available in the field today. The elements of the system, the methods, and the materials needed for learning and deploying visual order are clearly described in *Visual Systems*.

5S + 1 and visual systems, of which it is a part, are truly risk-free, low-cost, and worth millions. Everything needed to put them to work in your factory is contained in this book.

—Bruce E. Hamilton
Vice President of Operations
United Electric Controls Company
Watertown, Massachusetts

Chair of the Board of Examiners
The Shigeo Shingo Prize for Excellence in Manufacturing

A Foreword From an Educator

American manufacturing, once diagnosed as sick with such ills as long lead times, loads of inventory, and adversarial relationships between management and the workforce, is experiencing a rebirth of work spirit while it is solving the operational problems that affect production. In this book Dr. Gwendolyn Galsworth describes the first step in a methodology that builds information directly into the process of work so it can be shared visually. It's called visual systems and is a best practice of lean production. This method not only serves the bottom line, it leads to a resurgence of work spirit.

Companies have spent millions on programs designed to increase the enthusiasm and morale of the workforce. Visual systems deliver on that promise and they do it for free; it comes as an integral part of the process. How? The fundamental cause of low morale is fear: fear that we won't do a good job, fear that we don't know how to do good work, fear that we don't know. We ask ourselves: What can we learn, what knowledge would give us an edge, make us part of the in-group—what knowledge would allow us to perform in ways we only dream we can?

Because visual systems puts knowledge directly into the physical workplace, these fears are removed and the human potential of work is unleashed. For every action, there is an equal and opposite reaction. Remove the fear and the morale goes up. The simplicity of what visual systems can do for us in the workplace catches us off guard. We have been there too many times. We have seen programs come and go. We have been to the seminar where we walked on hot coals.

Why should visual systems be different? Surely a workplace technique can't deliver as much. Surely we can't increase throughput, cut lead times, and increase the morale of the workplace all at once. Simplicity eludes us because, as Galsworth points out, we value complexity. We want to dismiss the simple answer and spend millions on an MRP system instead or order something else newer, bigger. We are caught in the trap of our culture: The more it costs, the more we value it. We want to choose complexity over simplicity.

Yet, as you read this book, the simplicity of the methodology catches you up, it starts your own creative juices flowing. You begin to look for ways you can get this paycheck in your own organization. Where are the places of clutter and flow that look like a plate of spaghetti when the process is analyzed? Still, we hesitate to embrace the promise of the paycheck in workplace morale—how can it be? Suddenly the light breaks through: Visual systems can keep delivering and delivering and delivering because the method is not tied to some abstract mathematical equation or to a piece of equipment or to a computer program. It is tied directly to our creativity. Simplicity now has value—visual information sharing unleashes creativity and provides a way for human potential to tackle chaos in the workplace. We can see the payoff. Changing chaos to order delivers to the bottom line.

There it is. The cat is out of the bag. Galsworth has signed over the million-dollar idea to you. To cash the check of visual systems is to gain a better place to work, people who feel better, and more wealth to create even more jobs. To reap the rewards, we simply share information vital to the workplace—visually. *We let the workplace speak.* Suddenly what was not understood by the workforce and presumed to be held secret is visible. Our unspoken fear that "if the information is not available to me, then I must not be important enough to have it" disappears. The workforce understands, human potential is sparked, ideas start to flow and change—the thing you have been searching for happens automatically and, as Galsworth points out, eventually without a word being spoken. Fear is replaced by freedom.

Galsworth has done an amazing job of reminding us that reborn manufacturing means a revitalization in the workplace. Our imaginations take hold and the opportunities seem endless. The human potential to create a better workplace has great depth. As the information that has not been shared is shared, change, an often maligned term, takes on a new and positive meaning.

The 5S + 1 approach provides a structure and methodology for implementation that fits well with manufacturing. Steering teams composed of workforce associates provide a mechanism for choosing projects. Management champions are given the tools to reward the visual order effort in the workplace. The details of 5S + 1 are explained in lay terms so they are easily understood. The tools of visual order easily support the efforts of companies that have adopted lean manufacturing. For companies that have not started a lean manufacturing effort to remove waste, beginning with visual order presents a hidden advantage: Workplace disorder can hide the possibilities of cell design.

As with any methodology, training is important. It is necessary for your workforce to understand that visual order is important, that information sharing is valued, and that there is a systematic way to make it happen. As with any change process, management must role-model the effort. Your workforce will surprise and amaze you when they take the concepts and use the tools that make it happen. Set up a 5S corner, provide the training, support it with resources and management—and watch work spirit take off.

This book combines theory with an extremely practical approach to change. It is self-explaining and easy to follow. It leaves the reader with a haunting challenge as well as a promise. Galsworth admonishes us to develop a plan for improvement time. There it is again, a simple message with a powerful punch. If we only have time for production, there will be no improvement. Rise to the challenge. Take this book and schedule the improvement time to read it. Share it with your workforce and stick to the methodology. Marvel at the results your workforce can produce. Recapture what you once knew: There is joy in work. Becoming a reborn manufacturer is not that hard after all.

—Carol M. Shaw
Director, The Center for Competitive Change
Associate Dean of Continuing Education
The University of Dayton
Dayton, Ohio

Preface

Today, excellence in manufacturing means work that is done to a drumbeat, a drumbeat set by the customer. When demand increases, the drumbeat quickens; when it decreases, the drumbeat slows. Finding that drumbeat is the work of lean production; stabilizing and maximizing that drumbeat is the work of visual systems, visual order (5S + 1), and the visual workplace. Whether you are a traditional manufacturer or a leader in lean production, visual systems is a best practice.

Even if you come to this book already committed to implementing visual order and achieving a visual workplace, *read through it in its entirety before changing anything.* Pay special attention to Chapters 14 and 15, which contain the crucial preliminary steps to putting the concept into action. One of the beauties of 5S + 1 is that it is simple, low-cost, and straightforward—in other words, it is not rocket science. But implementing simple things effectively is rarely easy. The devil and the delight are in the details.

You will not be able to do it alone. If you are a manager in a position to open or close the improvement gate, think about opening it to 5S + 1 and keeping it open. Start a study group with your peers and consider the principles, methods, and outcomes described in this book and what impact they could have on your company and its profitability. Get operations involved, and involve the people who live every day with the effects of workplace confusion and information deficits.

Consider providing all associates[1] with copies of this book so that they can start their own study groups—and see them become energized as they realize that they can bring visual order to their own work areas themselves.

Expect to be surprised, even astonished, by the creativity, focus, and tenacity triggered in and around you by the methodology you read about here. Visual order will change your organization and your production performance for the better, and it will change you in the process. This change will happen because people want to do work that makes sense. Working alone or in teams, they will use the structure of 5S + 1 to find ways of making that happen.

The workforce will become precise and spirited in their involvement as they implement the steps of visual order, because the 5S + 1 methodology is both systematic and values-driven, with spirit as its core value. In 5S + 1, the true first *s* is for spirit—the spirit of the workplace itself and of each individual who works there. The centrality of this value to your success cannot be overemphasized. Like the individuals and teams who created the examples in this book, you and your colleagues will align yourselves to the

---

1. In order to recognize some measure of the value that people on the shop floor contribute to the corporate good, many companies refer to their employees as *associates,* an example I will follow in this book.

spirit of the workplace and discover ordinary and extraordinary ways to bring visual order to your work area. Through it, you will bring vastly increased profitability to your company.

Getting the Most Out of This Book

This book has four parts. Part One, *The Big Picture*, sets the context. Part Two, *The 5S Method*, presents the first five steps of the process. Part Three, *The +1 Method*, presents tools for building and sustaining the gains. And Part Four, *Go!*, addresses implementation issues and shows you how to get started.

And now for a quick chapter-by-chapter tour.

Part One: The Big Picture

The first three chapters of Part One give you background, context, definitions, and a list of underlying requirements.

Chapter 1 discusses the roots of the 5S + 1 methodology and places it within the larger context of visual systems, visual information sharing, and the end goal—a visual workplace. The chapter presents a vision of a visual workplace as it actually exists in a number of world-class companies and explains its strategic importance. Central to that strategy is a clear understanding of time as the shadow of motion and the distinction between the value-adding activity that customers will pay for and the non-value-adding (waste) activity that burdens your company with cost. Your first step in eliminating the waste of motion is to eliminate information deficits in the workplace, starting with deficits in location information, the job of 5S + 1.

Chapter 2 defines basic terms, concepts, and principles, beginning with a scan of everyday visual systems—on the highway, in the supermarket and hardware store, and all around us. The four types of visual devices are defined and placed on a ladder of control, culminating in devices that guarantee 100 percent adherence to standards. Some brilliant low-tech, high-effect, shopfloor examples are given.

Chapter 3 highlights the importance of a systematic, step-by-step approach to making this kind of strategic shift in a company. You will read about a company that chose a "blitz" approach to visual order—and what happened a year later. This leads directly to a discussion of the five start-up requirements for a successful implementation of visual order, including the 5S + 1 process.

Part Two: 5S Method

Part Two details the first five steps of 5S + 1.

Chapter 4 presents the first principle of visual order and introduces the ins and outs of the key technique called **3-Tagging.**

Chapter 5 discusses the next three principles of visual order, along with tools for implementing each.

Chapters 6 and 7 give you exact procedures for achieving **smart placement**—putting location information in place. Both are supported by dozens of actual examples.

Chapter 8 presents case examples of visual order principles as applied in four different manufacturing settings.

Chapter 9 discusses how some of these principles can be put into practice in nonproduction areas.

Part Three: The +1 Method

In Part Three, you learn about the nine +1 tools for building and sustaining the habit of visual order in the workplace. It is a common complaint in improvement initiatives that momentum drops off (or never gathers) and people drop out. Sooner or later every implementation faces that crucial problem, and the entire effort can flounder and fade if it is not handled carefully and with insight.

Chapter 10 discusses in detail the issues of resistance and inertia, and gives suggestions on how to handle them.

Specific remedies to resistance and inertia begin in *Chapter 11.* After the nine +1 sustaining tools are briefly introduced, four of them are treated in detail: the visual workplace code of conduct, the 5S corner, the 5S checklist, and the 5S patrol.

Chapter 12 discusses the next two tools, the visual workplace steering team and visual minisystems. It also talks about **resonance,** the hidden power behind leading by example.

Chapter 13 describes the final three tools, the visual workplace coordinator, the management champion, and the management watch, and links them back to steering team functions and other sustaining mechanisms so that you can see how the whole +1 system works.

Part Four: Go!

Part Four brings us to actually putting the concepts of the first three parts in place.

Chapter 14 explains the three outcomes you can expect from your first 5S+1 cycle: a showcase that demonstrates the practices and benefits of visual order, a quantified set of results, and direct experience on how the methodology works on *your* shop floor. As part of this, you learn about the **laminated map,** a final and indispensable 5S+1 tool for helping you to decide on the scope of your implementation and the specific areas to include.

Chapter 15 gives detailed information about awareness education and team training, and includes tips on whom to train and how to modularize the learning and share the gains. Also included is a sample module-by-module training calendar.

Chapter 16 catapults you out of the how-to details of the method into its broadest possible impact—a useful, refreshing, and, I hope, inspiring perspective.

Every chapter except for Chapter 16 is supported by lots of visual examples, including many drawings and photographs of actual devices and minisystems created by workplace associates and teams working at U.S. companies. There are also a number of appendixes to support the team-process and waste-reduction efforts, as well as a Glossary, Suggested Readings, a Resources section, and a useful Index.

☆ ☆ ☆ ☆ ☆

I sincerely hope you enjoy this book and find that what is presented here brings you to a deeper understanding of how to support excellence in yourself, in others, and in your company through the principles and practices of visual order.

Acknowledgments

A rough count of the people who have contributed to the making of this book reaches a thousand in no time. To them all I say thank you. I could not have done it without you. You inspired me. You informed me. You kept me going.

Thanks to Norman Bodek, president of Productivity Press and Productivity, Inc. In my position as head of his training and consulting group in the mid-1980s, I had the opportunity to work closely with two of the world's master practitioners of lean production: Dr. Ryuji Fukuda, the first person to introduce me to 5S and visual control systems, and Dr. Shigeo Shingo, one of the chief architects of the Toyota Production System, who stretched and tempered my conceptualization of these systems to encompass the entire spectrum of visual information sharing. My deep appreciation goes to all of them.

Then there are the companies, the real development sites of the visual workplace approach. Earliest was Packard Electric, in 1984, with manager John Croft, whose advanced understanding of standards and standardization seeded the methodology that followed. Through John Croft I had the great good fortune to meet James P. Walker. Thank you, Jim, for your unswerving support.

At Pratt & Whitney (a division of UTC) in East Hartford, Connecticut, I want to thank Paula Robbins, Chuck Atcherson, and Grace Reed for their contributions.

I owe Clark R. Shea a large debt for his support of 5S + 1, at both Pratt & Whitney and Hamilton Standard's Blade Company in Windsor Locks, Connecticut. I thank all the associates of Blade Company for their vital interest and participation, especially unit manager Stanley V. Mickens; associates Ed Brey, John Christian, Tom Dancy, Mike Feltrin, John Ghann, Al Lapa, Richard Scorzafava; visual workplace steering team members Tom Cormier, Lonzio (Gordy) Gordon, Cynthia Matroni, Theresa Paul, Brad Slater, John (Yago) Yacavone; and Howard Ferrara.

The next milestone was the 5S + 1 implementation at United Electric Controls Company (UE) in Watertown, Massachusetts, as of this writing the most comprehensive and mature application of visual order. Thank you to UE's president, David Reis, whose defined yet unobtrusive stand on continuous systematic improvement is fuel for UE's march to lean production. Dave's behind-the-scenes support of 5S + 1 worked in perfect partnership with the improvement pathway forged on the production floor by Bruce Hamilton, UE's vice president of operations. This partnership is the hidden strength behind UE's transformation.

UE associates were exceptional in the way they embraced both the letter and spirit of the 5S + 1 methodology. I thank every one of them. Special thanks to UE's first visual workplace steering team members—Randy Campbell, Luis Catatao, Michael Holmes, Beverly Scibilia, Mildred Williams—and to the team's visual minisystems superstars, Bill Antunes and John Pacheco. I also want to acknowledge the contributions of Cindy Barter,

Ellen Brill, Randy Brown, Maria Helena Cabral, Theresa Carroll, Harvey Chambers, Carlos Chaves, Bob Comeau, Mike Contardo, Tony Cruz, Maureen DiRusso, George Farraher, Dan Fleming, Krikor Frounjian, Shahag Hagopian, Vee Hagopian, Joan Hurton, Pam King, Doug Kuntz, Jesse MacArthur, Debbie Martin, Frank McKenna, Andrea Minasian, Mary Rose Mix, Manny Monteiro, Judy Moon, Ryta Mullen, Cheryl O'Connell, Lilia Orozco, Paul Plant, Janet Prescott, Bob Rando, Fred Ritzau, Lee Sacco, Regina Santos, Manny Sousa, Kelly Tonner, Steve Torres, Hieu Tran, Michael Vailliant, Glen Whittaker, and all other UE associates participating, directly or indirectly, in the implementation. Finally, for their resourcefulness and commitment, my gratitude to Annie Yu and Maureen Hamilton.

At Fleet Engineers and sister company Lee Industries (Muskegon, Michigan), thanks to Wes Eklund, Tim Olt, Garry Boos, and Mark DeWitt for their willingness to support a shopfloor-driven implementation and the readiness to open their doors to public scrutiny just six months into the change process.

An enthusiastic thank-you to every Fleet employee, and especially to steering team members Brett Balkema, Kenny Cain, Laura Dewald, Steven Hascher, Dan Herzhaft, and Craig Tobey; to Dennis Johnson, Larry Kaufman; to all associates in the FB 27 cell, Fleet's 5S + 1 flagship; to Fleet's quick changeover team—Gary Buys, Roscoe Clark, Greg Hancock, and Al Stone; Fleet associates Jeff Hamm, Robert Oldaker, and Roger Stalzer for their splendid artistic contributions; to Stefanie Bennett, Bruce Boos, Cindy Boos, Harold Coleman, Patti Falbe, Mike Hart, Diane Schmiedeknecht, George Stewart, and Terry Verhulst.

And at Alpha Industries (Woburn, Massachusetts), thanks to George Levan, Ken Bushmich, Ellen Babson, George Cassello, Russ McGibbon, Earl Scranton, Sau Tran, Bernice Pereira, and Beverly Fischer; at Curtis Screw Company, Inc. (Buffalo, New York), thanks to Carl Falletta, Bruce Kilbin, Dave Stanley, and Kent Young, the members of the visual workplace steering team and Curtis Screw shopfloor associates; at Greene Rubber (Woburn, Massachusetts), thanks to Patricia Broderick, Eladios Cruz, Ed Davis, Janine DeGusto, Carlos Gomes, Sheila Morton, Daniel Rossetti; at Lemco-Miller (Danvers, Massachusetts), thanks to Diana J. Bass, Barbara DiMento, Steve Fockens, and associates from the production floor; at TS Trim Industries (Canal Winchester, Ohio), thanks to Ron Servon; at Philips Automotive Electronics Co. (Fort Wayne, Indiana), thanks to Robert McKenzie and the associates who work there; at Trans-matic Manufacturing (Holland, Michigan), thanks to Amy Covault, Rob Ptacek, Bob Veurink, Mary Wiley, and all other associates who work there.

The University of Dayton's Center for Competitive Change (CCC) has been a strong supporter of the visual workplace approach, bringing it to the attention of the general public beginning in 1995. My thanks and appreciation to CCC Director Carol M. Shaw, and to the Center's exceptional staff, Jean C. Steele, Ruth V. Jackson, Ed Inesta, Laura Hopper, and Joan Wysong.

On the technical side, the staff of United Lithograph (Somerville, Massachusetts) turned 35mm slides into the superb black-and-white prints in the text, giving them a depth of readability and precision I never imagined possible. Heartfelt thanks to Jay Meiselman, United Lithograph's vice president of manufacturing, Thais Gloor, preflight coordinator, Ken Morse and Mark Durkee, scanner operators, and Paula Tognarelli, prepress manager.

Graphic artist John R. Clegg applied his considerable gifts to the book's many figures. Thank you, John.

On the editorial side I want to thank Tricia E. Moody for her guidance and encouragement; Anthony Vlamis, senior acquisitions editor at AMACOM Books, for believing in my book from the very beginning; AMACOM's Alex Saenz, Lydia Lewis, and Kate Pferdner and AMA's Edward L. Selig for their support and collaborative spirit; and finally, editor Aurelia T. Navarro for her skilled assistance in the developmental and editing phases of this book. Her unswerving belief in and support of this book kept me on task and true to its essence and mine. My thanks to you, Aurelia, is beyond measure.

Business friends and acquaintances helped so much along the way. While realistically there may be little chance I can name each one of them, the following list is my sincere attempt: Joseph E. Rizzo, Robert Butler, Robert W. Hall, Lea A. P. Tonkin, and the administrative staff of the Association of Manufacturing Excellence; Mark Orton, Sherry Gordon, Pat Wiggett, and Paul Demers of the New England Suppliers Institute; Michel Greif of ProConseil (Paris); Leslie Massa of Seton Nameplate Co.; Michael Rowney of Deltapoint; Connie Dyer, Karen Jones, and Tom Fabrizio of Productivity, Inc.; Brian Maskell of Brian Maskell and Associates; Scott Whitehurst of Prince Corporation; Paul Turner of Borg Warner; Robert Williamson of Strategic Work Systems; John Nanonsky of Packard Electric; Nicholas Vanderstoop of General Motors of Canada; Louis Stephenson of Gates Rubber; Mark R. Hamel of The Ensign-Bickford Company; Patricia Hawkins; and Jim Childs of John Wiley & Sons.

For their care of my body, mind, and spirit, I thank dear friends Janabai Raymundo, Joyce Tattleman, Clifflyn Bromling, Deborah Barlow, Larry Winer, Donalyn DiSpirito, Tonya Bednarick, Camilla England, Virginia Hallman, Sally Schwager, Mataare, Bill Mueller, and Jaimie, Jnan, and Alice Clegg.

For the gifts of solitude and beauty, my thanks to Pat Wardwell and her husband, Tom, and to Victor Oppenheimer. And for the space to write and electricity for my computer, thanks to head librarian Marcia Schatz and the board and staff of the public library in Blue Hill, Maine. And a special thank-you to Charles Addison Ditmas III.

To my family, for all you do, my thanks: my mother, Geraldine M. Galsworth; my brother, Gary L. Galsworth; my niece, Ondine Galsworth Atkinson; and my nephew, Daniel Spencer Galsworth.

And finally my eternal gratitude to Samuel N. Bear, Anderson Merlin, Philip Hylos, and friends for their creative encouragement and unwavering guidance. It is their song I sing.

One
The Big Picture

Chapter 1

Toward a Visual Workplace

The Foundation: Visual Order

This is a book about **visual order**: how to achieve and sustain a clear, clean, safe, and organized workplace. If you are new to the notion of visual order (sometimes referred to as industrial housekeeping or workplace organization), you may wonder why a whole book on this topic should be written. You will have no such question if you have already implemented visual order in your company or seen it in action.

If you have any doubts about the power of visual order in a work environment, look at the photograph of a workbench before visual order was implemented (Photo 1-1) and after (Photo 1-2). Without knowing any more than your eyes tell you, you know which bench is the more productive, more efficient, and less frustrating place to work.

Visual order is the foundation of excellence in manufacturing. When it is in place on the production floor, work gets done efficiently and effectively. When it is not in place, work still gets done—but at a level of cost that is hard to justify.

Visual order is not an end in itself. It is the indispensable first step of a more complete process called **visual information sharing** or **visual systems**. The ultimate outcome of this process is a **visual workplace**. There are no ands, ifs, or buts about it: You cannot achieve a visual workplace without first putting in place the principles and practices of visual order.

In this book, you learn how to implement visual order from start to finish through an approach called **5S + 1**. Implementing 5S + 1 is not a difficult process, but it is a systematic one. 5S + 1 is a set of principles and practices that, until recently, have not been well known in American business and industry. In the 1980s, **5S** (a narrower version of the approach) received wide attention when American companies began to send groups of managers and associates to Japan to tour that country's so-called **parlor factories**. The name derives from the fact that these plants are white-glove clean. No chips, no grease, no grime—and, in many instances, not a speck of dust, even in factories that machine parts. The floors shine. Safety records are flawless. Machinery is clean enough to show a single drop of oil—but of course there are no drops of oil. The American visitors were stunned, and they clamored to know how this could be. The secret, they were told, was 5S.

5S is the Japanese code name for cleanliness and order—*with a vengeance*. It is as far from the notion of spring cleaning as any activity can be. This is not putting things in order one week only to have that order disappear without a trace the next week, like a pebble in a pond. This is order to last, a key waste reduction strategy, and the foundation of the visual workplace.

The term *5S* is familiar throughout Japan and refers to the five housekeeping practices that are part of the daily routine of every Japanese household. In the mid-1950s, these practices became a corporate imperative. Here they are in Japanese, followed by an English pronunciation and their usual translation:

The Original 5Ss

seiri (say-ree):	proper arrangement
seiton (say-ton):	orderliness
seiso (say-so):	cleanliness
seiketsu (say-ket-soo):	cleaned up
shitsuke (she-soo-kay):	discipline

Unfortunately, something got lost in the translation and words that were meant to inspire us to action left us wondering what all the fuss was about.

5S + 1: Visual Order, American-Style

The approach used in this book, which has been developed and defined specifically for the American workplace, is called *5S + 1— the principles and practices of visual order.* Exhibit 1-1 lists the 5S + 1 principles.

1-1. Before Visual Order.

1-2. After Visual Order.

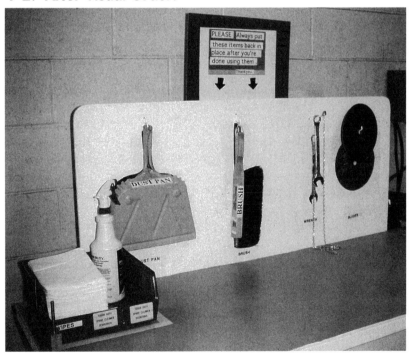

Exhibit 1-1. 5S + 1, American-Style.

5S + 1

S1:   Sort Through and Sort Out
S2:   Scrub the Workplace
S3:   Secure Safety
S4:   Select Locations
S5:   Set Locations
+ 1:   Sustain the 5S Habit

The result is a work environment that is clear, clean, safe, self-explaining, self-order-ing—and sustainable.

What Does Visual Order Look Like?

A company that has implemented 5S + 1 comprehensively displays a level of orderliness and clarity that most other organizations have never dreamed of, let alone experienced.

In the best of such companies, each work area contains only what is needed—nothing extra, nothing just in case: lean, elegant, essential. Tools, parts, dies, and fixtures are exactly at hand—and they are clean and safe. The floor is spotless, even in shops that machine metal. Equipment, workbenches, racks, shelving, and cabinets are white-glove clean, in, over, and under. Most cabinets don't have doors, and drawers are infrequently used.

Floor and bench surfaces are infused with meaning. Every workplace item has a designated location built directly into the workplace via borders and home addresses. Every item has an identifying label that acts as a type of dog tag. Raw material, parts, sub-assemblies, and finished goods are easily stocked and retrieved, even in traditional production systems.

Material handling flows smoothly, with no detours around anything—stacks of raw material, WIP, scrap, debris, or people. Clearly marked borders identify traffic lanes, walkways, and workways. You can tell by looking where it's safe to move and where you need to be especially alert. Forklift and tow motor drivers move in and out of work areas without ever having to ask anyone what needs to move or where it goes next. Addressed locations for incoming and outgoing WIP are standard.

No one has to wait to do his work. Materials arrive on time. Instruction, certification, schedule, and authorization to engage in the work is visibly in place in the work area. Everything is at point-of-use.

Each work area, whether on the shop floor or in an office, is visually indicated, along with a list of parts, products, and services for which that area is responsible. Every desk displays the name and photo of the person(s) working there, along with contact and back-up information. Each machine visually announces its function, what is made on it, and contact information in case of problems.

In the best visual order companies, a map of the work area locates you in the context of the entire building. You always know exactly where you are, and you can always get to your destination *on your own* because visual order points the way. Such visitor-friendly information sharing lets customers and callers feel safe, secure, and smart.

The workforce in such companies has learned to think visually, looking for a visual order solution to problems at the first sign of trouble. Costly secrets and surprises as well as the need for microsupervision have long since disappeared, and a common improvement language is visually in place that enables the workplace to communicate instantly and explicitly.

In sum, the workplace is clean, uncluttered, safe, and well ordered. Products and services flow at an accelerated rate. People are empowered, flexible in their skills, spirited, and involved. There is a rhythm to the work; this is a rhythm that rarely falters. People engage in daily tasks with clarity, precision, and confidence. In such companies, there is no part of the work environment that is not helping the company achieve its objectives—no tool, no bench, no machine, no part, no rack, no spot on the production floor that is not infused with meaning. The workplace speaks, linking people, process, and things—and waits for our ready reply.

Why Clean Up the Workplace?

People intuitively recognize that a clean, uncluttered, safe, and well-ordered workplace is a productive workplace. But does it really make that much difference? Why not, the logic goes, make do with a little less than a picture-perfect work space and just concentrate on getting product out the door?

These are important questions—and unless we answer them clearly and definitively, there may be lingering doubts about whether the considerable effort required to make the shop floor self-explaining and self-ordering is worth it.

Today's Customer Will Pay Only for Value, Not Cost

Although many businesses might prefer it otherwise, today's customers are willing to pay only for value—not for cost. It wasn't always that way. Even ten years ago, a company could get away with adding a margin of profit to the cost of making product and call that the product's price. Today, that same company must set the price at the outset—and then figure out how to squeeze *both* the cost of making product *and* the company's profit out of it.

This is what customers expect: excellent quality, on-time delivery, superior customer service, extensive choice, *plus* right pricing. And they'll wind up at your competitors' door if you can't give these to them. The paradigm for making a profit has been irreversibly altered.

It also used to be that a company would say that it was working all the time just because people were busy. *"We're busy all the time making products for our customers,"* says Joe Profit, CEO of BZ Machining, Inc. (BZ). In fact, everyone at BZ, from hourly associate to manager, agrees. Ask anyone how many hours out of a hundred he actually works,

Exhibit 1-2. "We Work 100 Hours Out of 100."

100% "Busy"

and every last person will say: "A hundred, of course!" Exhibit 1-2 shows how BZ and its employees see the situation.

Let's probe a little deeper and find out what the folks at BZ mean by "work." When BZ employees use the term *work*, they are referring to whatever they are doing at the time that does not include eating or taking a break. We hear the same from managers and hourly employees.

Those days are over. Today's customers will pay for the value that gets added—and nothing else. Your competitors are using a new definition of work, and it is time you did the same. The new definition of work is *moving in order to add value*. For example, every time Stan, lead machinist in commercial products at BZ, walks over to the table to get a tool, he is doing something for which the customer will *not* pay. This activity does not add any value to the product. Stamping adds value. Casting adds value. So do grinding, assembling, and coating. But moving to get something—a tool, a part, a work order, or instructions—does not.

Strictly speaking, when Stan does any of those things, he is moving *without* working, and that is called **motion**. By definition motion adds cost (not value) and that cost comes right out of the bottom line.

> To move and add value is called **work.** To move and *not* add value is called **motion**. *Motion*, then, means "moving without working, moving and adding cost."

The workplace is a living environment where millions of people spend the better part of their waking hours. The vast majority of these people come to work to work. *Moving without working* is not what a company pays its employees to do nor what employees show up for. But motion is precisely how too many people, associates and managers alike, are forced to spend their workdays. In far too many companies, motion is corporate enemy number one. Instead of working, people spend precious time searching, wandering, or waiting for the tools, materials, and information they need in order to do their work.

What Do I Need to Know?

The magnitude of detail that workers need to know on a daily basis—but do not know—is vividly reconfirmed nearly every time a company considers implementing visual order. In preparation for these implementations, I often call a data-gathering session and ask those who participate (usually a healthy cross section of departments and levels) to respond to a single question about their life at work: "What do I need to know?"

"What do I need to know that I do not know *right now* in order to do my work? What *don't* I know that I need to know to do the right work, at the right time, with the right tools, in the right quantity, of the right quality, etc.?"

It is the same question for everyone. People's answers, which they commit to paper, are telling—a quick diagnostic on the state of information sharing in that organization.

One of the most striking lists of answers was provided one hot July morning by Hank, an assembly operator in an electronics plant in the Midwest. His list appears in Exhibit 1-3.

When he was done with his list, Hank took me aside and said: "You should have asked what *don't* I need to know. It would have taken a lot less time and a lot less paper!" His point was clear.

Lists like Hank's are not the exception, they are the rule. Lists from associates look very much the same across industries and geographical regions, and lists from managers and supervisors everywhere also are remarkably alike. Some are identical.

Literally millions of employees start every workday with huge information deficits

Exhibit 1-3. Hank's List.

What Do I Need to Know?

- Where are my pliers?

- What am I supposed to make today?

- How many am I supposed to make?

- By when?

- Who will be picking it up when I'm done?

- Who's working with me today?

- Which parts do I use?

- What's today's quality spec?

- Which are my fixtures?

- Where are the parts that were supposed to be delivered yesterday?

- Where is my supervisor?

- Who is my supervisor?

Exhibit 1-4. The Reality: We work (add value) 5 hours out of 100 (not to scale).

95% NVA	5% VA

that they have come to accept—along with the searching, waiting, wondering, and wandering—as a way of life.

☆ ☆ ☆ ☆ ☆

Research shows us the truth about the relationship between value-adding activity and motion.[1] Based on a cross-industry study involving 120 companies, it was shown that people actually got to work only five hours out of every hundred, on average. That is, for every hundred hours they put in, only five of those hours added value to what they were doing. The other ninety-five hours were spent (yes, you guessed it) in motion, in generating waste, not in adding value. (See Appendix E for more on waste.) That's a ratio of 95/5: ninety-five hours of non-value-adding (NVA) to every five hours of value-adding (VA), and that was on average. Exhibit 1-4 presents one way for you to visualize the truth of what went on in those companies.

With a ratio like this, the strategic direction for the companies involved in this study was crystal clear: Get rid of the waste. Get rid of the motion. Let me explain in broad strokes.

The VA/NVA Ratio Sets Strategic Direction

When a company does not realize the link between **value-adding (VA)** and **non-value-adding (NVA)** activity, it can make disastrous decisions about its strategic direction. For example, BZ company, which knows nothing of its VA/NVA ratio, declares its intention to double shipments in the next twelve months and in the process buys a bank of new equipment—the latest and the greatest. A year later, CEO Joe Profit holds a victory dinner for his managers. "We made it!" he crows. "A year ago we shipped 75 truckloads of BZ widgits a day. Now we are shipping 150 loads daily!!" The company celebrates. But a person with VA/NVA awareness knows it is a defeat, a disaster. Exhibit 1-5 shows you what really happened.

Exhibit 1-4 showed you a 95/5 ratio: ninety-five hours of motion or non-value-adding activity for every five hours of work or value-adding activity. BZ, Inc., succeeded in doubling its output by *improving* its value-adding component. It added value to the value it was already generating, making what it did right even better. If you think this is an

---

1. Thanks to the Technical Transfer Council of Melbourne, Australia, and Norman Bodek, president of Productivity, Inc., and Productivity Press, for introducing me to this important research.

Exhibit 1-5. A Failed Growth Strategy: The ratio got worse instead of better (not to scale).

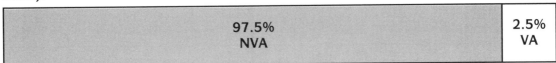

| 97.5%
NVA | 2.5%
VA |

unalloyed good, you are wrong. Instead of having increased the value portion, Joe Profit's action caused it to shrink. Look at the VA part of the ratio in Exhibit 1-5. Before it was 5 percent; now it is 2.5 percent, exactly half. It shrank by 50 percent when Joe succeeded in doubling the output. That's the way this ratio works.

And the non-value-adding portion grew by exactly the same percentage points: 2.5 percent. A waste ratio that had been 95 percent ballooned to 97.5 percent. Yes, BZ, Inc., succeeded—it succeeded in digging itself into an even deeper hole. If the company keeps on like this, it will soon be out of business.

When we understand the implications of the 95/5 ratio, our strategic direction is clear: attack motion. The world's best companies know this and stay the course until the waste portion of the ratio shrinks to the size of the value-adding portion (Exhibit 1-6). When you succeed in cutting that much non-value-adding activity out of your workday, you can invest in the value-adding portion with confidence. Until then, motion is still eating your bottom line.

Exhibit 1-6. A Company Strategically Positioned
to Invest in New Technology (not to scale).

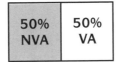

Attacking Motion Through Visual Systems

Time is called the shadow of motion (Exhibit 1-7). That is why all wastes can be collapsed into a single massive waste called motion. Motion calls loudly to us in the language of defects, rework, scrap, and overprocessing. It speaks to us as the material handling, delays, macrosearching, microwaiting, rummaging and reaching, walking and wandering, bending and turning, and looking and glancing that occur thousands of times in any given workday. They are forms of motion. They are all about time.

When we search for the source or cause of this motion, we find a strong link to information deficits in the workplace. And visual systems (beginning with visual order) are designed to put an end to these deficits.

The Core Issue: Information Deficits

Workplace information changes quickly and often: production schedules, customer requirements, engineering specifications, operational methods, tooling and fixtures, mate-

Exhibit 1-7. Time Is the Shadow of Motion.

rial procurement, work-in-process, and the thousand other details on which the daily life of the enterprise depends. Organizations need a way to ensure that this information gets shared rapidly, accurately, and completely as soon as it becomes available. Without this, the workplace is thrown into debilitating and long-lasting confusion, and the people who work there come to consider searching, waiting, wasting precious time, and making costly mistakes a way of life—a life of motion.

Information deficits in the workplace come in two varieties: deficits in location information and deficits in specification information.

Deficits in Location Information

Need-to-know lists like Hank's speak to a distinct and compelling need for the most basic type of information in the workplace. What could be more basic than knowing where your pliers are? This is **location information**. As its name suggests, location information answers the *where* question. When location information is in place, work can begin. When it is missing, work stops—or it never starts.

The stops may be microevents, lasting less than a minute but occurring hundreds of times in a single workday. Other stops are longer, consuming five to ten to forty-five minutes before they are resolved. If such stoppages are experienced by only 10 percent of the workforce (a conservative figure; the reality is closer to 40 or 60 percent), the result is a shop floor limping its way to the end of a shift. The lack of location information is a serious operational barrier that impacts all phases of production and profitability.

Deficits in Specification Information

The second category of missing information is called **specification information (spec information)**. Spec information refers to product and service **standards**: the detailed description of products or services and the manner in which they are made. These details include product requirements that relate to technical standards (tolerances, dimensions, etc.) and to procedural standards (operating procedures and methods). That is, once the pliers are in hand, spec information tells us how to use them to make product. Spec information is there to answer the *what, who, when, how,* and *how much* or *how many* questions related to work. When spec information is missing, employees do not know what is required of them.

Compensating Behaviors

Information deficits are a serious operational problem. Their existence can trigger a range of compensating behaviors that burden people and the production process as well as many other parts of the enterprise.

For example, missing information can put the emphasis on fire fighting instead of on long-term solution-making. Fire fighting is a Band-Aid approach that attacks the symptoms rather than the true causes of a problem. Fire fighting glorifies the failures of the system instead of taking steps to put a reliable, repeatable process in place—succeed at fire fighting and people call you a hero, even though you came up with a temporary half-measure. One of the main triggers of fire-fighting activity is the scarcity of accurate, relevant, complete, and easy-to-get information.

Information deficits can also cause the "busy syndrome"—the behavior of chronic motion. When information is needed but not available, we spend our time searching, asking, waiting, interrupting, looking, checking, and double-checking. These tasks consume our days. Because we are in a constant state of *doing* we assume that what we are doing must be important. This is a natural but mistaken conclusion. If we continue in this belief for too long, we may even conclude, for example, that "this company wouldn't have gotten through the day without me" or that "this darn business depends upon me." Chronic busyness gives us a false sense of importance, false because keeping busy is not work.

Furthermore, when information is scarce, knowledge becomes power. This leads to some curious notions about what and who is important and why. The material planner, for example, who carries by memory all the information on parts planning and scheduling for the company seems like a genius—she can answer all your questions. But you are powerless if that person is in a meeting, out sick, or on vacation.

Without easy access to information, people are forced to interpret what a thing *might* mean, instead of knowing what it *does* mean. Since it is often anybody's guess, everybody guesses. In the absence of facts, assumptions are everywhere. When needed information is not on hand, employees begin to rely on hunches (theirs and those of others), or to search out *insider information,* knowledge that has been secreted away. This is the way of the world, not because people prefer it, but because a viable alternative is lacking. As a result, those in the know become power brokers, and withholding information can become more important than sharing it.

The scarcer information becomes, the less employees trust each other or themselves. They begin to feel isolated, even immobilized. A sense of disempowerment follows that leads people to start worrying about making mistakes. In time, *not making mistakes* becomes the driving force. When this happens, initiative, responsiveness, and flexibility disappear—and mistakes are made.

Here we have the makings of a disempowered, sluggish, and disspirited workforce for whom the workday becomes as demoralizing as it is empty—the exact opposite of the clear, dynamic, and forward-moving enterprise that is needed in today's highly competitive marketplace. Information deficits do not just keep us making mistakes. They keep us from working.

Remedies That Don't Work

Some companies attempt to address information deficits through increased supervision, hoping that a closer policing of the process will improve its performance. Other organizations use report writing and report reading as substitutes, supported by a seemingly endless stream of memos. Meetings are often other attempts to remedy the need to know, and they usually end up triggering a lot of paper but not much news. In such work environments, the terms *disinformation* and *full disclosure* take on new and piercing significance. Looking for anything or anyone becomes everyone's worst nightmare, and changing a decision is the one decision you never want to make.

These mechanisms are attempts to spread a net large enough to catch detail and meaning—and they do not work. They are themselves forms of motion.

Many companies turn to computers for a solution to their information deficits. This *seems* logical. Computers are, after all, huge information stockpiles, capable of manipulating massive quantities of data at the stroke of a key. In addition, many of the best systems are designed with lots of involvement by the users themselves. Even when quality specifications can be accessed in a nanosecond, however, and current bills of material (BOMs) are available at the touch of a button, computers are at best only a partial solution to getting the information in—and the motion out—of the production process.

The problem here is two-sided. First, the information in computers is usually not what most employees need in order to do their work. Second, even if computers could supply the right kind of information, they could not supply it fast enough. The information is quite simply in the wrong location. It is in a box.

The problem with computers is both the medium and the message. To serve today's workforce, information must be moment-to-moment fresh *and* available at a glance. It must be part of the process—as physically close to the process as possible. In short, it must be at *point-of-use*.

Point-of-Use Information

At its best, **point-of-use information** is so close to the process, it is virtually indistinguishable from the process itself. This is information that can be pulled as needed, exactly where and when it is needed. Computers can never be close enough for that. Even when they are on-line on the line, they are too far away.

Information that is at the point of its use is the long-lasting solution to information deficits in the workplace. When information is that close, we can access it on demand. The information is part of the process, built into the items of the workplace—the tools, fixtures, machinery, documentation, and shelving. It is in the floor itself in the form of borders, indicators, and controls. When we need it, we pull it. We pull the exact messages we need from the workplace. This pulled information ensures quick, accurate, and complete work. Like the pull systems of just-in-time (JIT) and the lean production it supports, point-of-use information cuts the waste out of the system and enables the process to reach its highest level of function. The workplace speaks.

Here is an excellent example of a low-cost, frontline visual solution that allows the process to speak.

A Point-of-Use Visual Solution

The company is United Electric Controls Company (UE), a small manufacturer of switches and controls in Watertown, Massachusetts. Photo 1-3 shows you a bank of ordinary bins for holding small parts used in seven different subassemblies. Many of these parts look identical (but are not), and many of their part numbers differ by only one character. Up to this point, components for each subassembly were individually kitted in a central stockroom as a way to avoid parts mix-ups.

In the late 1980s, when UE eliminated its central stockroom as part of its JIT initiative, all components were moved to their point-of-use, right on the line of production. While this change decreased flow distance significantly, it simultaneously increased the fre-

1-3. Parts Mix-Ups (Before).

This shelf of bins holds small parts used in seven different products. Many parts seem identical, as do their part numbers, but they are not. Mix-ups were a common occurrence.

quency of parts mix-ups, even for the most conscientious operator. Although an operator had a computer-generated bill of material and work order with all the information needed to build a quality unit, the wrong parts still got picked. Worse than that, since the subassembly was enclosed in a housing, a defective unit could move downstream to final test before the defect was spotted. No amount of training, supervision, or operator diligence solved the problem. People were at their wits' end.

Photos 1-4 and 1-5 show you the visual solution that eliminated the problem 100 percent. This brilliant device came from Luis Catatao, a manufacturing support technician at UE. Here's how it works. Holes are cut into cardboard or particle board that correspond to the individual part bins required in a given subassembly. The template prevents the operator from picking any part but the ones used in that product. This is point-of-use information at its finest. Simple, low-cost, easy-to-implement, and 100 percent effective. The process itself speaks to us and helps us do the right thing. We know it. We have confidence in it. It supports our best intention and delivers to the customer what the customer is willing to pay for: added value.

☆   ☆   ☆   ☆   ☆

We may be shocked to see how much location and spec information is lacking during any given workday. It is equally astonishing to realize the levels of ingenuity and resourcefulness that employees exercise (as in Luis's case) in order to meet production objectives in the face of these glaring information deficits. One can only imagine the improved levels of output and performance that could be achieved if this burden was systematically and comprehensively lifted.

1-4. The End of Mix-Ups (After).

Mix-ups are now impossible because of the product-specific templates that operators use to block out all the parts the product does not contain. The cutouts in this cardboard act as visual guarantees **(poka-yoke)**, corresponding to the location of each bin of parts used in the J40-9613-9620 assembly, Notice how the numbers on the template match those on each bin—backup insurance on the process.

1-5. Further Mix-Up Prevention.

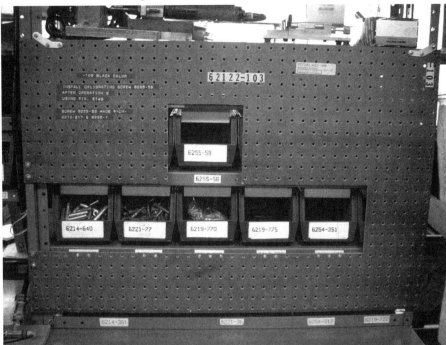

Here is the same template concept made of pegboard. Notice just above each bin the wooden blocks that force the bin to stay in place during refilling. Without the blocks, mix-ups might happen if bins were put back in the wrong shelf location.

That's the whole point. The solution to these deficits is not more or better supervision. Nor is it more or better training. The solution is not more classes in ESL (English as a second language) or improved interpersonal communication skills. Those have already been tried. While such remedies can be effective in addressing a certain group of problems, they are not designed, either singly or in combination, to solve the problems caused by the absence of point-of-use in the workplace. They cannot let the workplace speak.

Begin by Implementing 5S + 1: Visual Order

The purpose of visual order (5S + 1) is:

1. To prepare the physical work environment to hold location information and specification information
2. To install location information into the workplace—the information needed to find people, things, and places easily and quickly, and safely

Some companies think that they need to wait until they have their production system figured out before implementing 5S + 1. This is upside-down thinking, similar to the notion of cleaning up the house *before* the house cleaners arrive. While you have the option of implementing 5S + 1 on the heels of another improvement process, visual order is *at its shining best* when it forms the base on which all other improvement approaches are built. Visual order is a universal enabler. It is the first step of every improvement journey.

5S + 1 is a core competency needed to maximize benefit from other improvement tools—kanban, cellular manufacturing, quick equipment changeover, statistical process control (SPC), total quality control (TQC), zero quality control (ZQC), demand flow/pull systems, six-sigma quality, self-managed or self-directed work teams, and/or reengineering. Visual order is fundamental to them all.

Apply visual order to optimize traditional manufacturing, with its high volumes, long lead times, bottlenecks, complex material handling, and other high cost indicators. When the time comes, let 5S + 1 smooth the way for converting your shopfloor approach to lean production with a vastly accelerated and responsive flow rate. Not only will visual order help identify what needs to change, it will help maintain order and predictability while the change is in process.

Trackable, Bottom-Line Results

People intuitively recognize the value of a well-ordered, self-explaining, and self-regulating work area. When asked for precise benefits, these same people are often left speechless, mumbling something about "Well, it's really important, that's all. It's just plain common sense." Not a compelling argument for the skeptics among us. In too many cases, the absence of measurable financial and operational benefits can result in a decision against implementing the process.

The following is a list of individual results compiled from American companies across a range of industries that have effectively implemented visual order as the first step in their journey to a visual workplace.

Cut in floor space:	60%
Cut in flow distance:	80%
Cut in rack storage:	68%
Cut in number of forklifts:	45%
Cut in machine changeover time:	62%
Cut in annual physical inventory time:	50%
Cut in classroom training requirements:	55%
Cut in nonconformance in assembly:	96%
Increase in test yields:	50%
Late deliveries:	0%

Over, above, through, and under the results you see above is one clear and present awareness: *motion is time*. And since motion is time and time is money, we must attack motion—minimize it. For this, visual order is the tool of choice.

Work That Makes Sense: The Uncommon Solution

Implementing location information and the visual order that results impacts motion directly. It eliminates the cause of walking, searching, and other grosser forms of motion. By locating workplace items closer to their points-of-use, we automatically reduce the distance traveled. Over time, the area that we move within becomes more and more focused and requires less and less square footage. As our movements become more efficient and less scattered, we can begin to notice less obvious forms of motion—turning, reaching, stretching, bending—and we find ways to minimize these as well.

Cellular manufacturing has turned motion reduction into a science and an art. One of the requirements of a work cell is that all operations be executed as efficiently as possible. If you have ever observed or worked in a cell, you know that people must maneuver in a space that is defined by the value that gets added there—the work. All the waste has been removed from the process and motion is at an absolute minimum. In the best of cells, working looks more like dancing. Every step and each hand movement look choreographed—measured and intentional.

The same can be true of all work settings, including traditional manufacturing. Whether you work in a machine shop or stamping plant, on an assembly line or in purchasing, visual order is central to it and can create an entirely new level of work, one that blends focus and intention for outputs that are superior.

As your focus and intention become more precise, suddenly it's just you and your work. When all the unrelated movements are eliminated and all the tiny extraneous interruptions are removed, you can simply do your work. You are alert and relaxed as you bring a new dimension of attention to the task at hand. This state is possible at work, on the shop floor, in your company. You have experienced it before, but perhaps not yet at work. It is a state of intent stillness where all your resources are at your disposal and they surface to assist you when and as needed. They flow from you. Motion as you have known it no longer exists in any form. It is just you and the silent, steady rhythm of your breath as value is added. This is what you have always wanted work to feel like. This is what work is meant to be—the ease of your contribution flowing through you and into the process your company has asked you to perform. This is work that makes sense.

One: The Big Picture		
1. Toward a Visual Workplace	2. Visual Systems in Context	3. The Five Start-Up Requirements
Two: 5S Method		
4. S1/Sort Through and Sort Out	5. S2–S4/ Scrub, Secure Safety, and Select Locations	6. S5/Set Locations: Borders
7. S5/Set Locations: Addresses	8. 5S Stories From the Shop Floor	9. 5S+1 and White-Collar Applications
Three: +1 Method		
10. People: What to Expect	11. +1: Building and Sustaining the 5S Habit	12. +1: Leading by Example	13. +1: Leading Through Standards
Four: Go!		
14. Showcase, Scope, and the System	15. Training and Education	16. The Hundredth Monkey

Chapter 2

Visual Systems in Context

Visual systems are everywhere, and they have been around for a very long time. The world's best companies have been using them for decades—and they know why.

Toyota, Citizens Watch, Sony, Honda, Nissan, Matshushita, Akebono Brakes, Sumitomo, Panasonic, Hitachi, and Komatsu—some of the world's best companies—set the standard for visual excellence for the rest of the world over two decades ago. Pockets of this excellence are beginning to appear in organizations that have more recently adopted a visual approach. Packard Electric, Johnson Controls, AMP, Fleetguard (division of Cummins), Dana, Union Carbide, Boeing, Weyerhaeuser, Ford, Varian, Vintec, and United Electric Controls Company rank high among these—as well as Calsonic, Nummi, and other Pacific Rim transplants and joint ventures.

The best of these companies exude a visual competence that is unassailable. The production floor is more than just clean, neat, and orderly. It is more than a collection of posters, signs, arrows, and color-coded addresses. When visitors enter such a facility, they know they are witnessing something extraordinary, an exceptional competitive condition. They are witnessing a **visual workplace**.

> A **visual workplace** is a work environment that is self-explaining, self-ordering, self-regulating, and self-improving—where what is *supposed* to happen *does* happen, on time, every time, day or night.

The bedrock of manufacturing is standards: what is supposed to happen. The bedrock of *excellence* in manufacturing is adherence: the extent to which these standards are followed. A visual workplace is intentionally designed to ensure that standards are met. It creates an environment in which compliance is the natural and predictable response. And the road map for achieving such an environment is the Blueprint for a Visual Workplace (Exhibit 2-1). The Blueprint, the central organizing framework for achieving a visual workplace, is an eight-level model that can be divided into three stages.

Stage 1 (level 1) has two objectives: (1) preparing the workplace to hold two types of visual information—location information and specification information, and (2) putting location information in place. In other words, Stage 1 focuses on implementing visual order (5S + 1).

Stage 2 (levels 2–5) concentrates on increasing adherence to standards, first by visually sharing specification information on weak standards, scoreboarding the results, and then, if adherence remains incomplete, building standards directly into the physical workplace.

Stage 3 (levels 6–8) strives to eliminate all irregularities in the adherence chain by removing the option of compliance and building 100 percent source inspection directly into the process of work. The goal of this final stage is error- or mistake-proofing (also known as fail-safe or *poka-yoke* systems). In short, it is to ensure that *only* the right thing *can* happen—the desired outcome is visually guaranteed. As you can see, the road to a visual workplace begins and ends with visual information sharing—visual systems.

What Are Visual Systems?

Virtually every day we interact with powerful visual systems in our homes and in the community. Supermarkets, shopping malls, hardware stores, hospitals, kitchens, theaters, sport stadiums, post offices, roads and highways, and countless other everyday settings are brimming with visual systems and devices that are there to help us. Visual systems surround us, influencing when and how we get things done, guiding, directing, and, if need be, limiting our choices.

> A **visual system** is a group of visual devices that are intentionally designed to share information at a glance, without having to say a word. The term **visual information** includes messages communicated through any of the senses: taste, touch, smell, and hearing as well as sight.

Exhibit 2-1. Blueprint for a Visual Workplace.

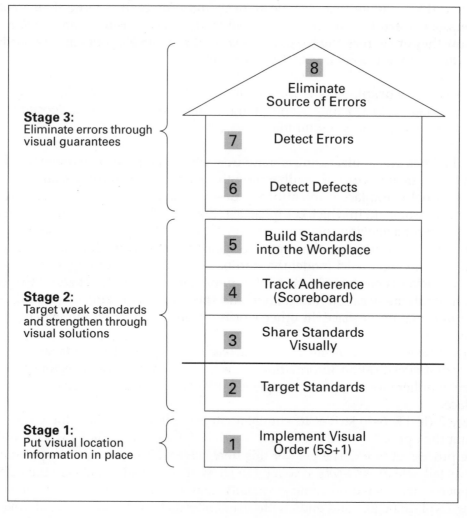

The heart of every visual system is information sharing that links what you intend to do (the task at hand) with the information you need to do it. And it does this at a glance, without having to say a word. Two characteristics distinguish visual information sharing from other forms of communicating, such as talking and writing: First, the information is entirely determined ahead of time—it is preset; second, it relies little or not at all on the spoken word.

Visual systems have us look at information in a new way, not so much as language but as bits of meaning or messages that get translated into a mechanism called a **visual device**.

> A **visual device** is a mechanism that is intentionally designed to share information vital to the task at hand at a glance—so that what is supposed to happen does happen.

Notice the emphasis on *intentionally*. The device is the result of a specific intention to send a message, to share information so the receiver of the information adjusts his behavior in response. That is the device's primary purpose. Yes, there are other messages we receive that cause us to adjust our behavior. Darkening clouds and a sudden wind in the trees, for example, warn us that it is likely to rain—so we grab an umbrella. Rain on the windshield sends the message that roads may be slick, so we slow down as we drive. These are highly valued pieces of information, but clouds, wind, and rain are naturally occurring conditions. They are not visual devices. They are not *intentionally designed* to trigger a change in our behavior.

Visual devices speed us along our way, even as they protect us from making sense-less—sometimes dangerous, often expensive—mistakes. They help us adhere to the standard way, the proven path. They help to make sure that what is supposed to happen *does* happen. They help us do the right thing. And they do this so seamlessly, we barely notice. Their power lies in the fact that, though we use them constantly, we are barely aware that they exist. We simply respond.

Let's take an everyday example of a visual device. You are on a turnpike in a nearby state on your way to a company function. This is your first time in the area and you are already ten minutes late. With just another few miles to go before your exit, you zoom into the toll plaza. You're wondering how much the toll is this time—twenty-five cents? thirty-five cents? fifty cents? Instead of consulting your highway guide or asking the toll

2-1. Toll Station.

The visual devices on this toll station make it self-explaining, allowing drivers to be self-regulating. No need to ask any questions; key information is visually shared and ready to be pulled as needed.

2-2. Example of a Pull System.

This store sign is "unseen" by nearly everyone—except by people needing to get a zipper repaired. They pull the message.

booth attendant, you head for the automatic toll booth, spot the 50¢ sign, toss two quarters in the slot, and continue on your way (Photo 2-1). The information was preset so it is there, when and as you need it, available at a glance, without asking—or for that matter thinking twice about it. You simply pull the information from the toll booth and act, without having to speak or hear a word.

Visual Information: A Pull System

The **pull system** is a unique characteristic of visual devices: The information in it is preset but the information is only shared when and if it is *pulled* by a user.[1] That is, if you want the message the device contains, you see it, notice it, and *pull* it into your awareness. If you don't see it or don't want to see it, the information simply sits there, waiting for a user. You are the customer of visual information. The message gets delivered only if you "buy" it. Photo 2-2 is a perfect example.

Or look again at the toll booth example. As a stranger to that area, you pulled the information about the toll amount (50 cents) because you didn't know how much to pay. A local driver can zoom through the toll booth without that need. She already knows the toll amount and probably puts two quarters on the dashboard before pulling out of the driveway at home.

Photos 2-3 through 2-6 show a number of everyday visual devices. See how easily they convey what we need to know, precisely *when* we need to know it. We interact with literally hundreds of such devices every day. Take a moment to think of others.

---

1. My thanks to Michel Greif, friend, colleague, and author of *The Visual Factory* (Portland, Ore: Productivity Press, 1991), for early and valuable discussions on visual information sharing as a pull system.

2-3. Bank Clock.

Do you wear a wristwatch every day? If so, you can appreciate the power of this bank clock, a visual device that shares information at a glance.

2-4. Kitchen Utensil Holder.

The utensil holder is a powerful visual control device, ensuring that knives, forks, and spoons get put back in exactly the right place—so that they are there the next time we need them.

2-5. Highway Sign.

Speed-limit signs are every-where on roads and highways. Though many may see the message, the sign has no power to make people respond and behave in accordance with it.

2-6. Lines on the Highway.

On roads and highways, our safety depends on the messages these simple lines power-fully share. In this case, the lines are telling us where to drive and when it is or is not safe to pass.

The Four Types of Visual Devices: Adherence by Degrees

There are four broad types of devices used in a visual workplace—the visual indicator, the visual signal, the visual control, and the visual guarantee—each of which exerts progressively more control. The degree of that control depends on two factors: (1) the extent to which the message it sends is likely to be obeyed and (2) the potential risk or loss if *we decide to ignore it*. The level of control a visual device exerts is called the device's **power index.**

Viewed as a group, the four types of visual devices become a kind of hierarchy or ladder of control. At the two lowest levels, a device merely suggests a certain behavior; adherence is optional. On the third and fourth levels, the device is designed to ensure that you adhere.

Visual Indicators

A **visual indicator** tells only. It shares information by displaying or showing it. It is passive. Visual indicators are used when compliance or adherence is voluntary. You can notice them or not, obey them or not. It is up to you. Generally speaking, if you don't, negative consequences are minimal.

2-7. Hardware at a Glance.

The bank of screw parts in this hardware store offers you so many visual cues that it is easy to locate precisely what you want. Notice how each of the dozens of bins is clearly marked (addressed) according to screw type, length, head type, and price.

2-8. Street Signs.

This system of visual indicators (a visual minisystem) makes critical information easy to access, depending on a person's varying needs. Not only can you easily locate the street you are on, the district you are in, and direction you are going, but you also know at a glance where and where not to park.

Common examples include all the signs that "speak" to us in supermarkets and retail stores (Photo 2-7). The visual indicators there tell us what, where, how much, and how many. These indicators require no apparent action from us—but we would surely miss them if they were not there. Look at Photo 2-8. How many different visual indicators can you see?

You will also find visual indicators in the workplace. The sign indicating the name of your department is a visual indicator (Photo 2-9). For a newcomer, visitor, or customer, for example, it contains a lot of valuable information that you and your associates may take for granted. Photo 2-10 shows you a visual indicator that reminds people to reorder

2-9. Location Indicator.

This visual indicator at Lee Industries in Muskegon, Michigan, tells us both the name of the cell and what is made there: a crank for semi-trailers.

2-10. Reorder Indicator.

This visual indicator is an invitation to do the right thing: reorder the plastic wrap. Will you pull the message from the device and take action? Let's hope so.

plastic wrap when it runs out. The indicator, which is waiting for you when the last bit of plastic is used, assumes a response: that you will take the trouble to reorder. Because a visual indicator tells only, however, it has no power to compel adherence, and its power index is minor.

Visual Signals

A **visual signal** is slightly more powerful than an indicator. A visual signal first catches our attention and then delivers its message.

2-11. Light Signals.

On this busy corner, you can see several visual signals and visual indicators. Can you name them?

2-12. Signal Plus Indicator.

Visual signals and indicators are often used together to make sure that what is supposed to happen really does happen. At this dangerous intersection, the flashing red light (visual signal) strengthens the message of the stop sign (visual indicator).

2-13. Sound Strip.

The conversation between you and the roadways is continual, with information pulled as needed. This highway sound strip, for example, may remain silent for literally hundreds of miles. But as we make our way back home from Thanksgiving dinner in another state, our stomachs full of turkey and mince pie, we are about to make the acquaintance of this powerful visual signal. Everyone is asleep, and the driver is beginning to follow suit. As the car heads for the shoulder, the sound strip springs into action: WAKE UP! WATCH OUT! it shouts, grabbing the driver's attention just in time.

Home and community examples are abundant. Red lights, caution lights, the light on your coffeemaker, and the fasten-seat-belts buzzer in your car are all visual signals. The power of a visual signal is this: *It changes.* The light is either red or green. The sound is either on or off. Because it changes, it catches our attention and we get the message.

How many visual indicators can you find in Photo 2-11—and how many visual signals? Photo 2-12 shows a dangerous intersection where a simple visual indicator—the stop sign—was not enough to ensure safety. The visual signal of a flashing red light was added as a backup.

Add to these the sound strip alongside the highway that sends you a wake-up call if you start dozing off while driving (Photo 2-13). This rumble strip is a perfect demonstration of the pull mechanism: The alert message of this strip is intentionally designed into the road. It lies there waiting until you need it and then it is instantly there at your service, precisely at the point of use.

What would it be like if vital messages were imbedded in a similar manner into your work area, allowing the production floor, for example, to assist you in your work—instead of just lying there, mute and helpless, as you and your co-workers spend precious time searching and making mistakes? What would it be like to layer information

2-14. Clothespin Signal.

A red clothespin is the visual signal used in the silent daily dialogue between Camilla (who prepares reports) and Nate (who picks them up). When the report is ready, Camilla attaches a red clothespin. When Nate comes by, he sees the pin, picks up the report, and by removing the pin, ''tells'' Camilla that he got it. No words are exchanged. The message is delivered at point of use.

into the work environment and let the workplace speak? Give it a voice? Make it a partner in the process of work, an accomplice in profit making?

Common visual signals in the work setting include flashing lights on machinery, annunciator buzzers on forklifts, and production boards with displays announcing output figures.

Like the highway sound strip, not all workplace signals are electronic. The visual signal in Photo 2-14 is the red clothespin that an associate clips on the tray when a report is ready; it sends the signal that the paperwork is ready. And when the report is picked up, the person who takes it removes the clothespin as a signal that the report has been retrieved. The transaction is complete, and everyone knows it, at a glance, without speaking a word.

Because a visual signal is more active in delivering its message than a visual indicator, its power index is moderate.

Visual Controls

Visual controls cross the line from optional to required behavior. With them, adherence begins to get built in.

Instead of merely displaying or sending out information, as with visual indicators and signals, visual controls attempt to impact our behavior directly. They do this by structuring or building the message directly into the physical environment. As a result, the number of ways we can respond is limited.

The power of a visual control is structural. That is, the physical structure of the device sends the message. Speed bumps are a good example of this. We see them coming and get their message immediately: slow down—or pay the consequences. No one is standing there to make us adhere or to punish us if we do not. We simply know we will ruin our suspension system if we choose to ignore the message.

Visual controls narrow our response options. They restrict our choices by putting physical limits in place—limits related to quantity, volume, or number and to size, height, width, length, or depth. These limits are part of the physical structure of the environment and the reason they can exert control over us. If, for example, we are stocking inventory and there are only nine hooks, each of which can hold only one unit, we can only stock nine items. The number of hooks determines our behavior and the limits of our response. The number of hooks is the control device—the visual control.

The same principle is in action in a car parking lot. Instead of hooks of a certain depth, the white parking lot lines are the control mechanism (Photo 2-15). The number of lines, the space between them, and their angle exert a powerful influence on our behavior. The predetermined pattern of those lines limits not only how many cars can be parked in the lot but also where and how individual drivers park. No one needs to tell us. We know. These lines go a long way to ensure that everyone parks in a uniform

2-15. The Power of Lines.

Lines can exert a powerful visual control on our behavior as shown by the ones in this parking lot. They demand compliance. Because they are self-explaining, they let us be self-regulating. Imagine the same parking lot without the lines. What would happen?

and orderly manner. (For another great community example of the power of lines, take a good look at the runway next time you are at the airport.)

If you doubt the power of lines, imagine the same parking lot you see in Photo 2-15 without the lines or covered with snow. Without the control information that is in the lines, either mayhem breaks out or we are forced to rely on a parking attendant to figure out a workable pattern. In either case, we are no longer self-regulating. With the lines in place, no one needs to tell us what to do; we simply respond to the information built into the asphalt.

The same principle applies to the forklifts parked in Photo 2-16. Four forklifts. Four spaces. If you park the wrong way or try to fit in a fifth forklift, it is immediately noticeable.

2-16. Forklift Parking.

The same control principle of lines applies to this small parking area for forklifts. No one needs to tell you how or where to park. Can you see how the area could be strengthened by including the visual indicator for a location address?

Lines of visual control are at the heart of all kanban and, as you will see in later chapters, have a key role to play in achieving visual order.

Because visual controls have a strong impact on our behavior, their power index is set at major.

Visual Guarantees

Visual guarantees are at the top of the power index. Also known as a mistake-proof, fail-safe, or *poka-yoke* device, a visual guarantee is designed to make sure that *only* the right thing can happen. It prevents us from doing the wrong thing. Prevention information is designed into the device.

We encounter dozens of mechanical and electronic visual guarantees in the community. The gas-pump handle at the neighborhood service station, for example, mechanically prevents you from putting back the pump the wrong way. Only one way will work—the right way. All the information you need to do the right thing is built into the handle itself. Similarly, many phone booth shelves are intentionally slanted to reduce the chance that you'll leave valuables there; you can't forget your things because they keep sliding off onto the floor.

The guarantee element of the above devices is mechanical, built directly into their architectures. Other devices are electronic. Returning to the gas station example, notice how the gas pump automatically shuts off, thanks to an electronic "visual" guarantee (a sensor device) in its nozzle. We simply cannot forget and overfill our gas tank—guaranteed.

Visual guarantees in the workplace are based on the principle of 100 percent source inspection. Their potential in eliminating quality defects is truly impressive. Though many companies confine their applications to sensors and limit switches, there are more than a dozen other subtypes of visual guarantees, the most common of which are locator pins, reference rods, templates, counters, odd-part-out devices, and detect chutes.

We already saw an example of a fabulous visual guarantee at UE in Luis Catatao's bin templates in Chapter 1 (Photos 1-3 through 1-5). Here is another excellent visual guarantee that a machine shop team developed, this one of a detect chute.

No Defects: A Visual Guarantee

The operator in Photo 2-17 is holding an over travel assembly plunger that has just been milled and which he will now drop into the small bin. Whenever the bin is filled, it is sent downstream and each plunger is inserted into its mating part, a brass bushing. From time to time, however, the outer diameter of the plunger is not machined properly; it is too large. If the operator doesn't notice this abnormality in a sampling inspection, a defective plunger travels downstream to the next operation undetected. Not until a different operator tries to insert the plunger into a bushing is the defect found and set aside.

Photo 2-18 shows the same bin, this time with a visual guarantee in place. A detect chute has been mounted on the bin itself, a small plate on which the mating part (brass bushing) is permanently fixed. When the operator finishes machining a plunger, it is dropped directly through the bushing into the bin. In the process, each and every part

2-17. Without Visual Guarantee.

The machining on this stainless-steel plunger is not always perfect. As a result, its outer diameter is sometimes too large. If the operator doesn't catch it, the defective part slips through, only to be discovered downstream when someone else tries to insert it into its mating part, a brass bushing.

2-18. With Visual Guarantee: Detect Chute.

A simple detect chute was made by mounting the brass bushing (the mating part) onto a plate that covered the top of the parts bin. The operator finishes machining a plunger and drops it through the bushing into the bin. It either passes the test or is set aside as defective. This is in-process, 100 percent source inspection that eliminates the possibility of this type of defect ever reaching a downstream operation.

is automatically 100 percent source inspected for that attribute—an oversized outer diameter. No other inspection is required. An oversized plunger is detected immediately and set aside. It cannot get through the bushing and therefore is never sent downstream. End of problem. (What does the team do, you may ask, if the plunger is too narrow? The answer: Develop a second visual guarantee to check for that attribute.)

This detect chute guarantee is a perfect demonstration of what is meant by "letting the workplace speak." The two parts (plunger and bushing) are actually exchanging information, talking to each other. As the plunger slips through the bushing on its way into the bin, it either says, "Oops, sorry, I'm too large; I can't get through"—or "There! Perfect fit. Send me downstream." All the information needed to validate that specification is at the point of use, visually shared.

Exhibit 2-2 summarizes the four types of visual devices.

Improving Your Visual Eyesight Through Noticing

Now that you know the four types of visual devices, be on the lookout for them. Doing this can improve your team's "visual eyesight" and go a long way in helping you under-

Exhibit 2-2. The Four Types of Visual Devices.

Type of Device	Power Index	Community Examples	Workplace Examples
Type 1 VISUAL INDICATOR (tells only)	Minor Power	• Street Signs • No-Parking Signs	• Re-Order Sign • Department Sign
Type 2 VISUAL SIGNAL (grabs attention)	Moderate Power	• Traffic Lights • Back-Up Lights • Brake Lights • Sound Strip	• Red Clothespin
Type 3 VISUAL CONTROL (limits behavior)	Major Power	• Parking Lot Lines • Grid Lock Lines	• Forklift Parking Lines
Type 4 VISUAL GUARANTEE (allows correct response *only*)	Maximum Power	• Gas-Pump-Handle • Automatic Gas-Pump Shutoff	• Assembly Template • Plunger Detect Chute

stand how these devices work in the community, your home, and the workplace. It can also trigger ideas for devices you can implement in your own work area.

To help in this, post a wall chart with the names of the four devices on it and common locations (Exhibit 2-3). Then go on a device hunt with your team and share your discoveries (you can use sticky notes to do this so you can reuse the chart). Don't be surprised if there are some lively debates about which kind of device this or that one is. The matter can often be cleared up with a little discussion. Other times, particularly in the case of controls and guarantees, the line stays blurred. In all cases, this exercise is an excellent tool for sharpening your eyesight and enlivening the learning process. It gets people thinking and talking about visual systems.

Visual Minisystems

Any and all of the four types of visual devices we just discussed can be used together to ensure a certain outcome. When they do, the cluster is called a visual minisystem:

A **visual minisystem** (or **minisystem**) is a cluster of two or more visual devices, intentionally designed to work together in support of a desired outcome.

Exhibit 2-3. Wall Chart for Examples of Visual Devices.

Type of Visual Device	Found in Home	Found in Community	Found in Workplace
INDICATOR (tells only)			
SIGNAL (grabs our attention)			
CONTROL (narrows response options)			
GUARANTEE (allows correct response *only*)			

A visual minisystem is a smaller version of a visual system. The toll station we discussed at the beginning of this chapter (Photo 2-1) is an excellent example of a minisystem. Photo 2-19 shows you that toll booth in the context of an entire toll plaza. There you can find many information-sharing devices—from indicators to signals to controls to guarantees—all working together to minimize the need for person-to-person interaction and to make it easy for us to pay the toll (or pick up the card) and move speedily on our way.

2-19. Toll Plaza: Visual Minisystem.

Every day, thousands of cars pass through this toll plaza, which is a visual minisystem that uses an assortment of visual devices to make sure drivers pass through safely and swiftly—and pay the toll.

2-20. School Bus: Visual Minisystem.

The community school bus is a moving visual minisystem. No matter where it goes when kids are on board, it sends the same vital message: Slow Down; Pay Attention.

The crayon-yellow school bus is another example of a community minisystem. Look closely at Photo 2-20. How many different visual devices can you count aimed at the single goal of getting children to and from school safely and on time?

Low-Tech Ideas That Work

Photo 2-21 shows an outstanding example of a workplace minisystem, developed by a shopfloor team at a GM supplier plant in Mississippi specializing in wiring components for electrical automobile harnesses. Wire drawing is a high-speed process, and machine dies frequently break from the strain. The team was looking for a way to make sure broken die parts were picked up and repaired in a timely manner, and with a minimum of chasing. Because these dies were delicate, the team also wanted to protect each die from further breakage in the pick-up process.

Their visual solution was a simple and brilliant minisystem: Get some clear plastic containers, put a label on each, and put them up on a shelf at eye level. When a die broke, the operator placed the broken die part in the plastic container (small enough to allow only one die per container), wrote on the label the machine number, date of breakage, and, if possible, cause of break, and then put the container up on the shelf. When

2-21. Broken Die Parts: Visual Minisystem.

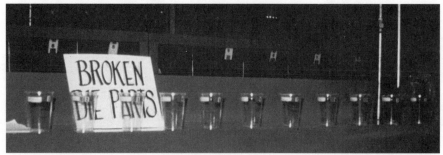

This simple, low-cost, high-results minisystem does what no computer can do: It shares vital operations-level communication at a glance. Operators, repair personnel, and the process itself become partners because people can tell—and act—by looking.

the die-repair associate came by to look for new work, he could tell simply by looking. The operators, in turn, could tell by looking if the repair team had been by for a pick-up. No one needed to chase after anyone. This low-cost/low-tech minisystem shared at a glance all the needed information on broken die parts, as part of the process.

Visual minisystems are critical for building visual order, and you will learn more about them in Chapter 12.

☆ ☆ ☆ ☆ ☆

In the next chapter, we'll look at the five start-up requirements for every successful implementation of visual order, the final piece of the big picture we are discussing in this first section of the book.

One: The Big Picture		
1. Toward a Visual Workplace	2. Visual Systems in Context	3. The Five Start-Up Requirements
Two: 5S Method		
4. S1/Sort Through and Sort Out	5. S2–S4/ Scrub, Secure Safety, and Select Locations	6. S5/Set Locations: Borders
7. S5/Set Locations: Addresses	8. 5S Stories From the Shop Floor	9. 5S+1 and White-Collar Applications
Three: +1 Method		
10. People: What to Expect	11. +1: Building and Sustaining the 5S Habit	12. +1: Leading by Example	13. +1: Leading Through Standards
Four: Go!		
14. Showcase, Scope, and the System	15. Training and Education	16. The Hundredth Monkey

Chapter 3

The Five Start-Up Requirements

Creating a visual workplace is not simply a matter of putting some visual devices and minisystems in place. These may get you started—but alone, they are not enough.

A case in point is ABC Manufacturing.

ABC Manufacturing: Blitz Aftermath

ABC had made impressive strides in productivity and quality as a result of converting to a lean production system. Lead times were down by 35–40 percent and markets were booming. Quality was competitive with the best in the industry, and the workforce was stable, hardworking, and excited about the changes.

A year before my visit, the president had attended a 5S improvement blitz at a nearby plant, organized by a well-known consulting group. The blitz promised to create a visual workplace in the host plant within five days. To quote the president, she was excited by the change she witnessed in the space of one week at the host plant. She decided to have the same thing done in her company. Now, twelve months later, she asked me to come in for a diagnosis.

While the weeklong blitz had produced results in her facility, they did not last, nor had they spread the way she had envisioned. A call to the nearby plant where the first blitz took place revealed that the same was true at that company. Over the long term, the results were disappointing, with little of the promised bottom line impact. Housekeeping levels were back to the previous levels or worse.

Let's walk the floor at ABC together. As we enter the main production area, we see the remnants of last year's housekeeping campaign: four-foot banners hang in practically every department, exhorting cleanliness, order, and discipline. Here and there, we see frayed lines of tape and wonder at their purpose. We see some silhouette tool boards, but in several cases the tool doesn't match the outline.

Several of the hundreds of processes in this facility are clearly labeled, along with a handful of shelving units. Ceiling signs in a stamping cell mark incoming/outgoing areas, and one die rack is color-coded with the press it supports. I see three visual minisystems, one for hand tools in manual assembly, one for international shipments in packing, and one for gauges in quality. Two quick changeover charts are posted on one of the dozen or so 5S bulletin boards, along with weekly SPC (statistical process control) charts; some of these are three to six months out-of-date. Several management memos on visual factory goals and objectives can also be seen.

Cleanliness levels are adequate but uneven. I skid across one floor that looks shiny but is instead slippery. While there is evidence of an effort toward order, unmarked piles of raw material, WIP (work in process), and overdue deliveries sit scattered throughout the plant. As I stop to chat with operators and supervisors along the way, few people have anything to say when asked for results they can see. Most shrug. One supervisor loudly declares that as far as he is concerned, 5S is a step backward.

What Went Wrong?

Three hours later, I return to the boardroom where the president and her direct reports are waiting. "Why isn't 5S working out in my company?" she asks. I tell them the unadorned truth:

> "Your instincts are right: Your company needs a comprehensive implementation of visual order. But what I saw on your shop floor will never get you there.
>
> "I saw a number of perfectly serviceable visual devices and a few minisystems that were scattered, stand-alone attempts. I saw a workforce that wants to improve but has no time to do so, and managers interested in the notion of a visual workplace but unclear about what that means or how to get there.

"In short, I saw an implementation without momentum because it has no roots, without direction because it has no vision, and without leadership because your approach to change has not been systematic—at least not to this point.

"You have many strengths in your favor, not the least of which is the energy and goodwill of your associates and supervisors. You can turn this around. But if you continue as you currently are, the possibility of ever achieving visual order, let alone a visual workplace, in this facility is at best remote—and at worst, a waste of time for you and everyone who works here."

The room is silent for a full minute. Then the president asks the right presidential questions: "What needs to change? How do we get there?" What I tell her is the subject of this chapter.

How to Get There: The Five Start-Up Requirements

The field of manufacturing improvement is strewn with broken dreams and progress that might have been but never was. All too many companies behave as though just thinking about "a change for the better" will make it so. Nothing could be farther from reality. For improvement to happen certain conditions or requirements must be met from the outset. If they are not, the effort fails and we seldom realize why.

The Five Start-Up Requirements

1. A clear, attainable vision
2. A specific role for the individual
3. An established improvement time policy
4. A set of defined performance measures
5. A step-by-step methodology

A Clear, Attainable Vision

When comprehensively implemented, visual information sharing provides solutions that, in their totality, can transform a company and radically improve its operational performance and competitive advantage. A worthy goal, you say. But before you embark on this extraordinary journey, make sure you know the destination. Make sure you have the vision. That's the first step. The name of the vision is: *a visual workplace*. Defined once again:

> A visual workplace is a work environment that is self-explaining, self-ordering, self-regulating, and self-improving—where what is *supposed* to happen *does* happen on time, every time, day or night.

This definition describes how your company will function when a visual workplace is achieved. This is what you are aiming for. It is your goal, your vision. Remember it.

Now you must make that vision come alive. Do this by finding an actual place that captures that vision for you. This is your vision place, a physical location that demonstrates the vision in action: where the principles and practice of visual systems function seamlessly and consistently. Because your vision place must act as a kind of homing device during the course of your implementation, choose a place that you know well, somewhere you have actually been and that you know firsthand.

Perhaps there is a factory nearby that captures the meaning of a visual workplace for you and shows you the results—a place that you and your associates can visit periodically for inspiration and ideas. Perhaps, it is a sister plant or a part of your own company that has already attained what you are after.

Your vision place need not be a workplace or factory. It could be some other type of facility in your own community. Some of the finest visual systems can be found in department stores, where self-regulation is at a premium. For example, Toys-R-Us (toy store) and Staples (office supply store) are outstanding in this respect as are most McDonald's outlets (both in front of and behind the counter).

Akebono Brakes (Japan) does it for me. That's my vision place. But the company is halfway around the world so I can't get there often enough. My substitute vision place is Disney World in Florida, for me the essence of a self-explaining, self-ordering, and self-regulating environment. Millions of people pass through there every year and the place runs like a top—even in the face of countless unforeseen abnormalities that crop up every day. Visual systems are in place and fully operational.

So identify a vision place where you can visit from time to time and be reminded of what you, your teammates, and your company are after in seeking to achieve a visual workplace. Hold that place vividly in your memory so you can access it anytime you need fresh inspiration. And ask your associates to do the same. (Note: You and your colleagues do not have to agree on a single place; it's strictly the more the merrier.)

A Specific Role for the Individual

Depending on your starting point, it can take from twelve to twenty-four months to achieve a workplace that can truly be described as visual. Yes, it is going to take time. You need a way, over the long haul, to keep you and your associates motivated, focused, and involved. You need a way to promote and support the involvement and contribution of the individual.

The visual workplace—and visual order, its first step—begins with the same question that Hank answered in Chapter 1:

"What do I need to know? What don't I know right now that I need to know to do my job?"

What information do you need at hand and available at a glance in order to do your work (Exhibit 3-1)? Answer that question down to the smallest detail and then convert each response into a visual device—one or more of the four kinds of devices discussed in the last chapter. The devices that result will ensure that the information will be there the next time you need it. Let the workplace speak.

Hank's first question was "Where are my pliers?" He knew if he didn't have his pliers in hand, he couldn't even start his work. What is at the top of your list? If it were posed to you, how would you answer the question, "What do I need to know?"

Notice that this question focuses squarely on *I*. It does not ask, "What do *we* need to know?" Visual order (and the visual workplace it supports) is an *I*-driven model. The individual is at its core. This must be so for a workplace to be self-explaining and self-regulating. The individual must decide what information is needed so that the message is there to pull when needed. In a visual workplace, the individual is both the designer and the user of the information that is visually shared. Notice the direction of the arrows in the above figure. In pull system terms, the individual is both the supplier and the customer of visual information-sharing systems.

Some may say this is a very self-centered approach to information sharing. Indeed it is, but it is not selfish. Visual information does not exclude anyone else because every workplace is a community of *I*'s, a network of individuals. Besides, the question "What do *I* need to know?" is only one side of the coin.

On the flip side is the second and equally important question, "What do *I* need to share?" Notice the direction of the arrows in Exhibit 3-2; they are pointing away from the individual.

"What do I need to share so that others may do their work—or do it better?" This question is a direct call for group-mindedness and team spirit. The question is still *I*-driven because it says that each one of us must take individual responsibility for sharing the information we know with others for the good of others, ourselves, and the company. It's easy to tell what needs to get shared first. Just notice why people interrupt you and what ques-

Exhibit 3-1. The First Question.

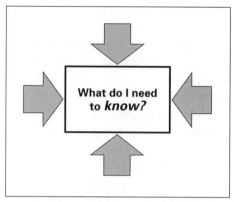

This question opens our awareness to all that we actually need to know, but do not currently know, in order to add value. Ask this question again and again to dig out the specifics for you. Then translate your answers into specific visual devices and minisystems.

Exhibit 3-2. The Second Question.

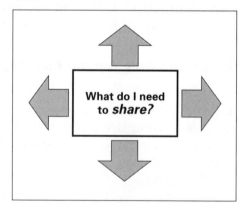

This second question opens us up to specific information that others need, but do not have, to help them add value. Ask yourself: What information do others need that I already know? If you still need help, ask people directly, then translate their answers into visual devices that share that missing information quickly and visually.

tions they ask. Translate those answers into visual devices so that others can pull these answers themselves, without your assistance. Help others become self-regulating.

There is really no conflict between the team and the individual in this methodology. The first cycle of work you will do in a 5S + 1 implementation will focus on what affects you directly, on your *locus of control.* Typically, this is your work area or bench (even in multishift operations). To experience visually what this means, imagine standing in your immediate work area with your arms outstretched; now pivot around in a circle. The area that you span with your outstretched arms is your *locus of control,* a sphere of influence inscribed by your fingertips. You can think of it like this, with you as the center:

Implementing visual order in your company begins when you take charge of your sphere of control and apply 5S + 1 within it. You do this as an individual. As you continue, your own individual effort eventually touches the individual effort of someone else. Your spheres touch or even overlap, one enriching the other, like this:

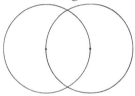

Each of you is independent but joined. Slowly and surely, these individual efforts will spread across your work area or department, connect, and overlap, like this:

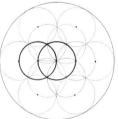

And as these overlapping rings of individual effort multiply and spread further, this gridlike pattern widens and eventually covers and connects all parts of the organization in a network pattern of effort. And you are joined, like this:

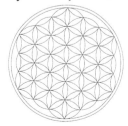

And it doesn't stop there. Individual spheres of creativity spill over the physical boundaries of the company and connect with individuals in other organizations—and the vision spreads, like this:

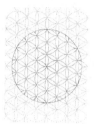

Be clear from the outset: the process of implementing visual order begins and ends with the individual, driven by the dual *I* question: "What do I need to know and to share?" The individual powers all change.

An Established Improvement Time Policy

The involvement of individual employees is key to the success of 5S + 1. Since this is so, we must know when this involvement will take place. An officially established improvement time policy is essential.

A company that has switched to lean manufacturing runs a tight production schedule. A company that has not yet switched also runs full tilt—but for other reasons. If either company does not establish an official improvement time policy, very little improvement will ever happen in that enterprise.

You see this everywhere, even in companies that loudly proclaim their commitment to continuous systematic improvement. Little or no actual time is set aside to do the very improvement activity the company says it wants.

It is an age-old battle—production time versus improvement time. Two worthy contenders attempting to occupy the same narrow twenty-four-hour space. The issue is not which is more important. Production will always win that argument, and this is as it should be; a company is in business to deliver. The danger, however, is that improvement will never happen. As mentioned, even organizations committed on paper and in public to a process of continuous systematic improvement are often hard-pressed to identify actual time for this to happen.

Too often improvement is left to chance and the ingenuity of those willing to eke out small pockets of time and make magic happen. We all know these people. They see the vision burning brightly before them and are determined to find a way. Time and again, these people prove—with their bodies, their energy, and all too often, their own lives—the age-old adage: Where there's a will, there's a way.

In a sad and important way, when these quiet heroes succeed, they do their companies and the rest of us some bit of harm. When they make magic happen, in the absence of a clearly defined improvement time policy, they unintentionally send the message that separate time is not needed. Wise, indeed, is the company that sees through this double think and takes steps to establish the policy nevertheless.

The lack of an established improvement time policy is one of the greatest corporate roadblocks to positive change today. The next step in your journey to a visual workplace is to make sure your company has an official improvement time policy in place. First write out a policy. Begin this by answering these three questions:

1. Who will participate in the first phase of the implementation?
2. How much improvement time is needed for these employees to make sure and steady inroads toward visual order on their way to a visual workplace? On a daily basis? On a weekly basis?
3. Given those two answers, how must the production schedule be adapted or adjusted to leave time for improvement?

Answering these questions can steer you in the direction of an improvement time policy that is right for your company. But coming up with a policy that looks good on paper is just the first step. It must be tested. Simply because your president agrees to let thirty minutes a day be set aside for *each* employee to work on improvement does not guarantee that it will happen. Far from it. The filing cabinets of companies everywhere are filled with such policies. Have they been deployed? Your company's improvement time policy must be *operationalized*, a word that is used often in this book. Thinking up a way to improve and actually operationalizing it so that improvement happens are two entirely separate events, with "thinking it up" the easier.

So let company policy makers (management, including union leadership where applicable) devise a policy they can accept — and then send that policy out to the production floor for testing. Do this in a confined, targeted area (not everywhere at once); this is a test. Let it run for a week or two. Observe what happens. Did everyone get in thirty minutes of uninterrupted improvement each day, if this is your stated policy? Two-and-a-half hours a week? Did *anyone*? Track this. Gather data. And be ready to go back to the drawing board to clear up mistaken assumptions and add the missing specifics that operationalizes the intent (see Appendix A for a useful improvement time measurement tool).

A Midwestern Company's Commitment to a Workable 5S + 1 Improvement Time Policy

For example, one very busy company in the Midwest was committed to a workable 5S + 1 improvement time policy. Management wrote up an inspiring preamble, declared it in writing, and then announced at a companywide meeting that improvement time would happen. Life went on as usual. Nothing changed. Production schedules were tight and product got shipped. 5S + 1 improvement did not happen.

Back at the drawing board, key adjustments were made. First, management and the visual workplace steering team (explained in Chapters 11 and 13) agreed that improvement time would indeed happen in weekly chunks of 2.5 hours each. Second, the company decided to bring in outside help once a week to run operations so that regular associates would be free to work as a team at least weekly. To support this, the shop floor was divided into specific work areas so that the outside help could rotate in a set pattern from area to area (see Chapter 14 for more on mapping).

Another innovative solution came from management directly. Top managers offered to be available for the cleanup work—and shopfloor teams accepted. Managers simply showed up in work clothes after hours, reported to associates for their orders, and got busy. I will never forget seeing the president/owner, comptroller, plant manager, and human resources director scrubbing the grime-coated floor and degreasing a stamping press. And associates managed to capture it all on videotape.

While this last was a temporary solution, it served a number of purposes in this plant:

1. It moved specific areas to a higher level of cleanliness.
2. It demonstrated management's willingness to act on its own pronouncements.
3. It caught the attention of the 5S + 1 skeptics.
4. It further fired the enthusiasm of 5S + 1 supporters.

Just as important, it was fun and turned out to be one of the first of many high moments during the course of this important transformation.

The short of it is this: Devising and operationalizing an improvement time policy is indispensable to implementing visual order and, ultimately, to achieving a visual workplace (see Appendix A for other improvement time policy material).

A Set of Defined Performance Measures

Making the shift from a traditional to a visual workplace does not happen overnight. It takes effort over an extended period. To keep you motivated and on track, you must define a set of performance measures that, from the outset, provides feedback on your progress.

The measures most responsive to the kinds of changes produced by improved visual order are linked to motion—the metrics of time and space. Here are six of them:

Six Measures Linked to Motion

1. *Floor space utilization.* How many square feet of floor space are covered with things versus how many are free for use; include all traffic and walkways, storage zones, and WIP locations.
2. *Material flow distance.* How far does the material have to travel as it makes its way to, through, and across operations; measure this in linear feet.
3. *Equipment changeover time.* How long do machine changeovers take in your area? Look at the range (high/low times) and the average.
4. *Search time.* How much time does each associate spend in looking for things, people, and/or information? Let each person keep track of their own metrics on this and then tally them on a daily and then weekly basis.
5. *Wait time.* How much time does each associate spend in waiting for things, people, and/or information? Again, let each person keep track of their own experience, then tally them.
6. *Interruption time.* How often is each associate interrupted, for how long, and for what reason? Track this individually and then tally collectively.

These are useful metrics, and you can use one, several, or all of them in support of your implementation. But whatever you decide, one measure is an absolute requirement:

the ratio of value-adding (VA) to non-value-adding (NVA) time. This is a measure so complete and powerful that all of my on-site clients must agree, as part of our contract, to compute it for *each* work area in the implementation. This computation is called a *value-adding analysis.* In a manner of speaking, they "can't leave home without it." Here is a walk-through of the analysis.

Calculating Your Area's VA/NVA Ratio

There are six steps to the process.

1. Begin by selecting the **work unit**, a specific product, component, or part.
2. Determine the work unit's **manufacturing lead time**, the time that elapses between the moment that work unit (material or WIP) enters your work area and the moment it finally leaves your area on its way to the next process or customer. In other words, estimate how long the work unit stays in your area.
3. Next identify each conversion operation that the work unit undergoes while in your area: each operation that transforms the unit and brings it closer to the customer's requirements.
4. Now determine how long it takes to perform each of these operations on a single work unit. Even if the batch size is 1,000, identify the time it takes to do the operation for a single unit. Let's say your lead time is one week, your lot size is 1,000, and you spend two full days stamping. How much of these two days is spent in stamping one unit—one second? two seconds? five? That is the number you need for the analysis.
5. The only exception to this is for a process such as heat treat or curing because the time is the same whether you treat or cure one work unit or a thousand. (If such an operation is part of your process, count in its full cycle time; *but* do not count in the loading time because loading and unloading is *strictly* motion—as explained in Chapter 1—however much you may see it as required at this time.)
6. Divide the total manufacturing lead time of this work unit (item 2 above) into the total of its value-adding time. When you have done this, change the result into a percentage by moving the decimal point over two spaces to the right. Now subtract that percentage from 100 percent and you will get your non-value-adding percentage.

Exhibit 3-3 is a worksheet for calculating this ratio, step-by-step. The Koala Pen-Clip case example that follows walks you through a complete analysis.

VA/NVA Analysis Case Example: The Pen-Clip Department at Koala, Inc.

A VA/NVA analysis was done in Koala's "clip" area, the department responsible for the metal clip on the pen cap for Product X-3 (Exhibit 3-4).

First, associates in the clip area established the manufacturing lead time. They were surprised to discover that it was four days. Probably no one would have believed it if they hadn't marked the metal coil with a streak of yellow paint when it first arrived in

Exhibit 3-3. Value-Adding Analysis Worksheet (Blank).

Value-Adding Analysis Worksheet

Step 1: Select a Product/Process Focus

1.1. Select a product or component manufactured in the area where you are about to implement visual order (5S + 1): _____

1.2. Indicate the time it takes for a single* unit of this product or component to cycle through this work area. In other words, indicate its lead time:** _____

Step 2: Determine the Value-Adding Time

2.1. In Column A (below), write down in sequence the steps or operations that this unit goes through as it is converted into something that is closer to the customer's specifications.

A. Value-Adding Operations in Sequence	B. Time	C. Convert
1) _____	_____	_____
2) _____	_____	_____
3) _____	_____	_____
4) _____	_____	_____
5) _____	_____	_____
6) _____	_____	_____

(Use another sheet of paper for more steps.)

Total _____ _____

2.2. In column B, mark down the time that each operation takes to complete. Add up the total.

2.3. Convert the time that each operation takes into the same measure (hours or minutes or seconds) and write these in Column C. Add up the total.

2.4. Convert the lead time (Item 1.2) into same unit of measure used in Item 2.1.C.: _

Step 3: Calculate Value-Adding vs. Non-Value-Adding Time

3.1. Divide the overall lead time into the value-adding time. Your answer is: _____

3.2. To get a percentage, move the decimal point in your Item 3.1 answer to the right two places and add a percent sign (%). This is your value-adding (VA) percentage = _____%.

3.3. Subtract this from 100% to get your non-value-adding (NVA) percentage. NVA = _____%.

3.4. Your VA:NVA ratio, then, is _____:_____.

* Even if your lot size is 1,000, calculate this lead time on a single unit, even as it waits for its 999 brothers before moving on.
** Don't know the lead time? Find out by noting when (day/hour) the unit/material physically enters area (even if queuing) and when it physically leaves (whether it moves to another area or gets shipped). Put a yellow mark, for example, on the unit itself to help you keep track.

Exhibit 3-4. Pen Clip.

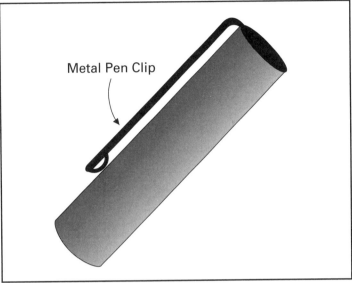

Metal Pen Clip

This is the component that was the focus of a value-adding analysis at Koala, Inc.

their area. They saw a spot of yellow paint on one of the clips as it was about to leave the area four days later.

Next they identified the following five value-adding operations in the process that transformed the metal coil into the clip on the pen cap:

1. Stamping
2. Forming
3. Deburring
4. Plating
5. Assembly

The third step was to determine the amount of time each of these steps took for one single clip. Even though the component moved through their area in lots of 500 units, they knew that to do the analysis correctly, they had to focus on the time each step took for just one work piece. How much time was required to perform each operation on a single unit? The associates understood that it was fine to estimate and round off at this stage.

These numbers are rounded up to the nearest second:

Operation	Value-Adding Time (Seconds)
1. Stamping	3
2. Forming	3
3. De-burring	62
4. Plating	38
5. Assembly	15
Total	121

Simple addition gave the team the total value-adding time per unit of 121 seconds. Then they converted their estimated lead time of 4 days into the same unit of measure as the value-adding time—seconds. Here are their calculations:

$$4 \text{ days } (\times 24 \text{ hr})^* = 96 \text{ hr}$$
$$96 \text{ hr } (\times 60 \text{ min}) = 5,760 \text{ min}$$
$$5,760 \text{ min } (\times 60 \text{ sec}) = 345,600 \text{ sec}$$

To calculate the VA percentage, they divided the total manufacturing lead time of 345,600 seconds into the value-adding time for one unit (121 sec).

$$\frac{121 \text{ sec}}{345,600 \text{ sec}} = 0.0003501, \text{ or } 0.03501\%$$

They rounded that up to 0.035 percent, and then to 0.04 percent. Finally, the team subtracted the value-adding percentage from the overall lead time (100% − .04%) for a non-value-adding percentage of 99.96 percent. Exhibit 3-5 shows you the team's completed analysis worksheet.

Twenty-Four Hours! Why?

I'm often asked why time is calculated on a 24-hour basis in the above analysis. The answer is that whether you are working or not, the unit is still waiting. Just because you are not at work does *not* stop that unit from costing the company. That cost does not stop accumulating until the unit is delivered to the external customer (and the payment received).

However, if you revolt against the notion of the non-value-adding clock running 24 hours a day, go ahead and calculate the ratio based on the number of hours per day your facility is up and running. The results remain shocking.

For an 8-hour shift, for example, overall lead time would be 115,200 seconds instead of 345,600 for our pen-clip example. When divided into 121 seconds, the result is .00105—or .11 percent (or an NVA of 99.89%). And while that is nearly triple the value calculated by using a 24-hour clock, the difference between .04 percent and .11 percent in terms of production value is nonexistent. Either way you slice it, you have a mountain of waste in your process, as you can see in Exhibit 3-6.

How to Use These Results

Like all powerful measures, the results of your value-adding analysis will show you exactly where your improvement direction lies. If your company is new to lean production and the motion reduction strategy that is its core, the ratio in your area is likely to approach the 95/5 we discussed in Chapter 1, i.e., 95 percent of non-value-adding activity (motion) and 5 percent of value-adding (work). It may turn out to be much worse.

It takes guts to actually calculate your VA/NVA ratio and look the truth of your process in the eye. And that sorry truth is: Any area with a ratio that is less than 50/50

Exhibit 3-5. Value-Adding Analysis Worksheet (Completed).

Value-Adding Analysis Worksheet

Step 1: Select a Product/Process Focus

1.1. Select a product or component manufactured in the area where you are about to implement visual order (5S+1): *Product X-3 Pen Clip*

1.2. Indicate the time it takes for a single unit of this product or component to cycle through this work area. In other words, indicate its lead time: *4 days*

Step 2: Determine the Value-Adding Time

2.1. In Column A (below), write down in sequence the steps or operations that this unit goes through as it is converted into something that is closer to the customer's specifications.

A. Value-Adding Operations in Sequence	B. Time	C. Convert
1) *Stamping*	*3 sec*	*3 sec*
2) *Forming*	*3 sec*	*3 sec*
3) *Deburring*	*1 min 2 secs*	*62 sec*
4) *Plating*	*38 sec*	*38 sec*
5) *Assembly*	*15 sec*	*15 sec*
6)		

(use another sheet of paper for more steps)

Total *2 min 1 sec* *121 sec*

2.2. In column B, mark down the time that each operation takes to complete. Add up the total.

2.3. Convert the time that each operation takes into the same measure (hours or minutes or seconds) and write these in Column C. Add up the total.

2.4. Convert the lead time (Item 1.2) into same unit of measure used in Item 2.1.C.: *345,600 sec*

Step 3: Calculate Value-Adding versus Non-Value-Adding Time

3.1. Divide the overall lead time into the value-adding time. Your answer is: *0.0003501*.

3.2. To get a percentage, move the decimal point in your Item 3.1 answer to the right two places and add a percentage (%). This is your value-adding (VA) percentage = *.035%*.

3.3. Subtract this from 100% to get your non-value-adding (NVA) percentage. NVA = *99.96%*.

3.4. Your VA:NVA ratio, then, is *0.04%*:*99.96%*.

Exhibit 3-6. Value-Adding vs. Non-Value-Adding Ratio: The Pen-Clip Team at Koala, Inc.

99.96% NVA (waste)   **0.04% VA↑**

percent (50 hours of value-adding versus 50 hours of non-value-adding in any 100 hours) is choking on the motion in its process; eating up the energy of the workforce and the profits of the company. If that is so, your corporate strategy is clear: Get rid of the motion. Operationalize that strategy now by embracing the fifth and final start-up requirement: a systematic methodology.

A Step-by-Step Methodology

However much you may want a visual workplace, you will never achieve it without a step-by-step methodology. The Blueprint for a Visual Workplace introduced in Chapter 2 is shown again in Exhibit 3-7. The accurate, complete, and rapid sharing of information is at the heart of a visual workplace. The first objective is a clear, clean, safe, and orderly

Exhibit 3-7. Blueprint for a Visual Workplace.

```
                         ╱‾‾‾‾‾‾‾╲
                        ╱    8    ╲
                       ╱ Eliminate ╲
                      ╱ Source of    ╲
                     ╱    Errors       ╲
                    ╱───────────────────╲
                    │  7   Detect Errors  │
                    ├─────────────────────┤
                    │  6   Detect Defects  │
                    ├─────────────────────┤
                    │  5   Build Standards │
                    │      into the Workplace │
                    ├─────────────────────┤
                    │  4   Track Adherence │
                    │      (Scoreboard)    │
                    ├─────────────────────┤
                    │  3   Share Standards │
                    │         Visually     │
                    ├─────────────────────┤
                    │  2   Target Standards│
                    ├─────────────────────┤
              ➤     │  1   Implement Visual│
                    │      Order (5S+1)    │
                    └─────────────────────┘
```

work area *because* only such an environment can hold the basic information vital to meeting the first requirement of production—knowing where things are. We call this visual order 5S + 1, and it is the foundation level of the Blueprint. With this information installed, the workplace becomes self-explaining and self-ordering—one step closer to self-regulating and self-improving.

In 5S + 1, we clear out the clutter, clean up what's left, make the objects of the workplace safe, arrange them along the line of flow, and anchor each item to a place with a border, an ID label, and a home address—simple visual indicators. At the completion of this process, the workplace has clarity of location, a long-neglected but crucial building block to excellence in manufacturing and accelerated throughput.

5S + 1 is a systematic approach for implementing visual order in American organizations. It has succeeded where other imported models have faltered. The what, why, and how of this process is the topic of the rest of this book. It's time for 5S + 1.

Two

The 5S Method

One: The Big Picture		
1. Toward a Visual Workplace	2. Visual Systems in Context	3. The Five Start-Up Requirements
Two: 5S Method		
4. S1/Sort Through and Sort Out	5. S2–S4/ Scrub, Secure Safety, and Select Locations	6. S5/Set Locations: Borders
7. S5/Set Locations: Addresses	8. 5S Stories From the Shop Floor	9. 5S+1 and White-Collar Applications
Three: +1 Method			
10. People: What to Expect	11. +1: Building and Sustaining the 5S Habit	12. +1: Leading by Example	13. +1: Leading Through Standards
Four: Go!		
14. Showcase, Scope, and the System	15. Training and Education	16. The Hundredth Monkey

Chapter 4

S1/Sort Through and Sort Out

In this chapter, we discuss the first principle of visual order: S1/Sort Through and Sort Out.

> *Reader's advisory*: While S1 as a technique is simple and straightforward, it is also perilous. Done correctly, S1 sets a tone of enthusiasm and optimism for the implementation and creates a base for teamwork that will feed benefits directly to the bottom line. Done poorly, however, the implementation risks becoming just another failed good idea. Make sure to read about 5S + 1 in its entirety (Chapters 4 through 12) before implementing S1/Sort Through and Sort Out.

The workplace can get overrun with *things*—parts, fixtures, shelves, bins, paper, pens, clipboards, desks, chairs, stools, racks, cabinets, phones, packing material, tools, equipment, machinery, material, scrap, and on and on. Some of these things are essential to workplace objectives but rarely everything. Piles of unneeded or infrequently used "stuff" get in the way of day-to-day operations and impede the flow of work. Speed is hampered and long lead times become chronic.

Let's face it. There are packrats among us, and they want to keep everything. Theirs is a just-in-case mentality. As a result, things begin to accumulate. Once-useful objects, now obsolete, are never discarded. The presence of all these unneeded items makes it harder to tell what is needed. As a result, we spend precious time trying to tell the difference. In addition, as unneeded items accumulate, they consume more and more precious floor and shelving space. Eventually, the clutter of nonessential items can lead us to conclude that more floor space is required as well as more shelving, extra pallets, carts, forklifts, and larger warehouses—not to mention more personnel to operate and manage them. Additionally, the health and safety hazards caused by clutter can be considerable.

No corner of an enterprise is immune to the clang, clutter, and crush of needless things. Stuff is everywhere, from the machine shop to the assembly floor, from customer service to the drafting department. Often the only places exempt from these incursions are the visitors' entrance and the boardroom, where corporate image is the prime consideration. These spaces are often remarkable in their spaciousness, polish, and elegance.

Clutter costs money, and it is the enemy of lean production. It's time to get rid of the debris.

Operationalizing S1: The 3-Tag Technique

5S + 1 begins with one simple action: clearing out the clutter. In S1, you decide what is needed and what is not—and then remove what is not. The tool for doing this is the *3-Tag Technique*. In it, you use different-color tags to identify what goes, what stays, and everything in between. A red, green, or yellow tag is applied to every item in the workplace, as summarized in Exhibit 4-1.

There are all kinds of ways to tag items. Office supply houses carry 1- × 2-inch or 2- × 3-inch tags that attach with string; or you could use self-stick dots, preferably large enough to write names and dates on. Another option is to mark the appropriate-color dot on an index card and tape the card onto the item. I would not, however, recommend using Post-its or other self-stick notes because they rapidly lose their sticking ability, especially in dusty areas.

Let's take a closer look at what each color tag means, and then see how they work together.

Red-Tagging

Red tags are posted on the items you want removed from your area. Some obvious examples would be:

Exhibit 4-1. The Three Tags.

```
┌─────────────────────────────────────────────────────────────────┐
│                                                                   │
│   ┌──────────────────────────┐     ┌──────────────────────────┐  │
│   │        RED TAG           │     │       GREEN TAG          │  │
│   │  1. I am sure that I do  │     │  1. I am sure that I do  │  │
│   │     not need or want     │     │     need or want this.   │  │
│   │     this.                │     │  2. I am going to keep   │  │
│   │  2. I am going to get    │     │     it.                  │  │
│   │     rid of it.           │     │                          │  │
│   └──────────────────────────┘     └──────────────────────────┘  │
│                                                                   │
│          ┌──────────────────────────────────────┐                │
│          │              YELLOW TAG               │                │
│          │  1. I am not sure yet if I need or    │                │
│          │     want this.                        │                │
│          │  2. I won't get rid of it—yet!        │                │
│          └──────────────────────────────────────┘                │
│                                                                   │
└─────────────────────────────────────────────────────────────────┘
```

- The seven boxes of spare parts for the product discontinued in 1967
- The twenty-five packing cartons you don't need anymore because packing got moved downstream
- The three bottles of dried-up glue

But there are less obvious items than these that can be discarded.

Know Your Requirements

Until and unless an item directly contributes to current workplace objectives, it is at best excess, and at worst clutter. If your company has already implemented JIT, your area is likely to be lean, with little evidence of these items—and this is even more likely to be the case if you have cells. If, on the other hand, yours is a traditional production system (whether job shop or high volume), expect to see piles of things that are simply not needed. Much of this will be junk—things that never have and never will serve any production purpose whatsoever. You don't want them and no one else does either. Get rid of them!

This refers to all items not associated with *near-term* production requirements (individually defined on the basis of batch size, machine changeover times, and so on, in your area), including:

- Raw material
- Components, subcomponents, or parts
- Tools
- Fixtures
- Carts or pallets
- Machinery
- Shelving or racks
- Office or clerical materials
- Packing or shipping material
- WIP and finished goods from previous production runs
- Scrap from previous production runs

Removal and Disposal Guidelines

As red-tagging gets under way, you will notice that some things can be thrown directly into the trash while others need further consideration. Some, for example, are not needed by you but may be of use somewhere else in the company. Or an item which is not needed now will be required in three months when you run that order again. Still other items are too big, too specialized, or too hazardous for easy disposal; their removal must be supervised.

In light of these variations, consider the following five supports for your red-tagging process:

1. Set up a red-tag removal location.
2. Schedule a red-tag pause.
3. Set up a capital assets disposal procedure.
4. Explore recycling options.
5. Measure red-tag volume.
6. Commit to regular red-tagging.

Setting Up a Red-Tag Removal Location

Deciding to get rid of an unneeded item and actually getting it out the door can be two different matters. To increase the likelihood that red-tag items actually leave your area, set up a red-tag removal location where you and others can put red-tagged items. This can be anything from a shelving unit (Photo 4-1) to a cart to a roped-off section of the floor. Some companies go a step further and schedule regular red-tag pick-ups and set up a central red-tag holding area.

Scheduling a Red-Tag Pause

You and your colleagues can set a time period during which red-tag items remain in the red-tag removal location before they are actually moved off the premises. This period, which usually ranges from two days to two weeks, gives people a chance to make disposal or recycling arrangements and/or get management authorization in the case of

4-1. Red-Tag Shelving.

In this company, red-tag items were stored on this metal shelving that was cleared off every two weeks.

red-tagged capital assets. This pause also gives managers and supervisors a chance to review items before they get tossed.

To facilitate this, have everyone date their red tags as they post them; then begin the countdown from those dates.

Exploring Recycling Options

Many unwanted items just don't look like junk. As a result, we hesitate to assign them to the trash bin. We prefer to find a way to avoid throwing away perfectly good stuff. The solution is recycling. Here are four ways to become a responsible corporate citizen and still move forward on S1:

1. *Recycle directly.* Make recycling arrangements for red-tag items. This simply means that employees need to separate red-tag items into recycle categories (plastic, paper,

metal) when they drop these off at removal locations. A local outside recycling vendor would then be happy to haul it away.

2. *Recycle to local schools.* Recycle red-tagged items to your local schools and get a tax write-off, plenty of goodwill, and possibly a write-up in the local newspaper. Teachers and students of vocational schools welcome obsolete tooling and old machines. Donor companies have been known to buy these back from the same school, refurbished. And elementary grades can never get too many bolts, nuts, housings, and other odds and ends for their art projects.

3. *Resell/barter.* Take a bite out of petty cash spending by setting up a barter program between departments. Red-tagged items from one department get sold to or bartered in another part of the company. If appropriate, invite sister plants to participate as well as your suppliers and customers.

4. *Hold a yard sale.* In the spirit of recycling and getting the things out the door, stage a yard sale for employees that lets them take home red-tagged items that would otherwise just get tossed.

Setting Up a Capital Assets Disposal Procedure

Some items are too expensive to simply remove or recycle. Their disposal must be closely monitored. In these cases, use a formal procedure that leaves an audit trail. Make the Red-Tag Disposal Form in Exhibit 4-2 (or some similar form) a part of your procedure.

Measuring Red-Tag Volume

Many companies are interested in tracking the level of red-tag items that get removed. Here are a few ways to do this:

1. Count the number of dumpsters that get filled.
2. Weigh the items.
3. Compute the dollar value of what was removed.
4. Track the number of liberated racks and shelves.
5. Calculate the liberated square footage of bench and floor space.

The figures can be impressive. For example, associates at Philips Automotive Electronics Co., an electronics manufacturer in Fort Wayne, Indiana, kept track of metal racks and cabinets. In the first four weeks of implementing S1, they carted away 37 standard metal shelving units, 9 metal cabinets, and 104 other racks. "They were all over the place!" one employee exclaimed. "All over the place!" You'll read more about S1 at Philips in Chapter 8.

Committing to Regular Red-Tagging

Many companies turn red-tagging into a workplace habit by doing it monthly—or even weekly. The red-tag cart comes around like clockwork on the last Thursday of the month, for example, and picks up what you no longer want. Like clockwork. It takes

Exhibit 4-2. Red-Tag Disposal Form.

Red-Tag Disposal Form	Today's Date _____	Additional Comments
Red-Tag File No. _____	Team/Person _____	
Item Category ___ 1. WIP ___ 9. Carts/Pallets ___ 2. Raw Material ___ 10. Fixtures & Tools ___ 3. Components ___ 11. Scrap ___ 4. Subcomponents ___ 12. Furniture ___ 5. Parts ___ 13. Machines ___ 6. Finished Goods ___ 14. Office Material ___ 7. Packing Material ___ 15. Shelving/Racks ___ 8. Equipment ___ 16. Other _____		
Item Name (include any item number) _____		
Unit Quantity _____		
Estimated Value ($$) _____		
Reason For Disposal _____ 1. Not needed _____ _____ 2. Defective _____ _____ 3. Surplus _____ _____ 4. Destination or use unknown _____ _____ 5. Other _____		
Disposal Date _____		
Disposal By (person/team) _____		
Disposal Method _____ 1. Discard _____ 2. Return to _____ _____ 3. Move to Disposal Area (location _____) _____ 4. Move to Temporary Storage (location _____) _____ 5. Other _____		
Signature (authorizing person) _____ Printed _____		
Actual Disposal Date _____		

Use this form (or one like it) to identify company assets that get red-tagged. Come up with a specific procedure that ensures their proper and trackable disposal.

guts to commit to red-tagging on a regular basis—and you'll love what it does for your work flow and the bottom line.

Yellow-Tagging

Yellow tags are used in two cases. First for things you need—but not now. They go into temporary storage: yellow-tag storage. They come back onto the floor only when there is a clear and present need. The second application is for borderline items, items you are not sure whether to get rid of or keep. You need to decide one way or the other. Until you do, the item gets a yellow tag (and a decide-by date). Here's a scenario to illustrate, with you as the operator.

Agnes's Story

Your name is Agnes, and you are an assembly operator for the XL product series, one of the 5S + 1 demo sites. You and a group of associates have just returned from the morning training session, armed with your assignment: Apply S1/Sort Through and Sort Out to your own workbench using the 3-Tag Technique. You are raring to go.

You begin to sort through the tools and materials on and under your bench. You pull out some red tags. "What don't I need? Get rid of these extra bins—red-tag! Get rid of these old parts; we haven't made any of those in months—red-tag! And all those soda cans that I've been collecting; time to turn them in—red-tag!"

"But what about this SRO fixture?" you ask yourself. You remember someone saying that the SRO line was closed down—or was that the ROS line? Better find out first. Those fixtures are not cheap. How to do that? Ahhh, you remember. This is a perfect application for a yellow tag. That yellow tag will buy you the time you need to get your answer. You write your name on a yellow tag and Friday's date as your decide-by deadline and tie the tag on the fixture (Exhibit 4-3).

Yellow tags buy you time to make a good decision, and the decide-by date lets you make sure you don't take forever. Yellow tagging allows you time to think. And it can open up the logjam caused by items that do not fall clearly into needed/unneeded categories. Here are some tips on using yellow tags.

Buddy Up

Sometimes we get overly invested in the objects around us and it's not easy to know whether the item is really needed or we just like to have it around. As we discuss later in this chapter, liking an item is a good enough reason to keep it; just get clear on your reason. But if you can't decide now, put a yellow tag on it and get a partner or buddy to help you get clear and decide. Put your name and your buddy's name on the yellow tag along with a decide-by date. Then when the date comes up, your buddy will get you to decide—or decide for you.

Exhibit 4-3. Yellow Tag.

Agnes put a yellow tag on this bin and a due-by date (3/7) to make sure she made a clear decision on keeping or disposing of that bin. For added insurance, she asked Miguel ("Mike") to be her backup to make sure she made the decision or to make it himself if she was stuck.

Yellow-Tag Temporary Storage

Yellow-tag storage is for the things that you want to remove from the regular work flow until you can decide whether to toss it or to keep it. Therefore, locate your yellow-tag storage area nearby. Find a shelf, cart, or floor section—or, if it's just for you, a spot under your bench. Putting items into this kind of temporary location can give you a chance to test your need for them. But remember: This is temporary storage; when the decide-by date comes up, the item either goes back into active use or gets red-tagged.

Green-Tagging

Use green tags on items you are certain you want to keep. A green tag item is an essential item. You want it. You need it. No bones about it.

Many people will red-tag and not green-tag at all. They say, "What's the point? Once I get rid of the stuff I don't need, everything that's left is what I do need." Other people prefer to see it just the other way around. They do green-tagging as a substitute for red-tagging. "Let me identify what I need, and get rid of everything else." Since the result is the same, respect personal preferences and get on with the task.

☆ ☆ ☆ ☆ ☆

S1 has another purpose: building employee involvement in the improvement process. Implementing visual order is not difficult or complex. The tasks imbedded in all of 5S + 1 are low-cost activities that make sense and have tangible results. In most workplaces, applying S1 produces many early victories. Anyone and everyone can play a part in improving visual order and take pride in what are often stunning results.

3-Tagging and the Territorial Imperative: Who Decides?

Some areas of the shop floor require agreement about what gets removed. These are the common areas in the workplace that are used by you as well as others. Packing areas, gauge and tool storage, parts containers, material storage, and the scrap bins are a few likely examples. Which items stay and which ones go will require a joint decision.

3-Tagging can become even more of an issue in multishift settings when workplace items and the physical layout itself are owned and used by people you may rarely see. Cellular manufacturing and the multiskilled workforce that supports it can put yet another spin on the ownership issue: All production items as well as the area itself are not only shared, they are held in common.

At the heart of each of these issues is the territorial imperative. Even though we rarely own the things we use to get our work done, we often feel a deep sense of ownership or territoriality when someone else messes with "our" things or tries to tell us what to do with them.

That is why, early in the implementation, people need to realize that *the first* s *is for* spirit—the spirit of the workplace and of each person who works there. In S1 this means letting each person decide what she wants to get rid of or keep.

The Majority Does Not *Rule*

Let's say there are seven of us working in a department and we are in the process of red-tagging shared items there. If six out of seven tags on an item are red, for example, and only one tag is green, the item stays. If six out of seven tags on an item are red and only one tag is yellow, the item is put into temporary storage. If the item has six yellow tags and a green one, the item stays. Action-wise, it's really that simple. But the impact of the values expressed by these actions are powerful and long lasting.

Diplomacy and resourcefulness can often ease the situation, as illustrated by the following example. An assembly associate was practically surrounded by a mountain of parts, but when it came time for S1, he didn't seem to want to remove any of them. "I just might need them," he said. His supervisor knew he was wrong (many of the parts were obsolete or damaged), but she didn't want to push the issue. Instead, she suggested that the associate put a green dot on a part when and if he touched it. He did, and at the end of a week began to realize that there were parts on his bench that he never touched—and never would. S1 began to make sense to him.

Charley's story, which took place in one of the ten focused factories (profit centers) of a large aerospace plant in New England, is based on an actual incident and did not have such a pleasant ending.

Charley's Story

The 5S + 1 implementation was in its ninth month and the shop floor was beginning to look and act really different. The clutter was gone. Floors and machines shone. Addresses and ID labels were in place for practically every tool, die, fixture, parts bin, pallet, container, and workbench. Teams were excited about the next steps.

Exhibit 4-4. Charley's Table.

Charley's prize table disappeared before we got a photo of it. This is a drawing of it as I remember it.

On Thursday the announcement came: The executive VP in charge of corporate marketing was coming on Tuesday. He wanted to tour the area and see a presentation by the steering team (a core group of shopfloor associates who led the 5S+1 process). That afternoon, the steering team met to plan for the visit and decided to make a before-and-after video of a work area so that the VP could see how the method worked, step-by-step. The problem was there were no "before" work areas. The whole floor looked terrific—except for Charley's corner. And there was a reason for that.

Charley was a loner and one of the grumpiest guys in the company. He didn't seem to like anyone; he just kept to himself and did his work. His area was an eyesore in comparison to the rest of the center, particularly that rickety old table that fit (to a T, you had to admit) in between the coiler and the gauge stand (Exhibit 4-4). People had let Charley and his table alone because, as they had learned in the training, the implementation could proceed and even succeed without him. They left him alone until the idea of the video came up.

When Jim, a machinist and point person for the steering team, approached Charley that fateful Friday morning, the rest of the team held its breath and hung out on the edges. "Hey, Charley," Jim said brightly, "remember yesterday's announcement? That corporate VP is going to be here early next week and we'd really like to do a great before-and-after video for the presentation. How about your area being it? What d'ya say?"

Charley stopped his work, looked up between his bushy eyebrows, and said, "No." He went back to work. The rest of the team went into a huddle. Then Geraldine, who had started work the same day as Charley seventeen years ago, said, "Hey, Charley, be a sport. We want to show ourselves proud next week—and your area could stand a change, don't you think? How 'bout it?" "No," repeated Charley as if it were an echo.

"Hey, Charley," Gary put in, "you don't want us to look bad, do you? What d'ya say? Majority rules?" Charley hesitated only a second and then repeated, "No."

"Well, then, I guess that's that," said Jim good-naturedly. "We aren't gonna force you, Charley. See you on Monday." The team spent the next few hours planning out a different presentation and went home at four o'clock along with everyone else—except for Geraldine, Henry, and Gary, who had a plan. They waited until Charley punched out; then they pulled out the video camera, took footage of his area in its dreadful "before" condition, and began to make magic. Four hours later, visual order ruled—and in the process, Charley's table went into the dumpster along with lots of other junk. In its place was a bright shiny metal table, with side racks and three drawers. It didn't fit quite as well as the old one, but it was close. Pleased as punch, the three team members went home, excited about the surprise that was waiting for Charley and the great videotape they would be able to show the guy from corporate.

On Monday, Jim made his way to the machine shop, passing Charley's area on the way. When he saw its new look, he was sure Charley had relented; and Jim worried a little that the pressure had finally gotten to the man. Then he saw Charley raving at the top of his lungs to Jim's boss. The day just kept getting worse from there—for everyone.

Lessons Learned From Charley

Charley's story is true, and it is not uncommon. What looked like a victory for the team turned into a setback. The workforce of Charley's company had been thoroughly trained in the 5S+1 technology. Although they were still in the applications cycle, they knew the process *and the values* for achieving a visual workplace. They just hadn't experienced them for themselves, so they tested out the model and made a mistake. They were on the verge of some new learning.

Charley never did get on board with visual order. Not that anyone really expected him to, but this was different. He opted entirely out of the system, even more than before. Charley kept his eyes down, and stayed on the edges where it was safe. But he was not alone. Others had been watching, others in the machining department and in other areas of the company. They saw what happened or heard about it, and they began to keep their eyes down, too, and stay on the edges where it was safe. People began to feel cautious and tense. S1 was becoming a battleground.

What happened to Charley had a harmful effect on the implementation at that company. The junk was taken away but, instead of feeling goodwill and satisfaction, the shop floor became divided over the incident. The very initiative that was supposed to bring the people together was tearing them apart.

Self-Driven Improvement

Visual order is a pull system. It is a self-driven model. The *self* referred to here is the same as found in the definition of a visual workplace: *self*-explaining, *self*-ordering, *self*-regulating, and *self*-improving. It begins with the *self* of the individual employee.

Letting people keep what is to them their cherished things will not ruin the visual order initiative. It will not even slow it down. On the contrary, it may well accelerate the rate because those who might normally work against the momentum, might even be on board—or at least on the sidelines.

Visual order can ignite a kind of missionary zeal in some of us. Managers, who sometimes tire of process-oriented improvement, hear about 5S + 1 and declare a war on junk, kamikaze style. "Get rid of everything in the area that even *looks like* clutter," they say. The area gets emptied fast. Scenes similar to Charley's story get played out in companies all over the world every day. And many times, the learning that comes out of them is limited, mostly due to a lack of understanding. In many cases, people walk away from the episode permanently angry at "Charley," self-righteous in their belief that they did the right thing, and stuck on the bumpy road to a contentious and adversarial implementation.

All in Good Time

The my-way-or-the-highway approach will not build the kind of participation you need for achieving a visual workplace. S1 is not the *end* of a process. It is the first step of a long journey. As we learn in the next chapters, deciding what to keep and what to toss is very much the beginning. In S2/Scrub the Workplace, we learn that if we keep it, we clean it. That is, if we want to hold on to a cherished thing (or things) that ignorant people may call junk, we will be obliged within the guidelines of the second principle of visual order to clean it up and make it proper. And then in S3, we are called on to make it safe; in S4, to find a home for it; and in S5, to give it an ID label and address. So, there is no harm in keeping it. The process will either move a thing out the door or up the ladder of visual order.

The work of S1 is—and should be—open to all. It can become a proving ground for the tasks that come after. Fail in S1 and the implementation could develop a limp that will always encumber it. Succeed in S1 and the implementation will gather momentum and become a channel for developing people and opening their spirits. And the benefits go straight to the bottom line.

One: The Big Picture		
1. Toward a Visual Workplace	2. Visual Systems in Context	3. The Five Start-Up Requirements
Two: 5S Method		
4. S1/Sort Through and Sort Out	5. S2–S4/ Scrub, Secure Safety, and Select Locations	6. S5/Set Locations: Borders
7. S5/Set Locations: Addresses	8. 5S Stories From the Shop Floor	9. 5S+1 and White-Collar Applications
Three: +1 Method		
10. People: What to Expect	11. +1: Building and Sustaining the 5S Habit	12. +1: Leading by Example	13. +1: Leading Through Standards
Four: Go!		
14. Showcase, Scope, and the System	15. Training and Education	16. The Hundredth Monkey

Chapter 5

S2 Through S4/Scrub, Secure Safety, and Select Locations

In this chapter, learning about 5S+1 continues, with the focus on the next three practices of visual order:

1. S2/Scrub the workplace.
2. S3/Secure safety.
3. S4/Select locations.

S2/Scrub the Workplace

Now that only the essential items remain in the workplace (*essential* as defined by each individual, not by group consensus), it is time to do a basic scrub and bring every item to a standard level of cleanliness. In S2, we clean. First, we clean all surfaces: workbenches, shelf and cabinet tops, lids, floor, steps, walls, and the outside of equipment. Then we clean the interiors: inside cabinets, shelves, drawers, closed boxes, the inside of machinery. When we do this on a regular basis, we come to understand that cleaning has broad implications for the bottom line.

Cleaning and the Bottom Line

Cleaning as Inspection

When cleaning is a part of every workday, we are obliged to take a closer look at tools and machinery. Routine cleaning helps us notice those all-important prefailure conditions that are missed when we wait to clean until something is dirty enough. Prefailure conditions are slight irregularities that, if noticed, give warning of a worsening condition. During the daily wipe-down of a CNC machine, for example, we smell something suspicious and call maintenance to check it out. Wiping down the press at the end of the day, we notice an oil drop that was not there yesterday—and we remember the motor burnout that shut down the line last month. Wasn't there some oil leakage in the weeks before that burnout? Hard to say . . . the machine was too grimy to tell. When cleaning is *not* a daily habit, such details escape our notice and become costly oversights. We miss the vital messages that the workplace sends us in its effort to assist.

New car and truck owners understand cleaning as inspection. When you are cleaning your new car, nothing escapes your searching eye, hand, and nose. The nicks, abrasions, and nearly invisible dents are all too evident. And you mourn every one of them.

This is precisely the dynamic that can occur when cleaning the workplace is a daily practice. The first time we do it simply shows us the level of accumulated neglect. With regular attention, however, we discover ways to maintain the item so less cleaning is required. When effectively implemented, S2 brings about an evolution in awareness and the benefit goes straight to the bottom line.

Cleaning for Throughput

You can expect the resistance to cleaning to range from strong to intense when you begin your S2 efforts. Hold on: This refers to the resistance *in you* as well as in your colleagues and managers.

Few people genuinely understand the incredible toll that a dirty work environment takes on employee morale—their own and that of others. Fewer still appreciate the measurable and negative impact dirt and grime have on the production process—on equipment utilization, product quality, yield, and overall manufacturing throughput. If we did, we would run, not walk, to the nearest broom, rag, and bucket and begin to scrub.

In the following discussion on chips, keep an eye on the bottom line. Take S2 for what it is: *cleaning for throughput.*

Chips

Chips (metal shavings) are an inevitable consequence of the machining process—and the curse of many a plant floor. They get everywhere and can create unsafe conditions that many shops tolerate as normal. One screw machine facility in upper New York State generates 35,000 pounds of chips a day on just one of its many products. While this company's underground removal system handles the vast majority of these chips, a single chip that escapes the process can—and does—cause equipment problems practically every day. For example, a single metal chip that strays into the one-inch area between the two plates of a proximity switch can shut production down as completely as a broken coil or worn tooling.

"Chips happen!" conventional thinkers insist. "If you want to remove metal from metal, you're gonna get mountains of chips and lots of stray chips getting into everything." But is this really inevitable? S2/Scrub the Workplace is intended to probe so-called conventional thinking and put our collective feet to the fire, with the emphasis on prevention, not coping.

Photo 5-1 shows an accumulation of chips around a milling machine that had to be swept up hourly to keep access to it clear. During S2, this repeated sweeping triggered an intense interest in chip containment. Area associates asked, "How can we contain chips closer to their source in the first place?"

5-1. Chips Everywhere.

Chips can be so much a part of a work area that associates will sometimes say, "We're in the chip-making business." The chips you see here flew 25/30 feet from the machine and had to be cleared at 45-minute intervals, or else operators could not get to their work.

5-2. Chip Prevention.

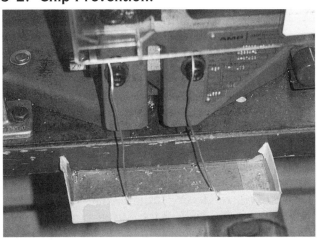

Here is the beginning of another chip-prevention device, this time on a small clipping machine in a wiring area. After the idea is fully tested, a permanent guard will be made and installed.

At first, they thought of putting a screen around the machine to keep the chips from flying out so far. But a closer look at the problem revealed a strange-looking device on the cutting wheel: a black rubber collar with a "thing" hanging from it (see Exhibit 5-1). Further detective work revealed that the thing was a rubber finger, one of a dozen that once encircled the collar and forced chips to fall straight down and not to fly off in all directions (Exhibit 5-2). When the broken collar was replaced with a new one, the chip problem came under control and only periodic sweeping was required. A big difference. Photo 5-2 shows you the beginnings of chip containment on a wire-cutting machine. Same principle, smaller version.

Exhibit 5-1. Mystery Device.

When associates began to look for ways to prevent chips from flying so far, they found this rubber collar with one rubber finger. "What's that for?" they asked.

Exhibit 5-2. Function Fully Restored.

They discovered that the collar once had a full circle of rubber fingers, specifically designed to make chips drop straight down, not out. Over time, the fingers broke off and no one remembered their original function. The new rubber collar cost $35, and chip containment became a breeze.

Cleaning as Ownership

CLEAN UP AFTER YOURSELF! I AIN'T YOUR MOTHER!
—Handwritten sign on a cutting-room wall

Investing personal effort and time in cleaning the items of our work—equipment, tools, racks, shelving, furniture, and floors—increases our value for them and for ourselves. Over time, we take responsibility for the level of cleanliness in our area and for sustaining it. When we engage in regular, routine cleaning, we come to understand *cleaning as ownership* and are filled with pride at the results.

You will read very little in this book about "discipline," even though 100 percent adherence to standards is the end-goal of the visual workplace. For many of us, discipline is too closely associated with obedience and punishment, a carryover from earlier days when bosses saw themselves as parent substitutes and their employees as so many children. As proven every day by the success of empowered teams, these terms and the concepts they describe are as out-of-date as they are ineffective.

Let's retire the word *discipline* from the business lexicon and use instead *building ownership*. Ownership is what happens when we engage in activities that make sense to us and speak to who we are on the inside. No one needs to persuade us or convince us to do these things. We do them willingly because they answer our own inner need for balance and order and our desire to be productive at work.

Operationalizing S2

Cleaning Supplies

If you want the workplace to be cleaned, you need to make cleaning supplies available. This may seem too obvious to mention, but far too many cleaning campaigns have faltered on this very simple point.

Basic S2 Supply List

- Broom
- Dustpan
- Hand brush
- Mop and bucket
- Bag of wiping rags
- Large trash bin

You can add to this list or get doubles and triples of each if your team is large, but these are the essentials. Cleaning supplies have a permanent role to play in visual order, and you will find a permanent addressed location for them in later 5S + 1 practices (S4/ Select Location and S5/Set Locations).

Exhibit 5-3. "Clean" Options.

Messy End	In Between	Clean End
Pigsty		Whistle-clean
Hell hole		White-glove clean
Filthy		Perfection
Disgusting		Heavenly
Revolting		Disneyland
Locker room		Over the top
Bordello		Mom's kitchen
Junkyard		You can eat off it
Dump		Spotless
Disaster		

What Does Clean *Mean?*

Before you get too far into S2, find out what *clean* means to you and your associates.

One way to do this is to develop a "clean scale." First, draw a line across a sheet of paper, flipchart, or white board and box in two columns at either end (Exhibit 5-3). Then ask people to describe both ends of the clean continuum in their own words: What does *really clean* mean to you? And what does *really not clean* mean to you? You are looking for a lot of different words for these concepts. On the positive end, for example, someone might start off with *whistle-clean.* At the other end of the spectrum, the word may be *pigsty.* Put each one of these into their rightful column, and leave plenty of space in between. Now start collecting other ideas. Have fun with this. Use it as another opportunity to build the spirit of the workplace.

Exhibit 5-3 reproduces the results of one brainstorming session. You and your team can fill in the space between the two columns with words or phrases that describe the levels of clean between one end and the other.

Exhibit 5-4 is the scale that one team came up with to get them launched. Everyone knew what the scale meant, and the intervals or levels were general enough for people to relate to without taking offense. It was revised within two weeks, but, in the meantime, the cleaning had gotten off the ground and everybody had a good feeling.

Exhibit 5-4. Sample "Clean" Scale.

What Clean Means (bottom is lowest)
   White-glove clean
↑ Clean enough for my mother
↑ Clean enough for my father
↑ Clean enough for my wife/husband
↑ Clean enough for me

Staying Flexible

One of the things you are likely to discover is that *not* everyone agrees with what clean should look like. This is perfectly natural and not a problem. So bear the following two things in mind.

1. Cleaning is an incremental process. Like all systematic improvement activities, a clean work area happens bit by bit. The goal gets reached by consistently applying the same principles and undertaking the same tasks over and over and over again.

Keep your eye on the progress you actually make today and this week, instead of the towering gain that might be achieved in six months. Focus on practical, doable, measurable progress so you and your associates have plenty of reason to celebrate along the way. And be sure to do that: Celebrate plenty along the way. You may make some big gains at the outset, but it is sure and steady that wins the race. And be ready to revise your clean scales often. Make them more lenient or more strict, depending on real-time cleaning progress.

2. It is important to clarify what is doable for your area. There is a huge difference in the meaning of *clean* in a semiconductor plant and *clean* in a stamping factory. Consider the current state of the workplace and calibrate from there. If there is a ten-year buildup of chips, coolant, oil, and grime, can you reasonably hope to achieve white-glove clean by the end of the month? Maybe all you can do is degrease machine surfaces and install some preliminary chip guards. Base the levels of your scale on what is realistic *for your area*. Schedule deep cleaning and machine painting after the first cycle is completed. Exhibit 5-5 is a sample for a machining area.

Measuring and Driving Improvement

The scale in Exhibit 5-5 is very specific to that individual work area. Like any good measurement device, this scale does not just assess the progress; it indicates the direction

Exhibit 5-5. What *Clean* Means in Machining.

What Clean Means—Machine Shop (bottom is lowest)

    Ready for paint!!!!
↑ Zero grease! Zero grime! Zero chips!
↑ Zero grease! Zero grime! Some chips remain.
↑ Zero grease! Some grime, and chips remain.
↑ Greasy, grimy, slippery, and covered in chips.

---

in which progress lies. When you and your associates achieve the top of the scale, consider revising the scale and launching a next round of deeper cleaning. And when cleanliness in the area reaches an acceptable level, let that level become standard, and turn your clean scale into an improvement maintenance device. Use it to maintain the standard level.

Another way to measure and drive improvement is to use a number scale. The six-point improvement scale shown in Exhibit 5-6 uses number values of zero through five.

Exhibit 5-6. Six-Point Scale.

0 = Zero Result	**1** = Slight Effort	**2** = Squeaks By	**3** = Satisfactory Results	**4** = Above-Average Results	**5** = Outstanding Results

Almost any scale can be used for improvement breakthrough or improvement maintenance. The important thing is for you and your associates to know where you are in the process. As you will discover in Chapter 11, scales can be combined with checklists as part of building the 5S + 1 habit.

☆ ☆ ☆ ☆ ☆

By now, a number of people are involved in the 5S + 1 process. A lot of red-tagging, cleaning, and scrubbing is going on. Management is wisely supporting the activity by providing teams with slots of improvement time and a budget per area ($50 to $100 is usual) to make it easy for associates to purchase the supplies they need to keep the momentum building—tags, brooms, soaps, and other cleanup items. All a team does to replenish its budget is hand in a bag of receipts. The place is hopping.

Managers are in the process of considering big-ticket improvement items. A plan for a new lighting system may be on the drawing board, for example, or machine degreasing, or a new paint job for the ceiling. People are beginning to see results. Slowly and surely, the first glimmers of visual order are becoming noticeable.

S2 and Painting

Once grease and grime levels are reduced through deep cleaning, you are ready to paint and seal the surfaces.

Photos 5-3 and 5-4 are before-and-after shots of a workbench at United Electric Controls Company. The clutter has been cleared out (S1) and the bench area has been freshly painted (S2). It is amazing what a fresh coat of paint can do. Fresh paint (especially white)

5-3. A Workbench Before Visual Order.

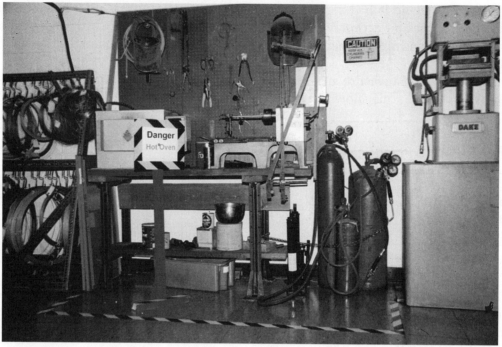

A workbench at UE before S1 and S2 were implemented. Notice the clutter and lack of uniformity.

brings in more light which, in turn, can have a significant positive impact on work patterns and productivity levels.[1]

Photo 5-5 shows Cynthia Matroni, leader of the visual workplace steering team at Hamilton Standard's Blade Company in Windsor Locks, Conn. Cynthia volunteered to paint the floor in her work area after she and her associates had thoroughly cleaned it. She wanted it done quickly and she wanted to do it herself. Stanley Mickens, Blade Company manager, lent his support to the implementation by getting a bank of foam machines painted during the same period (Photo 5-6).

An S2 Painting Example

A 5S + 1 team at Curtis Screw Company (a high-volume screw machine manufacturer in Buffalo, New York) got more than expected when associates asked manufacturing manager Carl Falletta to get the ceiling painted in the machining bay where S2 was under way.

1. For excellent insight into the impact of light and illumination on productivity, read the following two books on the so-called "Hawthorne Studies" conducted in a Western Electric facility in Hawthorne, Illinois, between 1927 and 1933: (1) Elton Mayo, *Human Problems of an Industrial Civilization* (New York: MacMillan, 1933); and (2) F. J. Roethlisberger and W. J. Dickson, *Management and the Worker* (Cambridge, Mass.: Harvard University Press, 1966).

5-4. The Same Workbench After Visual Order.

The clutter is gone and only the essentials remain, located in a bright, white, freshly painted area.

Carl said yes and stepped back to S1 on his way to S2. He had to because the ceiling was a rat's nest of pipes, airlines, conduits, and electrical wiring. As Carl put it, "We looked up at the ceiling and couldn't tell the difference between a live wire and a dead one. For starters, safety was an issue." By the time S1 was complete on this ceiling, three dozen lighting fixtures dating back to 1906 were removed, along with 20,000 linear feet of compressed-air lines that led nowhere (35% of the bay's total air line footage). Next the ceiling was given a fresh coat of white paint. Then all remaining lines, pipes, and conduits were placed at right angles to each other and painted bright red or blue to make them easy to trace.

The bill for this work came in at $10,000.

Was it worth it? Let's ask Carl:

"Those dollars were paid back three times over by the savings from our reduced usage of compressed air alone. Think of it. Each of our four machine bays in this plant has an air compressor, plus backups, at a purchase price of $50,000 to $60,000 each. Running them is also big bucks and a major part of our utility bill. With what we learned on this first round, we anticipate a 50 percent reduction in total compressed-air usage when we do the ceilings in the other three bays. The funny thing is that just before 5S + 1, we paid a top-flight engineering firm to do a compressed-air audit. They told us to reduce our system usage!

5-5. Setting an Example.

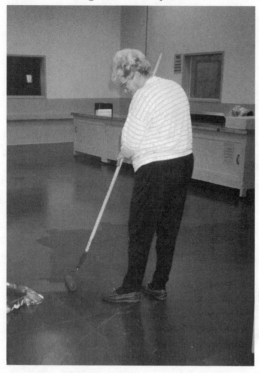

Cynthia Matroni, member of the VW steering team at Hamilton Standard, did not hesitate to set a positive example of what it takes for 5S + 1 success. She painted the floor herself, after she and her associates had cleared the area of clutter and scrubbed it down.

5-6. Fresh Paint!

Stanley Mickens, Cynthia's boss, gave the 5S + 1 implementation his enthusiastic support, as evidenced by the machine painting he approved in the early stages of the process.

That's just what we did—only not the way they thought we would. We did it through visual order."

The remarkable change on the ceiling gave an equally remarkable lift to production and ongoing improvement on the shop floor. It lets everyone know for certain that senior management supported 5S + 1—100 percent.

S2 and Equipment Maintenance

In many companies, equipment maintenance is so intimately connected to S2 cleanup issues that the two cannot be separated.

Especially in stamping plants and other settings that depend on heavy machinery, S2 helps everyone realize the destructive impact that dirt and grime can have on overall equipment effectiveness and manufacturing lead times. In such factories, it is not unusual for dirt and grime to get so thick that temperature, level, and pressure gauges are unreadable and just getting to gauge and lubrication points is the first challenge. Machine surfaces become so coated with grime that few associates would think of touching them, let alone take on the task of cleaning them. When dirt and grime reach these levels, it is no wonder that the parts produced by these machines also get contaminated.

Many companies have ongoing preventive and autonomous maintenance activities that address many S2 equipment concerns. Autonomous maintenance (AM) builds a partnership between the maintenance function and production by involving operators in the more routine tasks of equipment upkeep, such as daily wipe-downs, surface lubrication, and bolt tightening. AM is part of a larger and impressively effective maintenance approach called TPM (total productive maintenance). Use S2 with these other machine-support efforts and bring more sets of eyes and hands to the challenge of maximum equipment availability. (See Chapter 7 for more on equipment and visual order.)

S2 and Ventilation

No S2 discussion would be complete without a strong mention of the need for clean air in the workplace. For example, visit TS Trim Industries in Canal Winchester, Ohio, a Honda supplier specializing in interior trim and roof linings. You'll see potted plants throughout the facility. These are not plastic imitations. They are living, breathing organisms that depend on clean air for life. And that's the point. Whatever the added pleasure of having green things in the workplace, these plants provide real-time feedback on the air quality in the facility. If the plants begin to wilt, humans take notice.

In many factories, clogged air ducts are an important issue, a key cause of dust emission in the work environment. Because of the precision work, specialized equipment, and cost involved, getting the ducts cleaned is a perfect S2 task for middle and senior managers to undertake. As we have seen at Hamilton Standard and Curtis Screw, management is typically eager to take on projects like these to demonstrate support for associates and their improvement efforts.

Certain companies take the opportunity of S2 and the ventilation issue to get rid of drafty window (and door) systems that make utility bills soar in the summer and winter. If this also makes sense to you, consider glass blocks (transparent or translucent) as an inexpensive alternative to costly insulated window systems. Though glass-block units cannot themselves be opened and shut, you can install vent panels within the glass block array for increased circulation.

S3/Secure Safety

The safety impact of the first two principles of visual order is obvious to even the casual observer. Clearing out the clutter in S1 automatically eliminates many basic safety hazards. Removing grime from the floor in S2 can put an end to slipping. Even associates not actively involved in 5S+1 will appreciate these changes, not to mention your corporate insurance broker who typically uses the degree of clutter on the shop floor as an unofficial indicator of a company's entire safety effort. Implementing these first two steps makes it possible to see other less apparent risk conditions, preparing the way for S3.

S3/Secure Safety puts safety gains through visual order at the center of attention. Like air for breathing, safety is a workplace essential.

Be clear from the outset, however, that S3 is not a means of achieving 100 percent safety in your company. That is the charge of your safety officer and safety committee. S3 is there to assist by focusing awareness on a safer work environment as part of the visual order process in your work area. S3 puts the emphasis on safety gains through visual order.

For example, S3 prompts you and your colleagues to notice the hot solder iron on the workbench you just cleared and painted in S1 and S2. Its electrical cord is dangling dangerously above the cabinet doors where the cleaning supplies are stored. You see in a flash how easy it would be for someone to reach to open the cabinet doors and catch the end of the cord instead, bringing the hot iron down with burning surprise. S3 awareness will guide you to improve that one small placement—and move safety in your work area another step forward.

This same awareness will help you notice missing press guards, and motivate your team to redouble chip prevention efforts. OSHA and ANSI regulations take on new meaning as you and your group get the uprights in your area padded in order to prevent injuries from bumping into them. S3 can also be a major driver for environmental safety and the handling of hazardous waste. (Later, in S4 and S5, you will find ways to visually share safety location information and make sure the right waste gets into the right bin, and heavy lifting gets minimized through smart placement.)

S3 is a giant step toward a proactive, shopfloor-powered safety process. It begins with identifying and eliminating actual hazard conditions, and then searching out and preventing potential ones.

S3: Your Safety Infrastructure

Make no bones about it: Improved workplace safety requires high levels of technical expertise and resources. A distinct safety function is always needed. S3 is not enough.

Your company may already have a separate safety committee in place. Great! If so, consider linking it to your S3 activities. Send one or two steering team members to sit in on regular safety meetings so they can promote the visual order perspective. Another option is to invite management to head the S3 safety effort. Up until S3, management plays a supportive but behind-the scenes role in 5S + 1. S3 is a chance to get management more involved and let off some of the heat that gets ignited when highly skilled, action-oriented managers are asked to stand to the side and let shopfloor associates "lead" the 5S + 1 implementation.

A Recent Implementation

Sam, the plant manager of a small and successful metalworks facility, showed signs of frustration that he and his management staff were closed out of the lively 5S + 1 process that was taking place on the shop floor. At least that was his perception. While it was true that these teams were working strongly and well without him, Sam's input was still welcomed and needed. When he took on the leadership of the newly formed S3 Safety Team, his discomfort disappeared and he put his considerable skills to good use, without getting in the way of 5S + 1 shopfloor teams. The implementation benefited everyone as commitment and ownership were shared. However you work it out, remember that associates and managers together can make your workplace safer.

S4/Select Locations

To this point, we have identified essential workplace items and brought them up to standard levels of cleanliness and safety. Now we must find a home for them. In S4/ Select Locations, we determine where the items are best placed in the actual work environment. We call this **smart placement.**

Smart placement means aligning shopfloor items with the physical flow of work in order to accelerate that flow. This process begins by understanding how work flows right now. Based on that, you find ways to improve the flow. In S4, you don't actually change anything; it is a thinking and planning step. Figure out the smart placement for all workplace items; they will be physically moved in S5/Set Locations. Do not undervalue S4 just because no visible change results. It is an invisible but indispensable step in achieving visible order.

S4 is comparable to the thinking that goes on when you move to a new home or apartment. You need to spend some time figuring out *where things go*—where they are best placed relative to the other items in the area to maximize flow and function.

Imagine that you and your spouse have just moved into a new house. You are both avid football fans, so Sunday afternoon holds special meaning. That is why the placement of your couch, easy chairs, and television has got to be smart. But it doesn't end there. The functional flow between those items (couch, chairs, and TV) exists in association with another item: the refrigerator. The placement of all these items is based on the flow of function between them. This is exactly the intent when you apply S4 in your work area. Find the location that best expresses the functional flow between all the items in your work area.

Move through S4/Select Locations thoughtfully. It is a critical step, one that puts in place the concepts that you will operationalize in S5/Set Locations.

Operationalizing S4: The Maps

The process of selecting locations is supported by the use of two maps, the What-Is Map and the Could-Be Map. Both are simple floor diagrams of your work area that clarify the relationship between location, flow, and function. We will look at each map in detail.

The What-Is Map

Start with a big white sheet of paper. With a dark marker, outline the geography of your work area on it, exactly as it is now. Use solid lines to indicate permanent walls and other structural features. Use dashed lines to indicate partitions and walls that are movable. Mark off entrances, windows, and such areas as built-in closets. If there are doors, use a dashed line to show which way they open and how far they swing.

Next, write the name of each workplace item on a sticky note. Use different colors to differentiate between easy-to-move items (cabinets, carts, wastebaskets, and containers) and hard-to-move items (too heavy or bolted to the floor). Include anything that takes up space directly on the floor—CNC machine, die crib, workbench, parts racks, supply cabinet, chair, desk, bubble-wrap stand, stacks of WIP—anything with a footprint. (If you haven't already done so, standardize the names of things. Is it a workstation or a workbench? A tool or a fixture? A rack or shelving? These are simple decisions that can make it that much easier to focus on the real work.)

Show the relative size of these items by cutting the notes in proportion, or, for large items, using several notes to indicate relative size. Remember, S4 is about flow *and* relationship. If you work on a bench that is 20 × 3 feet, you may need five or six sticky notes to show the size of this table relative to the parts rack next to it, which may need only one note to suggest its size.

Make sure you make a separate note for each and every floor item in your area, each item that has a **footprint**. If you are working on this anywhere other than in the work area you are mapping, don't rely on memory to recall all the items. Go out on the floor and check.

One team did their mapping in a nearby conference room. When they thought they were done, they went out to check and got a surprise. Even though they worked in the area every day, the team had overlooked the following: one forklift, two gurneys, three ladders, one mammoth roll of bubble wrap, two trash bins, one scheduling board, and two stashes of WIP.

When you are sure you have made a complete set of sticky notes, make a second set, identical to the first. Set these aside; they will be used later in the second map.

Now put each sticky note on the white paper within the boundaries of your work area *exactly* as each item is located right now.

Next trace out the flow of work, information, and material as it actually occurs between these items. Map out the flow. In your mind's eye, walk through the sequence as work gets done in your area. Trace this out with red string, yarn, or self-stick arrows, or just draw it with a pencil or red pen.

5-7. The What-Is Map.

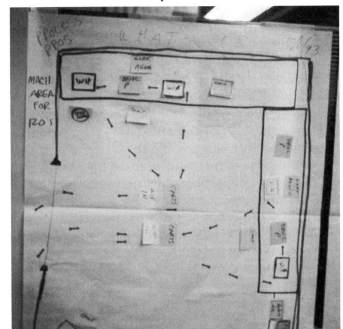

The What-Is Map captures the work area as it is, providing a baseline for change. Notice the arrows that show the direction and complexity of the flow.

Ask these questions: Where does the work enter the area? Where does it go next? And next? And next? Track the physical pattern that a work unit follows as it moves in and through your work area, step by step. Track it until it actually leaves your area completely.

When you are finished, your sheet of paper may look very much like a plate of spaghetti. This is your What-Is Map, and it serves as a snapshot of your current work pattern (Photo 5-7). Look at it, and you may see why the work does not flow very fast in your area.

Post the What-Is Map so everyone has a chance to consider it and perhaps suggest some changes. Expect adjustments if anyone in your area did not have a hand in creating the map. Welcome them. They are another indication that the 5S + 1 process is working.

The Could-Be Map

Now it is time to make the second map, the Could-Be Map. Start with a clean sheet of paper, the same size as before, and again draw in your work area boundaries. You and your co-workers will use this blank paper as the proving ground for a new and improved arrangement for workplace items. Take out your second set of sticky notes and arrange them on your new map so that they allow the best possible flow. Think about the floor layout in a new way. Be radical. Your guideline is: Water flows downhill.

Pulled by gravity alone, water runs an easy and efficient course. If rocks or trees get in its way (similar to the items in your work area), water will flow around them. This adds to its run time—which is not a concern in nature but which is the crux of the issue in the workplace. So, as you map, think about getting the rocks and trees out of the way. Locate them so that the flow is unblocked and can accelerate.

Ask yourself: How could area items be placed in better relationship to the flow so that the work moves more quickly through the area? Where might things be better placed? What are some possible new locations for items within the area?

The items you are relocating are identical to the ones on the What-Is Map. You have the same number of items and the same number of sticky notes. You are simply finding the best placement for them: locations that accelerate the flow of work instead of obstructing it. Do not get rid of any item during S4 unless it is removed with everyone's whole-hearted agreement (Charley's table still stays). And remember: S4 is a paper-only step. You do not get to actually move things until S5/Set Locations. S4 is a thinking step.

When you are done with this paper placement, test your thinking by tracing the new flow with arrows or red string. See if the flow is visibly improved. Make adjustments as you see new opportunities. Photo 5-8 is an example of a Could-Be Map.

5-8. The Could-Be Map.

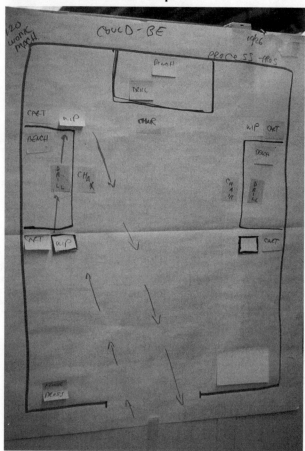

The Could-Be Map shows an improved physical layout and reduced motion based on the ideas of the associates who work there. Arrows show that the proposed plan can simplify the flow.

Implications of Selecting Locations to Reduce Motion

Some industries pay a higher price for motion than others. In semiconductor manufacturing, for example, any amount of motion can stop work entirely, if only for a few seconds. That is because many of the value-adding elements in the process take place under a microscope. Imagine this yourself. You are looking intently into the eyepiece of a microscope, bonding a lead onto a substrate. Anything that distracts you from that focus costs the process. Any interruption, any need to look up (even to pick up a pair of tweezers) takes your attention away from your value-adding work. To get back, you have to look through the eyepiece again, reorient your focus, and only then can you continue your work.

Motion takes different forms in different industries—reaching instead of walking, looking up instead of searching—but it is all still moving without adding value. The first step is to notice it and give it its correct name: Motion, moving without working. Then you can look for ways to eliminate it.

Exhibit 5-7 summarizes the S4 mapping procedure.

Fine-Tuning the S4 Process

S4 Mapping is a powerful process for appreciating and applying the principles of flow. Here are some tips:

1. This is a repeat because it is that important: *If you choose to develop the What-Is Map on your own or with a small core group of associates, make sure people know what you are doing and why.* When you are done, post the map so everyone in the area gets a chance to check out your thinking. Be prepared to explain your reasons for the new layout to your associates. And don't be surprised if they do not agree with you. Be prepared to modify the map in response.

2. *Get as many associates as possible involved in developing the Could-Be Map.* It should not be the work of just a few people unless trust levels in the area are extraordinarily high. You are probing into long-standing patterns, traditions, and habits, and people can start to feel territorial very fast. Make it comfortable for people to play around with options in rearranging the area.

3. Another repeat: *Leave the two maps up for a preannounced period of time (twenty-four-hour minimum) before moving to S5/Set Locations.* People need time to consider and absorb the proposed changes. That's right: At this stage they are only proposals.

4. *Make sure you designate a specific location for every item in the work area.* No exceptions. Sooner or later, this will mean a designated location for personal items (lunches, purses, books, etc.). Should these items be kept under the bench? over the bench? in lockers? Where? As in previous 5S + 1 steps, some people will see any such effort as "messing with my stuff" and will not feel motivated to cooperate.

Here again, if there are objections against this degree of orderliness (which some people genuinely experience as intrusion), let it go for now. At the outset (for the first two to four months), you are building support for visual order. If one or several people object to a proposed idea, go with the changes they are comfortable in making. Set a

Exhibit 5-7. S4 Procedure, Step-by-Step.

What-Is Map	
	Working with other associates:
1	Take a big sheet of white paper and put the name of your work area and the words *What-Is Map* in a corner.
2	Leaving a 1–2 inch margin, mark off the boundaries and entry points of that area. Use a solid line for walls and other unmovable structures, and dashed lines for partitions.
3	Write the name of each item in your work area on a self-stick note. Distinguish between movable and unmovable (or difficult to move items) by using a different-color note or placing a border around it.
4	Double-check to make sure you have a separate note for each and every workplace item that has a floor footprint.
5	Make a second, identical set of these notes and set it aside.
6	Place each note from the first set on the paper exactly as each item is currently situated.
7	Trace the flow of work, information, and material as it actually flows in relationship to each item and through your area. Use red pencil, arrows, or string to show this.
8	Post this map where all area associates (all shifts) can see it, and ask for their input. Is it accurate? Is it complete? Make adjustments until you reach agreement. Your What-Is Map is now complete.

Could-Be Map	
	Working with other associates:
1	Take a new sheet of blank paper. Put the name of your area on it plus the words *Could-Be Map*. Leave a margin and draw out the boundaries either as they are or as they will be when improved.
2	Study the What-Is Map and imagine how items could be placed differently on the Could-Be Map to improve/accelerate the flow.
3	Take the second set of self-stick notes and post them according to your new ideas.
4	Show the new flow in red pencil, arrows, or string.
5	When you are done, post this map where it can be seen and reviewed by everyone. Be prepared for other changes as people consider and reconsider their thinking. Invite outsiders to express their opinions. Modify the map in response to this.
6	Leave both maps posted for *at least* twenty-four hours before moving or changing *anything*.

timeline for reviewing the other changes after the dust settles. Make "the first S is for Spirit" an operational priority in your area. People are likely to become more open to change as the other parts of the workplace shift into a higher level of order and responsiveness.

5. You may find some proposed changes won't fly. For example, moving those CNC machines may make perfect sense but you'll need time to organize that. So *keep track of the idea, but don't let it stand in the way of implementing other improvements right away.* In other words, don't let the good fall victim to the perfect.

Before we move on to some general guidelines about smart placement, let's look at how S4 principles can be applied to cell design.

Special S4 Application: Cell Design and the Paper-Doll Layout

Cell Design

In case you are new to the concept, cellular manufacturing combines the value-adding activity of people and machines in a single operational sequence that puts the start of the process as close as possible to the end of the process (U-shaped). The ultimate goal of cell design is one-piece flow (manufacturing a single unit in an unbroken flow of work) versus the old way (a series of operations, isolated in function, time, and space). Instead of sending a housing unit to four different locations to be stamped, formed, drilled, and finished, you send it to a single location. As a result, a huge amount of time (motion) is saved and travel distance for people and material is cut to the bone. For this reason, the design or floor layout of a cell is critical to its success.

The general guidelines for cell design are nearly identical to the S4 principles of selecting the correct location for workplace items based on functional relationship and accelerated flow. Cell design is smart placement on a large scale. That Could-Be proposal to move the CNC machines that was rejected in S4 is accepted in cell design. And the paper-doll layout you are about to learn is the bridge.

Paper-Doll Layout

Even with the best Could-Be Maps, teams can get unpleasant surprises when they begin to implement a new layout. The **paper-doll layout** keeps these surprises to a minimum. Here is exactly how it is done.

1. Create a Could-Be Map as described earlier, using paper and sticky notes.

2. Gather the exact dimensions of the cell under design and the footprint of each workplace item that will be in it.

3. Find a large empty space—an empty section of the warehouse, for example, or an unused portion of the parking lot (weather permitting).

4. In that space, mark out an area in the exact dimensions of the cell under design. You can use tape, chalk line, or string to do this.

5. Cut out a piece of cardboard for each item you plan to locate in that space. Make sure the dimensions are exact.

6. Lay down the cardboard footprints (cutouts) exactly as shown on your Could-Be Map.

7. Check the layout. Walk through the paper-doll cell as it is now laid out. Test the flow of work against it. Were your computations correct? Is there enough space between machines? Is there excess space? Can an operator/operators work comfortably and efficiently within the space as it is laid out? Have you left enough room for point-of-use storage, racks, and shelving? For material handling? For walkways? Adjust the cardboard design as needed and record any changes on the Could-Be Map.

When the paper-doll layout corresponds exactly to what you want in the actual cell, you are ready to implement the design, with full confidence.

This paper-doll layout technique really works. In one company, for example, a shop-floor team thought they would need from 4,725 square feet for a cell. As a result of what they discovered in their paper-doll test, they reduced the cell to 1,100 square feet. That was a space savings of nearly 75 percent. Travel distance shrank from 890 to 140 linear feet, an 85 percent decrease.

You may find you change things half a dozen times in the process of your paper-doll layout. Clearly, it is better to do that on paper than to find mistakes after the machine has been moved and bolted in place. That kind of mistake need happen only once for you to swear to never set up a cell again without first doing a paper-doll layout.

Although S4/Select Locations is *not* designed to convert work areas to cells or cellular manufacturing, S4 is an excellent tool for introducing shopfloor associates to the principles of flow, long before the company may be ready to convert to cells. By the time that does happen, associates are with the program and can support the full change with greater understanding and enthusiasm.

Smart Placement Tips

Here are three things to bear in mind as you develop smart placement in your area.

1. *Make sure there is nothing directly on the floor.* This rule of thumb applies primarily to raw material, work pieces, and parts. Do not plan to place any of these directly on the floor. For maximum flexibility, consider putting all production floor items on wheels.

2. *Locate at point-of-use.* When identifying the best location, let *point-of-use* be your guide. Position the workplace items as follows:

- As close as possible to the actual location of their use.
- Within easy reach so that arms, and not legs, are used for getting and reaching.
- Facing you, in the order of use, so you don't have to change hands, and so you can put them away with one hand.
- So you have enough room to move and maneuver.

The above applies to many workplace items, especially hand tools. When tools are arranged in a precise order at point-of-use, operators soon memorize that placement and are able to take and return tools to their exact locations without looking. Like the surgeon's assistant in an operating room, they know the arrangement thoroughly. Consider tool belts and auto-return (just let go) cords to make smart replacement even easier.

3. *Locate precision items carefully.* Metal touching metal makes for a dull edge. Leave enough room around precision cutting tools to keep them from touching anything. The same with gauges. Consider the use of felt, foam, cut-outs, or ridged insets to deal with this.

Three Smart Placement Options for Inventory

Haphazard, jumbled piles of inventory are a major shopfloor stumbling block. Literally. Besides being inefficient, those piles of stock can be dangerous. Here are three smart placement options for stocking and stacking raw material and parts inventory: LIFO, FIFO, and stocking by code. As you will see, these are simple, logical procedures. However, a stocking/stacking approach is meaningless unless it is selected in advance—and everyone understands it. In many plants, this is not done. Instead the way things are stocked and stacked depends entirely on who is doing the handling at the time. There is no accepted approach. This is not too much of a problem when things get put away, but it becomes a nightmare when it's time to retrieve them. For starters, one often does not know where to begin to look.

The short of it is: Putting/picking and storing/retrieval are two sides of the same coin. As you are about to read, random stacking and stocking not only add considerably to overall lead time but also directly create defects, especially when freshness is at issue.

1. **LIFO** stands for "last in, first out" and refers to the simple procedure of stocking items from the bottom up and taking them from the top down (see Exhibit 5-8).

2. **FIFO** stands for "first in, first out" and refers to a placement approach that ensures that items are used in a specific order or chronology. FIFO is particularly important with dated material, when freshness is a stocking/retrieval issue. FIFO is important, for example, in preventing age-related deterioration of inventory by ensuring that what arrives first gets used first. Photo 5-9 shows a common FIFO mechanism: gravity-feed shelving that is stocked from the back and picked from the front.

3. **Stocking by code** means using a code, instead of the full name of an item, when stocking and retrieving it. Generally, you have three choices when stocking by code: (a) by function, (b) by product, or (c) by customer.

    a. *Stocking by function.* When you stock by function, you are grouping inventory together based on part type. Housings get stocked with housings, fasteners with fasteners, coils with coils, springs with springs, motors with motors, printed circuit boards with printed circuit boards, and so on. Generally speaking, stocking by function is a sound choice for mid- and high-volume production facilities.

    b. *Stocking by product.* Sometimes called *marshaling* or *kitting*, this stocking approach organizes inventory according to bills of material. That is, the part

Exhibit 5-8. LIFO.

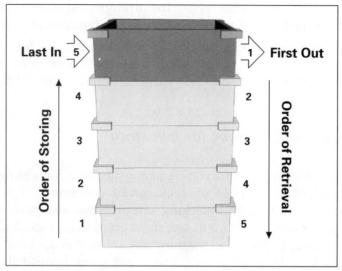

Last in/first out (LIFO) is one way to safely and systematically stock and retreive material. This figure shows you how to put it and how to pick it.

5-9. FIFO: Gravity Feed.

First in/first out (FIFO) is primarily used when order and/or freshness is an issue. The photo shows an easy way to do this: Stock from the back and let gravity be your ally for picking.

numbers required for a given product are placed in the same location. While some extra time to organize is required up front, the process of putting/picking parts can be quite efficient. Stocking by product is a popular approach in assembly plants.

c. *Stocking by customer.* In this approach, inventory is organized by customer. A supplier of automotive interiors, for example, divided its storage into three sections: one for Ford, one for Chrysler, and one for GM. Customer-specific inventory storage is a good choice for focused factories and other customer-driven organizations.

The careful thinking about smart placement that you do in S4/Select Locations will make S5/Set Locations easier to implement, and more successful in differentiating item variety and preventing mix-ups. This will become more critical as you move in the direction of pull systems, one-piece flow, and lean production.

In S4, we do not simply set things in order—at best a temporary solution. We map out the existing conditions to better understand the practical relationship between the items of the workplace. We do this on maps of our own making. The point of S4 is to understand and plan a layout of workplace items that is ordered by smart placement: the logic of an accelerating work flow.

Your S4 thinking bears fruit in S5 when locations are set based on S4 findings.

One: The Big Picture		
1. Toward a Visual Workplace	2. Visual Systems in Context	3. The Five Start-Up Requirements
Two: 5S Method		
4. S1/Sort Through and Sort Out	5. S2–S4/ Scrub, Secure Safety, and Select Locations	6. S5/Set Locations: Borders
7. S5/Set Locations: Addresses	8. 5S Stories From the Shop Floor	9. 5S+1 and White-Collar Applications
Three: +1 Method			
10. People: What to Expect	11. +1: Building and Sustaining the 5S Habit	12. +1: Leading by Example	13. +1: Leading Through Standards
Four: Go!		
14. Showcase, Scope, and the System	15. Training and Education	16. The Hundredth Monkey

Chapter 6

S5/Set Locations: Borders

Don't put it down! Put it away!
—Patti Falbe, Associate
Fleet Engineers, Inc.

''A Place for Everything'' Is Only Half the Equation

Now that you know where things should go, it's time to ensure that you actually put them there. It's time for S5/Set Locations. The intent in S5 is to make the location of things so clear and evident that everyone knows where to go to find what they need and where to return it. Location information makes it easy for *anyone* to find *anything, anytime.*

In addition to minimizing such an obvious form of waste as searching, putting things back in their proper location can bolster yields and reduce many types of product defects that are linked, for example, to errors in tool and parts selection or to an inadequate maintenance of verniers, calipers, micrometers, and other types of inspection gauges.

The well-worn saying "a place for everything and everything in its place" is only half of the workplace equation. The goal of 5S + 1 is to make sure that every item that leaves its designated location (because it is in use) will spring back into that location. This is known as *item recoil*—and it happens naturally when S5 is successfully implemented.

> **Item recoil** is the capacity of an object to find its way back to its designated location (home), solely on the basis of the location information built into its border, home address, and ID label.

Operationalizing S5/Set Locations

Achieving item recoil is an eight-step process, with the first six steps relating to borders. This chapter will focus on these six steps. Chapter 7 will discuss the other two elements of home addresses and ID labels.

Eight Steps for Setting Location

1. Locate all items based on the Could-Be Map.
2. Put borders in place for traffic lanes.
3. Put borders in place for unmovable floor items.
4. Put borders in place for movable floor items.
5. Put borders in place for walkways and workways.
6. Put borders in place for work surface items.
7. Give each bordered location a home address.
8. Give each item an ID label.

Bordering: The First Six Steps

Step 1: Locate All Items Based on the Could-Be Map

Use your finalized Could-Be Map to guide the correct placement of each workplace item.

Step 2: Put Borders in Place for Traffic Lanes

If your plant has a lot of heavy material handling, mark off borders on traffic lanes for forklifts and tow motors first (Photo 6-1). The safety implications of this step are obvious: People must know where it is safe to move and where they are sharing space with vehicles. As part of this, make sure to apply borders to any areas used for vehicle turning.

6-1. Borders: Where to Walk.

The first step in S5/Set Locations is to define where it is safe and permitted to walk. Here is a clear example that includes door information.

Tips

1. At the start of the bordering process, outline boundaries in plain masking or duct tape. When you have verified the placement, switch to heavy plastic tape, paint, or, in cases of heavy traffic, a paint/sealant combination (see the case example below for special instructions).

2. Color, in the form of paint or tape, can add a lot to borders. In addition to colored tapes, you can also buy checkered and zebra-striped tape. Take a look at a catalogue from a supplier specializing in identification products (see Resources section).

3. Whatever you decide, make sure to follow OSHA and ANSI specifications in the process. Exhibit 6-1 provides an overview of those standards. Check your OSHA and ANSI manuals for useful information on aisle widths, shelf height, exit placement, and the like.

4. In some cases, using self-adhesive plastic circles instead of a solid line of tape is preferable. For one thing, it is easier to replace three or four damaged plastic circles than to replace a whole line of solid tape because one portion is damaged.

5. Build deeper levels of meaning into your traffic-lane bordering through the creative use of lines. Our roads and highways, for example, use double lines to mean "don't pass" and dashed lines to indicate it is all right to pass or to trace out a vehicle path when wide turns are required. Are there areas in your workplace where this kind of border might be applied?

Exhibit 6-1. OSHA and ANSI Color Reference Guide.

Color	Meaning	Application
Red	Fire	To indicate the location of fire protection equipment and apparatus, including fire-alarm boxes, fire blankets, fire extinguishers, fire-hose locations, fire pumps, and fire-exit signs.
	Danger	To identify danger signs, safety cans or other portable containers of flammable liquids, and lights at barricades and at temporary obstructions.
	Stop	To mark emergency stop bars and stop buttons on hazardous machines.
Orange	Hazardous Bio-Hazardous	To designate dangerous parts of machinery and equipment that may cut, crush, shock or otherwise injure. An intermediate level of hazard. Fluorescent orange and orange-red are used to signify biological hazards.
Yellow Yellow/Black	Caution	To mark physical hazards that might result in stumbling, falling, tripping, striking against or being caught between.
Magenta/ Yellow	Radiation	To mark X-ray, alpha, beta, gamma, neutron, and proton radiation.
Blue	Warning	To warn of X-ray, alpha, beta, gamma, neutron, and proton radiation.
Green	Safety	To mark the location of first aid and safety equipment.
Black/White	Boundaries	To designate traffic aisles, housekeeping markings, stairways (risers, direction and border limit lines), and directional signs. Many other striped border combinations, in addition to the black/white variety, are available. Contact your local supplier.

For more detail, see: OSHA 29 CFR 1910-144; ANSI A13.1-1981; ANSI Z5351.1-1991.

Where forklift traffic is heavy, getting border lines to stay clear, clean, and in place can be a challenge. Tape (plastic or other material) will not last. The visual workplace steering team at Fleet Engineers, Inc., found a solution that worked for them.[1] Here is an adaptation of the guidelines they developed:

A Technique for Creating Clear Borders in Heavy-Traffic Areas

1. Before you change anything, research and verify the right approach for your plant. Always, always follow safety procedures exactly. Do it the smart way: Put safety first.

2. Make sure the floor is scrupulously clean. If your floors are concrete and your operations are greasy, you may have to go over the floor twice with an industrial strength degreaser and then follow that with a heavy-duty, solvent-based industrial cleaner. Getting the floor clean enough to hold paint can take a full 50 percent of your border application time.

3. Be careful about the paint and sealant you choose as well as the method of application. Spray cans of traffic paint are easy to apply but the lines can get covered over with dirt and grime within days due to the grinding weight of heavy forklift traffic. At that point, these lines will be hard, if not impossible, to scrub clean.

4. A urethane sealant may be the answer for you, but check with a reputable paint supply house first because certain combinations of paint and sealant do not work together. For example, when Fleet applied an oil-base sealant over an oil-base paint, the paint underneath bubbled.

5. If this happens to you, you may have to do what Fleet did: Remove the sealer and the painted lines, clean the surface thoroughly again (even to the point of applying that heavy-duty cleaner again), and start all over.

6. If you use latex paint for your lines, you may need several coats to get an even, solid color.

7. Many latex paints come in gallons and not in spray cans. Fleet had good luck using a 4-inch roller to lay down lines. The team used masking tape (¾") to help keep the line edge clean and sharp.

8. Latex needs to be dry to the touch before the next coat of latex paint is laid. In general that takes about thirty minutes, depending on weather conditions. By the time one coat is finished, the start of the line may already be dried for you to begin again at that point right away.

9. Be careful: Multiple coats of latex paint can produce a rubbery finish. Fleet took great care to pull up the masking tape (that they laid to keep edges clean) *as soon as* the last coat was *set*, not dry. They found that if they waited until the coat was dry, the paint would pull up with the tape.

10. There may be some seepage when you apply paint over the masking tape. According to Fleet, if this happens, you should be able to scrape the excess off.

11. After removing the masking tape, let the latex dry for eight to twelve hours.

1. Many thanks to Brett Balkema, Greg Hancock, Steve Hascher, Craig Tobey, and the other Fleet associates who helped develop and document this bordering process.

Make sure it is well set before applying the sealant. Rope off the area if you need to protect the finish.

12. When you are ready for the urethane sealer, put on a hefty coat. You can apply this freehand with a 4-inch roller. Make sure to overlap the sealant generously on both sides of the line (at least 1 inch on each side). You may want to apply a second coat after four hours for extra insurance.

As of the writing of this book, nearly nine months have passed since the Fleet team completed its bordering process. How are things holding up? Let's hear from Brett:

> "The lines are holding up amazingly well—we haven't had to redo a single line. We'd have been happy if they lasted six months but at this rate, they'll look great a lot longer than that. And because the lines are staying clean and visible, the areas are staying orderly. We are especially happy with the way shopfloor associates have taken to it. They were involved in the process from the start, and now they own it. This could never have happened if the process had been management-directed. It was really worth it!"

Thanks, Fleet! And if you, the reader, come up with a special solution to a border challenge, please share it with us so we can pass it along to others. We'd be delighted to hear from you (contact information is in the Resources Section).

Step 3: Put Borders Around Nonmovable (Stationary) Floor Items

Tape a boundary around each object in the area that cannot be moved. Nonmovable items include machines, permanent shelving, and any other item that rests on the floor and cannot be easily moved because it is either too heavy or bolted in place. Begin with duct or masking tape, and then switch to plastic tape or paint after the placement is validated (Photo 6-2).

Tips

1. Borders should not be flush against an item. Leave at least 2 to 4 inches between the object and its boundary. With heavy equipment, a wider margin can be left; in some cases, a margin of 8 to 10 inches may be warranted.

2. "Which way does that

6-2. Borders: Nonmovable Items.

Put a clear border around stationary equipment and other hard-to-move items and give safety a boost. Use borders to mark floor areas that are periodically traversed by moving machine parts.

Exhibit 6-2. Borders:
The Swing of a Door.

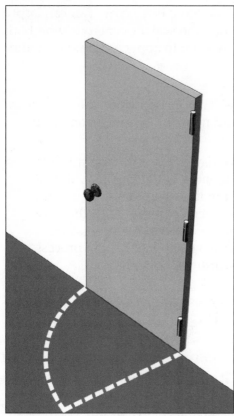

Safety first! Here is the same idea as in Photo 6-1, only this time dashed lines are used.

swing?'' you may have once asked yourself as you approached a door, only to find out seconds later when it bashed you off your feet. You never even suspected any danger. Outline the swing of the doors in your area to give everyone fair warning to stay alert. Dashed lines are often used in these cases when the use of floor space is predictable but not regular, as shown in Exhibit 6-2.

3. In the same vein, make sure your bordering traces the boundary around machine parts that move (travelers). This is important since border lines are meant to identify the safe zone around machinery.

4. Some nonmovable items do not seem to lend themselves to the logic of borders. For example, you may find yourself questioning the wisdom of putting a boundary around a permanent storage unit. Let your answers to the following two questions help you decide whether or not to put down a border. First, would it improve safety and reduce risk? Second, would a border add to the operational efficiency of your area? If either answer is yes (or even maybe), put them in place.

For example, at Greene Rubber Company, a fabricator and distributor of rubber products in Woburn, Massachusetts, the borders around its 30-foot cutting tables were instrumental in keeping rolls of stock off the floor and the way clear for an associate to access these surfaces from any point around them.

6-3. Borders: Movable Items.

By its very nature, WIP comes and goes—and it always has a home in this area thanks to these zebra-striped borders.

Step 4: Put Borders in Place for Movable Floor Items

Place a visible boundary around all the moveable objects on the floor of the area (as compared to movable items on work surfaces; that comes later). These objects include floor pallets, containers, bins, boxes, carts, gurneys, forklifts, and tow motors. See the borders around small bins of WIP in Photo 6-3 and large pallets of raw material in Photo 6-4.

Highly movable items (such as the ones named above) do not require a complete boundary outline around them. Use, instead, border strips at the angles of the item (called *commas*). By the same token, a large colored dot (plastic or painted) or small square or rectangle can designate locations for chairs, trash containers, wastepaper baskets, buckets,

6-4. Kanban Borders: Material Placement.

Visual order and kanban are natural partners. The kanban level in this area calls for five pallet slots—and visual borders mark the spot.

6-5. S5 Miniborders: Tables.

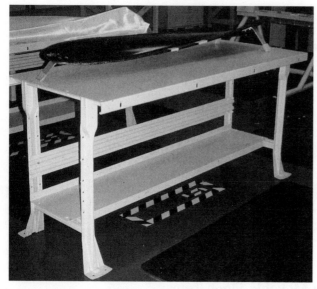

You do not need to surround every movable item with a complete boundary. The small rectangle under the table marks its spot. Large plastic dots can also be used.

and the like. Just make sure that whatever you do use meets the smart placement objective of giving meaning to the word *empty* (Photo 6-5).

Step 5: Put Borders in Place for Walkways and Workways

When you put borders down in step 2 to mark off traffic lanes, you probably also cleared up where people should walk. If more clarity is needed, lay down borders that specifically differentiate walkways from workways. A walkway border shows you exactly where people are supposed to walk. When that is clear, people will not misuse the walkways (by using them for storage, for example).

A workway border shows exactly where work is meant to take place. At a workbench, for example, a workway border reminds the operator where she is supposed to stand and move in reference to the bench. The two examples that follow demonstrate how powerful walkways and workways can be.

Bordering: As Trigger for Improvement. Associates on the assembly line in XYZ Company wanted a way to identify as many forms of minute motion as possible so they could then eliminate them. They used borders to help.

First, instead of laying down borders of all the same color, the team assigned a different-color border to each workstation on the line. The difference in the colors between each station let associates notice when they moved out of their designated workway, an abnormality.

In spotting this instantly, individual operators would ask themselves why and come up with real-time answers. *Why* did I cross the boundary between the workbenches? Is my work space too confined? If I was reaching to borrow a tool, what happened to mine? If I was stretching to put a unit down, why not move the incoming spot closer to me? The colored borders were used to trigger improvement questions.

6-6. Conventional Borders: Warehouse.

The line borders on this shipping and receiving dock are better than no lines at all. But much more is possible. Look at Photo 6-7.

Bordering: In a Warehouse. What comes up in your mind's eye when you hear the words *warehouse, loading dock,* or *shipping and receiving*? If you are like most people, you see stacks and stacks of "stuff"—stacks of temporary storage that are often as deep and wide as they are high.

Stacks can challenge us in ways we would rather not face. For example, what happens if you need to retrieve a certain unit from a stack or check to make sure a unit was included? Getting to that unit is usually a nightmare of moving everything out, getting what you are after, and then moving everything back. Photo 6-6 is a shot of a conventional loading/unloading dock at a moment when the stacks are mercifully low. Notice the narrow borders between the lanes.

A shopfloor team in a GM supplier warehouse in El Paso, Texas, came up with a better solution by installing walkways that doubled as workways.[2] The team left enough room for one person to walk and work between each stack—and painted the space yellow. Photo 6-7 shows the width very clearly, and Photo 6-8 shows the Texas warehouse layout. Wide yellow walkways/workways can be seen everywhere in this facility. For this and many other reasons, I like to call it the best little warehouse in Texas.

Step 6: Put Borders in Place for All Work Surface Items

Based on your Could-Be Map for the work surfaces, place small workbench items in their designated locations and put a border around each of them.

As with floor bordering, putting a tape or painted boundary around bench items is the first step in installing meaning there. Pay attention to the top of work surfaces and

2. My deepest appreciation to James P. Walker, former director of International Operations in a supplier division at GM, for supporting my research at this and other GM supplier sites in the United States and Mexico.

6-7. Improved Borders: Warehouse.

We can forget how difficult it is to check material when it is stacked deep and high—until we need to. When you lay down borders that are personwide, you create visual order and physical access.

6-8. Personwidth Borders.

Here is what person-width aisles look like on a full-scale shipping/receiving dock. Neat, orderly, and fully functional.

6-9. Work Surface Borders at Alpha.

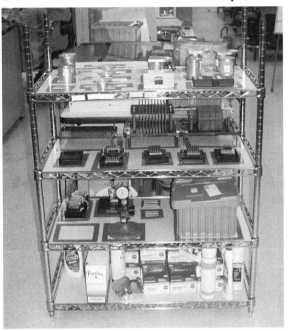

The team in this semiconductor cell at Alpha used bright-red plastic tape to make homes for its various platforms and die holders—and yet more motion was cut out of the process.

to the area underneath. If there is a shelf that is not in use, backtrack to S1 and get rid of it. Do the same for racks and any other kind of holding area—put down boundaries and eliminate any unnecessary items. Then go inside cabinets and drawers and establish borders for supplies and other items.

Photo 6-9 shows you the first bordering effort in a work cell at Alpha Industries, a semiconductor manufacturer in Woburn, Massachusetts. The team had to use special antistatic plastic tape in giving permanent homes to the many work items that were previously stashed in drawers and on shelves throughout the area. This simple bordering effort had a measurable positive impact on lead time in that cell. And that was just for starters. You can read more about this Alpha cell in Chapter 14.

Borders can do more than simply indicate the home locations of things. Because they are fundamentally a visual control device, they can also show minimum/maximum supply levels. Exhibit 6-3 shows a border application with a control dimension at The Ensign-Bickford Company, a leader in the design and manufacture of blast initiation systems in Simsbury, Connecticut. As the address indicates, this bordered area is specifically for Line 9, the blue line. The border not only marks where empty cord spools are to be stored but also defines the maximum number of spools to be stacked there: seventy-five.

You can use the profile or silhouette of an item as its home border. Photo 6-10 shows this concept applied to cleanup tools in the FB-127 Cell at Fleet Engineers, Inc. The shadows are just barely visible because the tools are at home.

Another way to achieve the border function without tape is by using cutouts. Cut the shape of the item out of foam or wood and let that define its home. This approach

Exhibit 6-3. Borders as Information.

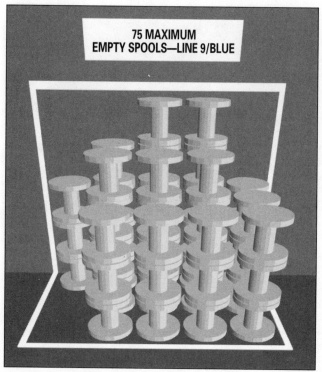

75 MAXIMUM
EMPTY SPOOLS—LINE 9/BLUE

Here are border lines doing double duty as visual indicators and controls. The shape and size the lines trace out tell us exactly where spools get placed—and what *full* means. The fact that the lines are blue provides yet another information detail: ''Only spools from Line 9 belong here.''

is particularly useful in machining operations that process a high variety of products, requiring a wide range of small dies, parts, and other tooling.

Borders in Multishift Operations

A frequently asked question in organizations that run two or three shifts is: What happens if the people sharing a workbench cannot agree on where things should be put? Some people would like to settle the dispute by voting. I cannot support voting as a solution because of the damage it can do to the spirit of the workplace. (I am not opposed to voting. I have simply found that the trust level in a group must be very high to support it. And the trust level of a group in the early stages of 5S + 1 is usually not high enough, unless the company has had teams in place for several years.) Other people favor prolonged negotiations and bargaining.

A simpler and more practical solution is to make a different location template for each person.

Location Templates

A location template is a mat made out of cardboard, Plexiglas, rubber, or any other material with a smooth surface that holds up under repeated use and can carry information.

6-10. Shadow Borders: Fleet's S2/Scrub Board.

This bold presentation of cleanup tools at Fleet Engineers makes no bones about the importance of S2 in the FB-127 cell. Shadow borders under each item mark home locations and ensure item recoil.

The template is sized to fit the work surface. All required location information is placed directly on it by tape, paint, or cutout, and with written address labels. Each operator has his/her own template with their placement preferences.

If Nina (who works the first shift) likes her solder paste on the right, so be it. Her template will reflect it. If Victor (second shift) prefers his solder on the left, he makes a home for it there on his template. If William (night shift) wants the solder paste squarely in the center of his workbench, he can have it. No negotiations are necessary when everyone can get exactly what they prefer.

When Nina leaves, she removes the tools and items from her template, sets them in a designated location, and stores her template in the holder behind the bench. When Victor arrives, he pulls out his template, lays it on the waiting bench surface, and arranges the tools and items according to the location information on his template. Same goes for William. No fuss. No bother. Just switch it over.

6-11. Two Overlapping Borders.

Location templates also offer a handy solution in multishift operations where left-handedness/right-handedness is an issue.

Variation on the Theme of Multiples

Borders can respond to other situations requiring multiple solutions. For example, how do borders get handled when the same machine is fed from two different rack positions? This is the question that Fleet's FB-27 welding team faced when they were putting floor borders in place in that cell. Their solution was brilliant, as seen in Photo 6-11: Simply designate two overlapping borders, one for each rack position.

Borders Give Meaning to Empty Space

Whether for floor or work surface items, putting borders in place gives meaning to the word *empty*. Knowing when a space is or is not empty is one of the main reasons for smart placement to begin with. Without a border, there is no way to tell that the space is a designated location when an item is not "at home."

Look at the sequence in Exhibit 6-4. You see a barrel in the first frame (A), sitting on an unmarked spot on the floor. Then you see that unmarked spot on the floor when the barrel has been removed (B). In this condition, the floor is without information. It is

Exhibit 6-4. When *Empty* Has Meaning.

| This is where the barrel belongs. | But when it is elsewhere, we don't know that this spot on the floor is its home. The spot has no meaning. | A simple border is the first step toward building *meaning* into the shop floor. | When the barrel is elsewhere, we still know something belongs in this spot. Adding a home address will further increase our understanding of this location. |

mute. It is silent. It has nothing to say to us about its intended use. It is empty, but how can we tell? The next frame (C) shows us a barrel sitting in a spot defined by a simple border. When the barrel is not at home (D), you can still tell—at a glance—that something "lives" there. We know the spot is empty. Few of us would dare put something else in that spot. That would be trespassing.

The absence of meaning on workbenches and the shop floor is one of the main obstacles to an accelerated work flow in today's workplace. When everything looks the same, associates struggle to grasp the distinctions that underlie varying functions. The workplace is mute because there are no visible cues of meaning. Borders address this issue and therefore can have a direct and measurable impact on lead time and quality. Without bordering, the physical environment is silent—and we don't know that we don't know.

Floor Borders: A Special Note

I encourage companies to put traffic, walkway, and workway borders in place early in an implementation. But not every company agrees, often with some reason.

For instance, a factory may have already attempted to put down floor borders, and after a good amount of effort, saw them erode practically overnight in heavy forklift traffic. Notwithstanding the excellent procedure discussed earlier that Fleet developed, their reluctance to do it again as part of their 5S+1 implementation is understandable.

In other companies, the layout of the production floor is in such a state of flux (such as when the system is shifting to cellular manufacturing) that floor borders may not seem to make sense in the near term. This may be a valid reason to postpone bordering—but let it only be a postponement. In both traditional and lean systems, factory after factory has reported that floor borders are definitely worth it, even when the floor plan is changing. The sooner they are put in place, the better.

Without them, it's business as usual and undesignated space is up for grabs for any of a number of competing uses. The result is not just the confusion of dissimilar material haphazardly placed but growing conflicts and hostilities as people compete for seemingly unclaimed territory. Vestiges of the wild Wild West.

☆   ☆   ☆   ☆   ☆

Now let's learn about the final two steps of S5/Set Locations: Putting home addresses and ID labels in place.

One: The Big Picture		
1. Toward a Visual Workplace	2. Visual Systems in Context	3. The Five Start-Up Requirements
Two: 5S Method		
4. S1/Sort Through and Sort Out	5. S2–S4/ Scrub, Secure Safety, and Select Locations	6. S5/Set Locations: Borders
7. S5/Set Locations: Addresses	8. 5S Stories From the Shop Floor	9. 5S+1 and White-Collar Applications
Three: +1 Method		
10. People: What to Expect	11. +1: Building and Sustaining the 5S Habit	12. +1: Leading by Example	13. +1: Leading Through Standards
Four: Go!		
14. Showcase, Scope, and the System	15. Training and Education	16. The Hundredth Monkey

Chapter 7

S5/Set Locations: Addresses

Finishing Touches: Implementing Home Addresses and ID Labels

In Chapter 6, we discussed the first six steps of the S5/Set Locations process, how and why to put borders in place. This chapter describes the final two steps, implementing home addresses and ID labels, putting the finishing touches on clarity of location, ensuring item recoil.

> **Item recoil** is the capacity of an object to find its way back to its designated location (home), solely on the basis of the location information built into its border, home address, and ID label.

Bordering: The Last Two Steps

Step 7: Give Each Location a Home Address

Now that each item has a bordered location, put an address on it. This is the item's home address, the location to which it returns at the end of each workday.

Make Address Bold and Dark. Make your addresses bold and dark enough to read at a distance of 4 to 5 feet. The key is high contrast. Research shows that the most readable combination is black letters on a yellow background. The second choice is black letters on a white background—but the letters have to be bold, dark, and visible at a distance. Thin black marker, ballpoint, or computer printouts are simply not visible enough.

Examples of Readability

• Photo 7-1 shows a rack of spring storage bins before S5/Set Locations. Photo 7-2 shows it after addresses were added: black part numbers on a yellow background and clear plastic lids on each bin to prevent springs from falling into the wrong bin in the picking process.

• Photos 7-3 and 7-4 show clear addresses on two operations in a multioperation process at Curtis Screw Company in Buffalo, New York. In addition to part numbers,

7-1. UE Parts Storage: Before.

These bins were supposed to be home for parts but became catchalls for whatever anyone might want to put in them.

7-2. UE Parts Storage: After.

Black-on-yellow addresses transformed the bins into near point-of-use storage for the nearby cells. The team added Plexiglas covers because, in the picking process, errors of look-alike springs falling into open bins continued.

7-3. In-Process Indicators.

Each WIP address in this process at Curtis Screw repeats the product number—M8219—the operation just performed—WASH/COUNT—and the one that comes next—TUMBLE. (See Photo 7-4.)

7-4. WIP on the Move.

This—TUMBLE—is the present WIP address in the process. The next operation—HEAT TREAT—is once again clearly named. It's easy to see how this address approach can make short work of material handling at Curtis Screw.

each address shows the current status of the WIP (work-in-process) plus where the parts go next ("waiting for"). This clever addition ensures accurate material handling, even for a new employee. Curtis uses bold white letters on a cerulean blue (computer-screen blue) background.

• Grinding wheels, blades, and cams vary in size, thickness, surface, and in a dozen other ways that are hard to detect by the naked eye. Mix-ups are common, and far too many people rely on memory or sight to spot these differences. When I asked one machinist how he told the difference between the more than seventy-five wheels hanging on Peg-Boards in his grinding cell, he proudly explained, "I can tell which is which because I put them there."

7-5. Cam Storage.

The shape and size of a cam carries its ID information. Differences between cams are so tiny that it is often a struggle to tell them apart. When a team in the Davenport department at Curtis Screw organized its cams onto this large board, the battle was almost won.

7-6. Cam Storage: Close-Up.

In this close-up shot, you can see how the cam pegs and fraction addresses make it easier to pick the right cam. A vast improvement, although there is still some room for error.

Mistakes can be costly, especially where cams are concerned. If you use the wrong cam and you are lucky, you'll get a quality defect. If the stars are against you, the wrong cam can destroy an entire machine. Anything that increases the accuracy of picking and putting such tools is good news for the company.

A team from the Davenport area at Curtis Screw took on the cam challenge. First, they organized some 800 cams (20% of those used at that plant) by size and assigned each a home on a large 15- × 8-foot board that was painted white on the top and cerulean blue on the bottom. Each of the two hundred pegs on that board was given a home address based on size ($\frac{1}{32}$, $\frac{7}{32}$, $\frac{1}{16}$, $\frac{3}{16}$), with one to ten cams hung on each peg (see Photos 7-5 and 7-6). This is a simple and effective remedy to one of the biggest headaches in machining. (Exhibit 7-1 illustrates a variation on this application.)

Use Word Substitutes. Long part numbers are common in manufacturing and one of the reasons for parts mix-ups. It is easy to think part numbers are identical when they differ only in one or two characters (see Photo 7-7).

7-7. The Unending Part Number.

Using a part number (PN) as a home address may seem like a great idea, but long ones, like those shown here, make mix-ups easy.

7-8. Number-Plus Drawings.

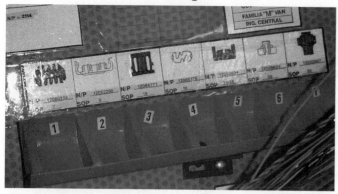

Use the part number and add a second handle to make ID easier. Here drawings help define what long PNs really mean.

Make it easy to tell the difference at a glance by using word substitutes in your addresses. Think of these substitutes as "visual handles" (as in handles on a soup pot). **Visual handles** give people different ways to identify *meaning*. In addition to standard names and part numbers, use one or more of the following: symbols, icons, photos, drawings, silhouettes, and shadow profiles.

Examples of Handles

• In Photo 7-8, this GM supplier makes good use of drawings for the quick and accurate identification of the tiny clips used in automobile electrical harnesses, the company's specialty. Once again, relying on long part numbers alone practically guarantees mix-ups.

7-9. Number-Plus Shadow Profile.

This shadow board is simple, homemade, and it works. ID numbers are included to ensure item recoil.

• Photo 7-9 is a fine example of a home address that combines shadow profiles (border) with numbers. Each tool has its own footprint for easy relocation, and the numbers help us confirm the right match.

• Remember our discussion on cams and how easy it is for mix-ups to happen? Exhibit 7-1 shows you an outstanding cam storage approach. The visual order devices you see there virtually eliminate the possibility of a mix-up. At least six different devices are used, including brightly painted bins that are color-coordinated to match the colored home addresses on the sign over the rack. Can you find five other visual order devices in this cam minisystem?

• Photo 7-10 shows you an innovative approach to home addresses for tools developed by UE associate Bob Comeau: photocopies. Put your tool or group of tools on the glass of a photocopy machine (carefully), push the copy button, and you have an instant

Exhibit 7-1. The Ultimate Cam Storage.

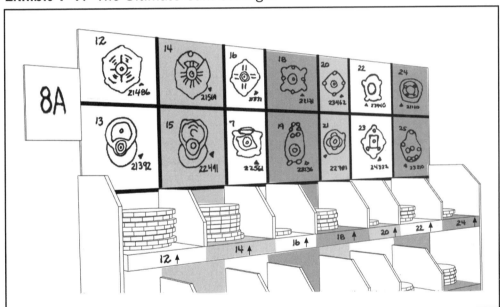

Many different visual devices work together in this minisystem to reduce mix-ups.

On the wall:

1. Cam part number address (e.g., 21486, 21392)
2. Cam outline address
3. Storage bin address (e.g., 12, 13, 14)
4. Red, yellow, blue, green coded addresses (shading on bins 14/15, 18/19, 20/21, 24/26)
5. Black borders to clearly separate cam addresses

On the shelf:

6. Color-coded bins
7. Wide/narrow bins
8. Bin addresses on the shelf ledge
9. Arrows below each address, pointing to the correct bin

7-10. A Photocopy Address—Worth a Thousand Words.

UE's Bob Comeau wanted a way to know that all the needed tools were in the bin. The result: the world's first photocopied tool address. What a concept!

address. The example shown in the photograph is the set of small tools needed for a Molex machine. They get stored in the plastic bin next to the photocopied address. You know the set is complete when the bin contents match up with the address. Wonderful!

Bob's idea spread through UE like wildfire. In the application shown in Photo 7-11, a sheet of Plexiglas protects the photocopied addresses from wear and tear as tools are placed and replaced over the course of the workday. Can you tell which tool is not at home?

7-11. Photocopy Address Plus Plexiglas.

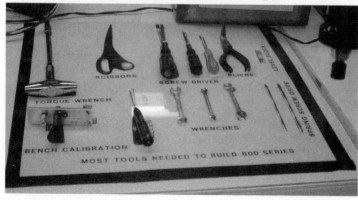

This team went one step further. Photocopy the tools, name each and lay down its address, and then cover it with Plexiglas. Can you tell which tool is not at home?

Step 8: Give Each Item an ID Label

The final step in the S5/Set Locations process is to put an identifying (ID) label on the item itself. Similar to a soldier's dog tag, this ID label moves with the item because it is *on* it (Exhibit 7-2). *All* workplace items—movable and nonmovable—are labeled, including:

- *Floor items*—e.g., machinery, cabinets, racks, shelving, bins, tables, benches, chairs, buckets, and wastepaper baskets
- *Bench items*—e.g., hand tools, gauges, oil cans, work instructions, part bins, consumable supplies such as paste, solder, and tape

Working together, borders, home addresses, and ID labels ensure item recoil (Photo 7-12). If the item gets lost or "wanders off" during the course of the day/shift, it can find its way back home, using the arms and the legs of a human partner. Use common names in your ID labels (unless exact part numbers are required), plus plenty of visual handles: symbols, photos, drawings, and silhouettes.

Exhibit 7-2. A Hammer Is a Hammer Is a Hammer.

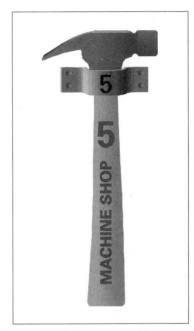

Put an ID label on every object to ensure item recoil—and improve your chances of finding this hammer, every time you need it.

Department ID. As part of your address/ID campaign, remember to include your department. You may know where it is and where you are, but visitors, newcomers, and customers can almost always use the help. The ID signs in Photo 7-13 show us both the name of the department and a specific operation of that department. Go all the way on this one and name every operation in the process. You will be positively amazed what a help it is to everyone.

One more thing about department signs: Although you can have them made professionally, think about letting an artist in the workforce create something special. Almost every company boasts a handful of people who can and love to draw. Ask them to try their hand at your department sign. This is yet another way that 5S + 1 can build interest, involvement, ownership, and reward—the spirit of the workplace.

Examples of Department Signs

- United Electric production technician Michael Contardo made the sign shown in Photo 7-14. Mike combined a blow-out of the parts list of the cell's main product with the cell's name: Spectra 10.
- The professional-level graphics of the sign for the FB-127 Cell at Fleet Engineers, Inc. (Photo 7-15), was designed and executed by Fleet associates Jeff Hamm and

7-12. The Three-Part Address.

Here you see the three elements of a complete address: the border around the barrel, the home address above the barrel, and the ID tag on the barrel itself.

7-13. Visitors Welcome!

What a relief to newcomers and visitors to UE's Bantam cell to find not only the name of the area they landed in but the name of every single operation as well—so simply done with a plastic sleeve, a hole-punch, and some string.

7-14. Spectra 10 Spectacular.

UE's Mike Contardo put the name of his cell--SPECTRA 10—on cardboard along with an engineering drawing of the parts blow-out. Then he took it all to shipping for shrink wrap.

7-15. Fleet's Fabulous FB-27 Cell.

This splendid sign was designed by Fleet's Jeff Hamm and Roger Stalzer for the FB-27 cell that was just completing its 5S + 1 transformation.

7-16. Battle of Titans at Fleet's Cutoff Area.

Roger Stalzer teamed up with Robert Ol-daker to design and execute this ingenious area sign, giving us all a lesson in art appreciation on the shop floor.

Roger L. Stalzer. A few months later, Roger teamed up with Fleet associate Robert C. Oldaker to do the sign for Fleet's Cut-Off department shown in Photo 7-16.

You-Are-Here Maps. Some plants are huge—a mile square or more. Have you ever noticed the way newcomers and visitors brighten up when they spot a You-Are-Here Map? We all take comfort in knowing exactly where we are at any given moment. Maps are fabulous visual location devices.

There are many ways that a map can enhance production objectives as well. The most obvious is as a support to material handling and safety. Maps can also provide the context for associates to recognize that they are part of a much larger activity, a fact that is often hard to grasp in the rush of everyday work. In this way, maps help build a sense of community in the workplace.

Thanks to CAD (computer-aided design), facility and work area maps are fairly easy to obtain. Think about introducing these kinds of maps early in your 5S + 1 implementation and look for ways they can be adapted to support the process. You may be surprised at the results.

☆   ☆   ☆   ☆   ☆

This concludes the eight steps of the S5/Set Locations process. Before we conclude the chapter, let's look at some of the broader implications of location information.

What Makes a Good Address?

An effective location address depends both on *what* information is shared and *how* it is shared. In far too many companies, for example, the way parts and material are stored and addressed is nothing short of a disaster. It is not enough to throw parts onto some shelves, hang a sign that says PARTS STORAGE, and leave associates to figure it out. That is just an example of bad shelving and a sure prescription for lots of motion and predictably long lead times. Like a road map without names on it, bad shelving may hold items we vitally need—but we have no way of finding them without clear addresses.

What: *Driver's License Level Information*

A good address is one that shares all the information you need to locate an item with an absolute minimum of motion. Take a look at your driver's license. There's your name, photo, home address, birth date, height, vehicle restrictions, driving restrictions, and the license number itself—all the information needed for positive identification. In the same way, a good shopfloor address shares many levels of information about its resident. The more complicated or look-alike an item on the shop floor, the more specific information is needed in order to find that item quickly, without the slightest possibility of a mix-up. Photo 7-17 shows the address for the copper and stainless-steel tubing. The address is plain and clear, and provides all the detail needed to make stocking and retrieval easy, quick, and reliable. Providing driver-license level information can reduce picking errors, speed up handling, and prevent stock-outs. Look for ways to adapt and apply these principles to other situations that need clear addresses.

How: *Finding Your Way by Sorts*

Now that you have decided on what information to include in your address, you must also decide how to display it. Consider using a technique called "Sorts." **Sorting** means separating things into finer and finer groups of meaning. Shopfloor life is made much

7-17. Shopfloor Address as an Item's "Driver's License."

Think of a shopfloor address as the item's driver's license. How much vital information can you share visually? The home addresses shown here point us in the right direction.

easier if this sorting process is intentional and designed directly into the workplace. Here are two examples—one where sorting is weak, and the other where sorting is a key support.

Weak Sorting

You are a material handler in an automotive supplier plant whose major customers are Ford, Honda, Chrysler, and Volkswagen. After seven years, you have gotten good at your job. Right now, you are on your way to get a bin of ⅝" hex-head screws for the Ford line—PN/6564-33. Since the parts inventory in this plant is stocked first by part type and then by customer (discussed in previous chapter), all you have to do is get to the screw section and then find the Ford stack.

You pat the sample screw—PN/6564-33—that you tucked into your pocket when you left the Ford assembly area twenty minutes ago and turn and face the waiting aisles, your computer slip in hand. Yes, there is the sign SMALL PARTS STORAGE: the first major sort, the first tiny step on your journey to PN/6564-33. But that's all there is. No other visual indicator is in sight. You and your pretty-good memory are on your own. Just go down that shelving aisle in front of you—and, by the way, good luck!

Now let's take you on a different journey to locate the same part number, PN/6564-33. This time, you'll have the benefit of major and minor sorts.

Clear, Intentional Sorting

You jump onto your tow motor, computer slip in hand: "Small Parts, Ford, F6/Screws, HH, A2." Yes, this plant only uses that dreadfully long part number (PN/6564-33) in its ordering procedure, but not in stocking and retrieval. So you head for the small parts section, your first major sort. You can see the bright black-on-yellow hanging sign: SMALL PARTS STORAGE. Ahhhhh. A few feet further and you see the big, clear sign announcing FORD, your second major sort.

You approach the shelving aisles with some hesitation. There are so many stacks. How are you going to find the screws? But just a minute. "Screws" is not your next sort; your next sort is "F6" (*F* is for Ford). There it is: a stand-up indicator in perfect numerical order on top of a four-tier rack—F6. Right below it is a tab for screws, your fourth sort. Now all you have to do is find the spot where A and 2 cross. There! There's the address, right on the bin *and* there's that long part number. You notice the small arrow pointing up that confirms you are picking the right bin of parts. A perfect match—and you know it (Exhibit 7-3).

☆   ☆   ☆   ☆   ☆

The difference between these two examples is clear: silent disorder on one end, informative visual order on the other. The first work environment offers little location information to support the material handling needs of production. The second shows an environment where location information is fully and powerfully a production support—and lead times show it. Notice how orderly and logical the system of addresses

Exhibit 7-3. Good Shelf Addressing.

The logic of this area's sorting approach is obvious from the addresses on these shelves. Look at all the useful information these shelves share visually.

is there. Notice the way location information is repeated so that stocking and retrieval are both easy and self-confirming. This is called "redundancy" in the process, one of the visual keys to self-regulation and a workplace where picking/putting mistakes are as rare as snowballs in a heat wave.

Compare this approach with the one used on your shop floor. See if you and your associates can develop ways to improve your current system further, with the goal of matching and then surpassing the best of the above.

When Volume and Units Are Variable

Bordering and location information can be problematic in one area of the shop floor: where the volume and type of units vary widely from day to day. Loading docks and shipping/receiving are two examples. The solution is the use of standing signs, ropes, and indicator blankets.

Standing Signs and Ropes

A **standing sign** is an easy-to-move stand that can be used to provide a home address to material of an indefinite size and type (Photo 7-18).

7-18. Standing Sign.

Use standing signs to deal with material that varies a lot in volume. Include several "handles" to make correct ID easier. This example uses part number, common name, and photograph. If mix-ups persist, consider attaching the part itself to the sign.

Here are a few things to remember in using standing signs.

1. Make sure the sign part of the stand shows all the information needed to make a correct identification.
2. Use the exact part number and improve recognition by adding some visual handles: the part's common name, a photo of the part, the part itself affixed to the sign.
3. Add ropes to section off the units if you need to safeguard them. Some say this is overkill—I say it's smart if only one error is avoided. *Redundancy is the name of the game in visual order.* Location information is one of those situations where more is better.

If you can anticipate the kind of unit coming into the area, do the following for instant and flexible ID:

1. Make an index card for each type of unit (again consider including part number, common name, and a photo).

2. Put all the cards on a ring and secure the set to the top of the stand.
3. When units arrive, flip to its card, secure the card with a clothespin so it doesn't flip over, and you are set. (For a variation, see George's story in Chapter 8).

Visual Blankets

A **visual blanket** is a piece of heavy cloth, rubber, plastic, or other material used to cover a stack of units when ropes or standing signs are not workable. Just mark the face of the blanket with the information needed: for example, J-54 WIP, DON'T TOUCH, or FOR HEAT TREAT PICK-UP. Then throw it over the units and you are set.

Broader Implications of Location Information

Safety

The impact of each 5S + 1 principle on safety issues can be significant. This is particularly evident in S5/Set Locations. Bordering, home addresses, and ID labels help us know where it is safe and not safe to walk and put our hands. Location information can take much of the risk out of handling hazardous materials by preventing the kinds of mishaps and mix-ups that can occur in nonaddressed work environments.

Addressing can also be the key to finding safety equipment fast—for example, locating a fire extinguisher when you need one. When that need arises, it is always urgent, with every instant of delay increasing the risk of loss. In moments of danger, lead time needs to be 100 percent value-adding. What is the use of having a hundred fire extinguishers in a facility if you can't get your hands on one when you need it? Photo 7-19 shows

7-19. Safety Location/Red Dot.

In case of fire, look for the bright-red dot. That's all. You'll find help there.

you one simple and effective solution. In this GM supplier plant in Mexico, a big, bright red dot marks the home for fire extinguishers. This plantwide standard makes it easy for everyone to know where to go to find safety equipment.

Take your cue from this approach and look for ways to make OSHA/ANSI regulations and other safety guidelines come alive in your workplace.

Equipment Maintenance

Visual location information can make a big difference in high-risk equipment maintenance situations. Let's say you are a new maintenance associate in an aluminum processing mill. Your first assignment is to find the source of a fluid failure on a five-machine coating line—fast! By the time you arrive, the rest of your crew is already at work on the bottom floor of a four-story maintenance pit beneath the line.

"How long will it take us to solve the 'mystery of the pipes'?" the head of the crew, Catherine, asks wryly. "We always make a bet when we get called on this machine." You look around and see why. A dense network of pipes, conduits, and channels criss-cross every surface in the pit. Not a single visual indicator is in sight (Photo 7-20).

How long will it take to determine exactly what is in each pipe? There is a big

7-20. Before S5: Pipes, Conduits, Channels.

What is in these pipes? In the total absence of location information, you can at best make only an educated guess.

difference between coolant and air, plain water and de-ionized water, water and steam. Are you prepared to turn on that unmarked valve to find out which is which? Even when you know the contents, you will still need to know:

- Where does each set of pipes, conduits, and channels originate?
- Where does each set go?
- Which set supports which machine section?
- What is the direction of fluid flow in each?

In the absence of visual indicators, you and the crew will have to depend strictly on memory, another way of saying "trial-and-error." Expect lots of motion. Getting concrete, reliable answers to any (let alone all) of the above questions could take a very long time. You are about to experience firsthand just how time-consuming, frustrating, and potentially dangerous a job can be without visible, point-of-use location information.

The lack of visual location information presents a special challenge in plants where those who diagnose the problem (usually the engineering staff) are not the same people who do the actual repair work (usually a maintenance crew from the shop floor). In the absence of ID labels, difficult work can quickly become a nightmare. Even the simplest technical details become a challenge to explain, and mid-process feedback is nearly out of the question. Things can go from bad to worse in a fire or in the case of a chemical spill. Unmarked pipes and valves take on a deadly significance when fire or chemical response teams must act quickly. This is information deficit at its worst.

The reverse is also true. Visual location information can lend an enormous hand to achieving fast, safe, and complete solutions to machine maintenance problems. The message is clear: Only an environment that is self-explaining can become self-regulating. The following is a basic list of location information that supports routine machine maintenance and machine utilization. Use it as a checklist to see where you might enhance your current level of visual ID information on your equipment:

Visual ID Information Checklist

- ☐ ID labels on direction of rotation on drives, belts, chains, and motors
- ☐ ID labels on content and direction of flow on all piping and hoses
- ☐ ID labels on replacement part numbers of drives, belts, chains, motors, guards, hoses, piping
- ☐ ID labels on rotation direction of drives, belts, chains, and motors
- ☐ ID labels on panels, boxes, motors, filters, cabinets, chains, belts, guards
- ☐ Control panels with layout diagrams or maps indicating lubrication fill points and frequencies, product codes, and location of backup control drawings
- ☐ ID labels on panels, boxes, motors, filters, cabinets, chains, belts, guards
- ☐ ID labels for lube points of panels, boxes, motors, filters, chains, belts, guards
- ☐ ID match markings for all fixed, adjustable, or critical fasteners, such as nuts, bolts, and screws
- ☐ ID match markings for all control adjustments (pressure, flow, speed, temperature, level, voltage, and current)
- ☐ Gauges labeled with system name and function

☐ Location diagram on machine for lock-out/tag-out points, drives, moving parts, hydraulics, electronics, control panels, lube points, chains, hoses, guards, motors, pneumatic/air devices, etc.

☐ ID color coding for lube containers and tools matched with machine lube points

ANSI leads the field in the set of highly systematic safety standards it has developed related to piping and valve identification. Most local and catalogue suppliers offer a range of products that meet ANSI requirements, including attachable flow arrows, preprinted, customized, or blank pipe markers, both the snap-around and decal variety (see the Resources section at the back of book).

From the Customer's Perspective

Location information can make an important, if unexpected, contribution to building your customer base. The same maps that can give the workforce a greater sense of safety, security, and context, for example, can have a similar impact on customers visiting a plant.

Customer visits are usually linked either to the status of business you are currently doing for them or to the possibility of new business. My own informal research strongly suggests that the safer and more secure customers feel, the more relaxed they become—and the more confident they are in your ability to meet their requirements. Maps have an obvious role to play here, and there is more that location information can offer.

Cycle through your work area when you and your team think visual order is in place. Only this time, look with the eyes of a customer. Is there location information that you take for granted that could be shared visually for the sake of your customers? How about addressing and labeling those CNC machines? Think about helping the customer "get smart" about your process by posting the name of each machine (technical and common name) on the machine itself. Indicate the products that each machine routinely makes—and, if it fits, add the customers for those products. Post the name of the operator or operators who run the machine, and consider including a photograph along with the number of years each person has worked for the company.

Sharing this information visually can go a long way in helping customers understand the process and the quality work that you and your colleagues produce on their behalf. This 5S-for-the-customer approach gives visitors enough information to pose specific questions (instead of vague and general ones) as they move through an area. Location information geared to the concerns of visitors helps them feel "smart"—and rightly so. With location information in place, the customer stands a real chance of understanding the process. Without it, a satisfying exchange is far less likely to occur.

Photo 7-21 is of a standing sign that the area team designed for the benefit of customers and visitors. It shows a photo of what the material looks like when it enters the department—and what it looks like when it leaves. The sign itself was professionally done and the impact on customers has been very positive.

As a customer of that plant explained when he awarded a $3.5 million contract to it instead of a rival:

"Both your companies have just about identical processes and identical quality. But your plant looks as if your people really know what they are doing. Better

7-21. Standing Sign at Hamilton Standard.

This sign was made for the benefit of customers. It shows the product before and after it was processed in this work area.

than that: Your plant made me look as if *I knew* what you were doing. That is the difference."

That's a difference you can take to the bank.

Finally, anticipating the visual needs of the customer is a sure way to keep visual order alive and growing. This is called "going to green" in the 5S + 1 methodology: when you and your associates hit the jackpot and the implementation shifts from great to fabulous. You'll get details on this in Chapter 14.

How Much Is Too Much?

A question that comes up frequently in shopfloor address campaigns is, "How much is too much?" When I hear this question, I always think about the great Gary Larson cartoon you see in Exhibit 7-4. You may think this shows an extreme—but obviously someone thought it was just enough.

Exhibit 7-4. How Much Is Too Much?

"Now! ... *That* should clear up
a few things around here!"

The real answer to this question is as short as it is true: It depends. It depends on the performance needs and expectations of your own work area. If your company is in the process of switching over to cell design, you may have less of a need for addresses, simply because your operations are physically so much closer together. Motion has been reduced to a minimum, shopfloor processes have been highly standardized, and adherence is vastly improved. You will need less location information to bring a state of visual order to production.

This level of "enough-ness," however, would not work for companies that have just switched to lean production—or are still waiting to commit. And the majority of organizations are in one of those two groups. Others still follow a highly traditional approach to getting product out the door. Large lot sizes, long changeover times, mountains of WIP, and lots of material handling. If that is your company, then you will need a wide range of visual location information devices to bring some clarity and logic to an otherwise chaotic shop floor. This is the kingdom of the hot lists. Nothing is predictable. Indeed, little is known in advance because the operating assumptions of the production system are constantly changing. A thorough implementation of 5S+1 in this kind of enterprise can go a long way in helping you and your associates cope with the constant change and keep it from tipping over into turmoil.

What should your work area look like? The answer lies in the link with motion. Ask yourself, "How much time in the course of my work is spent searching, wondering, wandering, and waiting—or bending, reaching, stretching, lifting, dragging, pushing, and turning? Or doing anything that shifts my attention away from the core activity of the corporation—adding value?" If you still spend a lot of time in motion, think about

Exhibit 7-5. The First Five Principles of Visual Order.

5S + 1	Principle	Description	Reminders
S1	Sort Through and Sort Out	Clear out the clutter; remove all non-required items. Keep only what's needed. *Get rid of the junk.*	Make sure to let the values of The Code guide you (remember Charley's Table).
S2	Scrub the Workplace	Define what *clean* means. Then clean all workplace surfaces and items. Paint as needed. *Cleaning is ownership.*	Make sure cleaning extends into cabinets and drawers and under machines and work-benches.
S3	Secure Safety	Make safety gains through visual order. *Make it safer to work.*	Don't overload S3 with all the unaddressed safety issues in your area. Form separate safety team if needed.
S4	Select Locations	Designate a location for each remaining item, based on the flow of material and information. *Design out the waste of motion.*	Do the What-Is/Could-Be Maps; double-check to ensure you've included *all* items with a footprint. Question your assumptions.
S5	Set Locations	Give each location a border, home address, and ID label. *A place for everything and everything in its place.*	Putting location information in place is a gradual process. Do it in small steps and in depth. Focus on item recoil.

putting more location information in place. Others may call it "going overboard." I call it "just enough."

Don't hesitate to encourage associates and teams to go overboard at the outset of a 5S + 1 implementation. Letting people go overboard gives permission to each person to do what they need to do to meet the visual requirements of their own work.

The question is not what "should" the workplace look like but:

• Does this current level of visual order serve my purpose?
• Am I able to meet what my work, my company, and my associates require of me?

The Hidden Benefit of a Clean, Safe, Orderly Workplace

When an area is clean, safe, and orderly, we can relax and do our work. Visual order lets us focus our full attention on the job at hand.

This state of focused attention can have a subtle and profound impact on the workplace, the company, and us. Visual order allows us to more fully engage in the value-adding work our customers are willing to pay for and our company has hired us to do. Instead of a jagged, interrupted, and reactive pattern of performance, there is a rhythm to our work that is as sure, steady, and fluid as our breath. The result, which we can witness in the world's best companies, is a much higher level of work and much finer degree of personal satisfaction.

☆   ☆   ☆   ☆   ☆

Before we go on to *+1 (sustaining the 5S habit)* and find out what to expect of people during an implementation, we'll read some stories about how several American companies applied the first five principles of visual order on the shop floor (Chapter 8) and in office areas (Chapter 9).

One: The Big Picture		
1. Toward a Visual Workplace	2. Visual Systems in Context	3. The Five Start-Up Requirements
Two: 5S Method		
4. S1/Sort Through and Sort Out	5. S2–S4/ Scrub, Secure Safety, and Select Locations	6. S5/Set Locations: Borders
7. S5/Set Locations: Addresses	8. 5S Stories From the Shop Floor	9. 5S+1 and White-Collar Applications
Three: +1 Method		
10. People: What to Expect	11. +1: Building and Sustaining the 5S Habit	12. +1: Leading by Example	13. +1: Leading Through Standards
Four: Go!		
14. Showcase, Scope, and the System	15. Training and Education	16. The Hundredth Monkey

Chapter 8

5S Stories From the Shop Floor

Visual order can solve many everyday shopfloor problems, the small and the irksome as well as the chronic and the complex. Visual order is part of practically every shopfloor solution.

The case examples in this chapter describe shopfloor visual solutions in four companies. Only one of these companies (Fleet Engineers, Inc.) moved ahead with a systematic implementation of 5S+1. The other three (Philips Automotive Electronics Co., Jackson Corrugated Container Inc., and United Tool and Die Company) applied the principles of visual order to specific workplace conditions. The four stories are:

1. 5S and space utilization/4,150 square feet freed
2. 5S and warehouse material handling/Barney's World

5S Frees 4,150 Square Feet

The first hands-on tool in the 5S+1 process is 3-Tagging: tagging what you want to keep, what you want to get rid of, and what you are not sure about. When you succeed at 3-Tagging, the work area contains only what is needed. The debris is gone. Red-tag success always make us feel great because we are reminded of the powerful benefit that getting simple can have on our work, our lives, and ourselves.

S1/Sort Through and Sort Out was first implemented at Philips Automotive Electronics Co.'s 65,000-square-foot facility in Fort Wayne, Indiana, after Vice President of Operations Robert McKenzie returned from a 5S+1 workshop at the University of Dayton. Here's how Bob described what he came back to and what he did first:

> "Cabinets, racks, and bins were all over the plant, in every corner. So I called a team together and we went out and identified exactly what we needed and what we didn't. Our goal was to free up square footage."

The tags came out. Actually they were stickers, big, round self-stick stickers. Red meant it goes, green meant it stayed, and orange (they couldn't find yellow stickers) meant the thing went into temporary storage. The Philips team moved out "a mountain of stuff," as Bob tells it: 37 metal shelving units, 9 cabinets, and 104 assorted racks (40 of which were sold off). And they did not stop there.

One of the challenges was to find a location for temporary storage, a place to put the parts, tools, and fixtures that would be needed again in six months but were not in use now. This led the team to attack the current storage areas. Once more, they pulled out their stickers, and they hit the jackpot again. A mountain of dark, dusty debris that had cluttered up the back spaces of the factory for decades moved toward the door.

The first cycle of S1 resulted in 2,750 square feet of "new" floor space—or, using Philips's $30-per-square-foot yardstick, $82,000 worth of usable space.

People at Philips were just getting energized, so Bob asked himself, "What can I do to keep the energy going and show people the real power of this method?" In answer, the team turned their attention to the plant's administrative offices.

The facility's nonproduction areas were divided in two: (1) manufacturing support next to the shop floor and (2) engineering, quality, and accounting on the other side of the building. As the team roamed through the two spaces, they saw piles of stuff against practically every wall and in every corner: engineering samples, sales brochures, product sample warrants (PSWs), procedures manuals, fixtures, and excess parts. Unoccupied office cubicles were filled with vacant desks, old computers and printers, sagging bookcases, mimeograph machines and other obsolete equipment, and filing cabinets, lots of filing cabinets, some of which were filled with quote binders that dated as far back as the 1970s. The place was crammed.

The stickers came out again and the facility's twenty office associates learned how to use them. Each person was asked to put a sticker on any thing *or space* s/he needed or wanted for work—and to initial it. The team was shocked to see that entire work areas went unclaimed. "Who owns this stuff? Who owns this space?" they asked. Most of the time, no one knew the answer. After three weeks, anything without a sticker was red-tagged and removed.

In addition, the team discovered that the square footage of most active offices had been partitioned off into spaces that were much larger than the people working there needed or wanted. Applying the flow principles of S4, the team helped slim these areas down to size and made the office work flow more efficient in the process. The result was the liberation of an additional 1,400 square feet, bringing Philips's total reclaimed space to 4,150 square feet, or over 6 percent of the entire facility.

Bob McKenzie says it would have been enough just to get rid of the junk, but the icing on the cake was yet to come. The new square footage was converted into new production space which, in turn, provided the company with the room it needed to bid on a $20 million *new* contract that had previously been passed on because it would have required capital expansion. Philips won the contract. Not bad for getting rid of some "stuff"!

5S and Warehouse Material Handling

In some warehouses, material handling can look like a game of 52-card-pick-up, with inventory instead of cards falling where they may. In many such facilities, pickers, packers, and forklift drivers learn to manage.

The following 5S story takes place in a traditional put/pick/pack warehouse that decided to apply the principles of visual order to one small corner of the building.[1]

Barney's World

Jackson Corrugated Container, Inc., in Middletown, Connecticut, is a small manufacturer of specialized corrugated cardboard shipping cartons. The company's warehouse is a classic. Built in the early 1900s, the 63,000-square-foot facility can house as many as 520,000 pieces of corrugated paper in silos that nearly touch the building's 15-foot ceiling. The place looks like chaos to a newcomer. One small corner of the warehouse (about 10,000 feet) is reserved for the inventory of Wiremold, a nearby wiring systems manufacturer.

Barney Moore is responsible for the Wiremold inventory and he is a master at what he does. Barney works alone, and before 5S + 1, relied strictly on memory to find what he needed as he traveled more than a mile a day by foot or tow motor.

Three things made material handling difficult in Barney's world. First, there was only a single route into the stacks and out again; it was one and the same. Second, all tow motor turns had to be made at a right angle (short square stacks may make sense in a grocery store but not in a warehouse). Third, no visual location information was in

1. Adapted from Gwendolyn D. Galsworth and Lea A. P. Tonkin, "Invasion of the Kaizen Blitzers," *Target: Innovation at Work*, the periodical of the Association for Manufacturing Excellence, vol. 11, no. 2 (March/April 1995).

8-1. Barney's World Before 5S + 1.

Stacks as far as the eye can see.

place to help Barney find his way. Photo 8-1 gives you an idea of what Barney used to face.

Add to these the fact that Wiremold, a JIT facility, regularly changed its orders several times a day. Phone messages and faxes with the latest requirements were constantly landing on Barney's "desk." And that's another thing: The quotes around the word *desk* were there because Barney did all his paperwork on a 4-foot stack of cardboard in the center of the area. Though the Wiremold orders always got filled accurately and on time, it usually took the whole day.

Barney and his boss were skeptical when they first heard about the concept of visual order but agreed to give it a try, on the condition that Barney's pick/put time would be significantly reduced in the process. The boss gave Barney and a small team of outsiders three days to make the change.

The first thing the team did was to remove all unneeded items from the area (S1), including obsolete Wiremold inventory and a 1967 red Ford Mustang that belonged to the owner. Then the area layout was redefined, and as many 90-degree angles as possible were removed, changing the flow from angular to diagonal (S4). In addition, the team discovered an unused loading dock 40 percent closer to the Wiremold inventory and prepared it for use.

Then the inventory itself was recategorized and clustered, with the most frequently ordered items placed nearest the dock and the less popular ones stacked further away. The slowest-moving items were moved out of the mainstream entirely. Each stack then got its own large ceiling sign, with a corresponding inventory part number on it. Preliminary location information was in place. And the icing on Barney's cake was a brand-new workstation, a standing desk constructed just for him, with a place for everything built into the work surface.

The impact of these simple improvements was impressive. Flow distance decreased by 105 feet, overall trip time was reduced by 25 percent, and Barney and his tow motor enjoyed far greater maneuverability.

Epilogue. About eighteen months after this improvement blitz hit Barney's world, I visited Jackson Corrugated for an update. What I saw did not surprise me. The ceiling signs were still in place, and Barney's new desk was still standing, but the clear traffic lanes had completely eroded and the desk was surrounded with damaged cartons, old tools, and general debris. All this confirmed my own experience that an improvement blitz can promise a lot and yet deliver little in the long run. That is why, as you will read in Chapter 15, I do not recommend the blitz, however seductive its promise. Instead, I recommend a methodical, step-by-step implementation of 5S + 1 as detailed in this book.

5S and Shopfloor Material Handling

United Tool and Die Company (UTD) is a tube-forming manufacturer in West Hartford, Connecticut, whose customers include Pratt & Whitney, Boeing, and Hamilton Standard. In 1994, UTD got on the improvement bandwagon by overhauling its die storage, mapping out a demand-flow system and implementing visual order in its pressure test area. It also came up with a creative solution to a worrisome problem for the whole plant: material handling.

George's Dilemma

George (not his real name) is in charge of material handling at UTD. George, who has been at UTD for over twenty years, is known by everyone to be hardworking, loyal, cheerful, and always willing to lend a hand. His is not an easy job, since, on any given day, pick-ups and deliveries can happen anywhere on the three floors of UTD's sprawling 145,000-square-foot facility.

Material handling is a challenge for George for another reason—he forgets and he knows he forgets. Pick-up and delivery mistakes were made and George got in the habit of getting someone else to double-check his work. When I entered the scene, that person was Victor Garo, UTD's plant manager. George wanted Vic to verify virtually every move of the day. No amount of personal support and reassurance seemed enough to build George's confidence and put him at ease with his abilities.

With the business expanding and the production system moving toward a higher level of output variety, UTD and George were at a crossroads.

Mistake-Proof Material Handling. Vic and his staff decided to put their heads together to find a visual solution to George's dilemma. They put themselves in George's shoes to answer the two core questions:

Exhibit 8-1. George's New Cart.

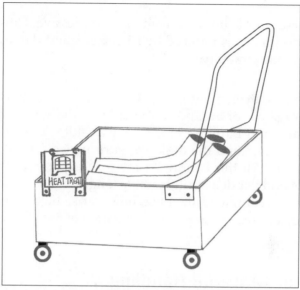

This is a drawing of one of George's carts, with the useful addition of a pack of location icon cards. When the cart is ready, the associate simply flips to the icon for the next downstream process—George's instructions when he arrives for the pick-up.

1. What does George need to know?
2. What does George need to share?

Their answers were translated into an innovative visual minisystem that eliminated the problem 100 percent.

The center of the solution is a booklet of laminated cards, each with an icon for each of the UTD departments on George's material flow route. A set of these cards was attached to each handling cart. When a UTD associate finished an operation, she put the completed work in a cart and flipped to the icon for the next operation, the downstream process. To make sure the cards didn't accidentally flip over and send the wrong signal, the operator clipped the card in place with a clothespin. When George came by, he could tell at a glance where the cart was supposed to go next, and he would take it there, confidently, without the need to double-check with anyone (Exhibit 8-1).

The icons that UTD chose were very specific to its process and to George. Heat-treat, for example, was easy to render by drawing an oven. Welding could be indicated by a torch. But how should they show the difference between nondestructive and pressure testing? The team's answers were ingenious. Nondestructive testing was indicated by an elevator with an arrow pointing down, because that process was located in UTD's basement, which George reached by elevator. A pay phone became the icon for pressure testing—the phone George used at lunch to call his wife. See these icons in Exhibit 8-2.

The new visual minisystem worked perfectly. No need for George to check with anyone. Confident in what his eyes told him, George responded with dignity and speed.

Exhibit 8-2. George's Icons.

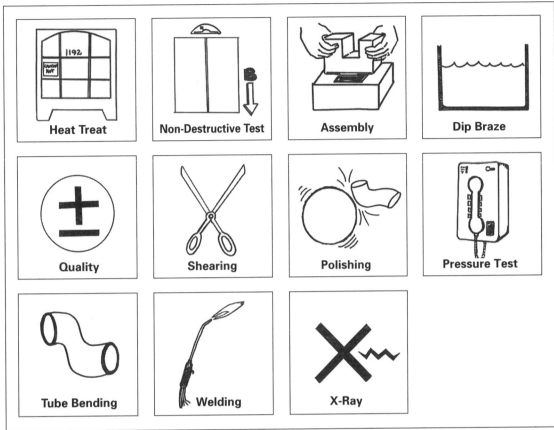

Heat Treat	Non-Destructive Test	Assembly	Dip Braze
Quality	Shearing	Polishing	Pressure Test
Tube Bending	Welding	X-Ray	

Here are the eleven icons that George used for about a year, until the process evolved, along with George's job description.

At last report, the icon minisystem has given way to progress. UTD is converting to a kanban-driven system. George's job description is also changing—and he is ready for it.

5S and Quick Equipment Changeover

Equipment can add value to production only when it is available. One of the times a machine is not available is when it is being changed over to run a different product.

> Equipment changeover time is the time that elapses between the last good piece of one run and the first good piece of the next run.

Long changeovers can take a big bite out of machine utilization time. But changeovers don't need to take a long time. Thanks to a four-step technique called Quick Changeover (QCO), long changeovers have become a thing of the past in thousands of plants all over

Exhibit 8-3. Four Basic Steps to Quick Changeover.

Step 1: Document	Document the *what-is* state. Record your changeover exactly as it is currently being performed. Do this by video; then register every single element or step on a linear flowchart, along with the time each step *actually* took to complete. These data provide you with your improvement focus and the raw material for your analysis.
Step 2: Analyze	Distinguish between the changeover steps that were actually done when the machine was running (called ''external elements'') and the steps that were done when the machine was not running (called ''internal elements'').
Step 3: Convert	Convert as many internal elements as possible into external elements. Do this by questioning every assumption you and your team have about why each internal element must be done when the machine is off—and why each external step cannot be eliminated entirely. Push up against every assumption you can find and seek to change each in favor of reduced changeover time.
Step 4: Streamline	Take every bit of motion (non-value-adding activity) out of all external elements and internal elements. To assist, apply 5S + 1: the principles and practices of visual order.

---

the world. Changeovers that used to take three hours (or even three days) in the 1980s can now be completed in thirty minutes or ten minutes or even three minutes. And a growing number of changeovers are completed in 100 seconds or less. The QCO method was developed by Dr. Shigeo Shingo in the 1950s at Toyota Motor Company. For details, read Dr. Shingo's classic, *SMED: A Revolution in Manufacturing* (Portland, Ore.: Productivity Press, 1985).

Quick changeover is a fundamental building block of lean production. Without it, the switch from high inventory (traditional) to just-in-time manufacturing could never happen.

The key to quick changeover is making the distinction between setup tasks that can be done while the machine is still running (staging tools and dies) and those that can be done only when the machine is shut down (tightening bolts). First separate external tasks (machine is running) from internal tasks (machine is off), then convert as many internal activities as possible into external ones, and then work to streamline both of them. It all comes down to this: Get rid of the motion. And visual order is vital to that process: Searching for tools during a changeover is like a surgeon looking for clamps while the patient is open and bleeding on the operating table. Teams that diligently apply the QCO method typically see a reduction in changeover time that ranges from 70 to 95 percent. Exhibit 8-3 summarizes the four basic steps of QCO.

Fleet's Bliss

Fleet Engineers, Inc., is a small stamping plant in Muskegon, Michigan, that supplies components and stampings for the automotive and heavy truck industry. Fleet has been in the high-volume/high-inventory stamping business for over three decades.

In 1994, Fleet management began to look for ways to implement lean production and change forever the way the company did business. During the next six months, Fleet had some success. A group of employees learned some things about cell design and put one cell in place, and learned some things about quick changeover—and got nowhere. It bears mentioning that this fledgling effort was the first time anyone at Fleet had any experience working in teams.

In 1995, Fleet decided to backtrack and implement the principles of visual order. A shopfloor steering team was formed and several 5S+1 projects were launched. Shortly after that, interest in quick changeover revived and a five-member QCO team began to meet (see Photo 8-2 for a combined picture of Fleet's 5S+1 steering and QCO teams).

The QCO team chose to begin on the 500-ton Bliss stamping press. Called P-1, this press handles thirty separate Fleet products, running about fifteen different products per month with outputs between 10,000 and 30,000 pieces per run. The net effect is that P-1 gets changed over four to five times a week. At the time the team began meeting, a P-1 changeover took one person from 1.5 hours to 4.0 hours to complete. Photo 8-3 will give a sense of the P-1 area before 5S+1.

8-2. Combined Fleet QCO and Visual Workplace Steering Team.

Front row (*left to right*): Roscoe Clark, Laura Dewald, Dan Herzshaft, and Brett Balkema. Back row (*left to right*): Gary Buys, Greg Hancock, Craig Tobey, Steven Hascher, and Kenny Cain.

8-3. Fleet's Press-1 Area: Before.

It is always a good idea to document an area by videotape or photographs before you implement visual order. Here is Fleet's Press-1 area shortly before the team began its work. Dark, disorganized, cluttered—a potential trigger for waste and accidents.

Last Things First. The first thing that members of Fleet's QCO team decided to do was *not* the first of the four basic steps presented in Exhibit 8-3. They did not document existing procedures. They did not distinguish between internal and external tasks, nor did they attempt to convert internal activity to external. They began by applying visual order to the dies storage area.

The reason they chose to do this is as important as the results they achieved. In the words of one of the team's associates, "Our biggest concern was getting five people to be able to look each other in the eye and work as a team. If we couldn't paint dies as a team, we sure couldn't reduce changeover time as a team."

To the team, that meant two things: (1) sharing the load and (2) no in-fighting. The associates on that team began with 5S + 1 exactly because they were not yet a team. They knew 5S + 1 was a simple, straightforward activity that allowed everyone to contribute something. No one would feel outdistanced or intimidated. Implementing visual order as a first step would either turn them into a team or show them that they could not be one.

This proved a wise choice for several reasons. First of all, two of the two team members were new to the P-1 area. Two others had been doing P-1 changeovers for decades, only solo. Gary Buys, who had been with Fleet for seventeen years, was the main setup operator for the first shift. Roscoe Clark, the second-shift setup specialist, was in his eighth year with the company. They were expert. Both these men knew they knew their stuff *and* they preferred to work alone. The fifth team member was brand-new to Fleet. That much difference in experience on a team can create a distance between its members that is often hard to bridge.

5S + 1 Task 1: Reorganizing Dies. It was unanimous. The team would begin by reorganizing the dies and tooling. P-1 required a lot of each for the thirty different products it ran. Plus, many dies were progressive, weighing from 5,000 to 8,000 pounds each and requiring multiple tools. Not a single die or tool had a home address or an ID label. In many cases, P-1 dies and tools were not even stored in the same location, let alone the same storage crib. As a result, a forklift had to be available during practically every changeover to help in the searching game.

During its first month together, the QCO team applied S1 through S5. They located, centralized, cleaned, painted, and labeled the thirty P-1 dies and the rack that held them. In the process, the team confronted their first hurdle—two people were doing most of the work. The load was not getting shared. And the two men doing the work began to grump and complain—to everyone but their fellow team members. The prediction was turning out to be true: They couldn't even get paint on the dies. That is when these five separate people instituted their first group norm (rule of conduct): *Show up; speak the truth; state how you feel.*

That's when the magic began to happen. The members of the group began to air their differences and pulled together. They were becoming a team. Besides the major die reorganization, the racks got a fresh coat of white paint, the P-1 dies were painted blue,

8-4. New Die Rack System.

In addition to a fresh coat of paint and significant reorganization of dies, the Fleet team switched the die rack layout from a straight line to an L-shape so they would have a ready-made corner for staging in the crook of the L.

and the tooling was color-coordinated to the dies. In addition, the QCO team changed the rack layout from a straight line to an L-shape in order to stake out a die-staging area in the crook of the L. See Photo 8-4 for the die rack's new look.

5S + 1 Task 2: Tool Carts. The next task brought the team closer to the actual changeover process. They began to apply visual order to the press area itself. After removing bins of debris that had collected over the years, the team determined: (1) which hand tools were actually needed in the vicinity of the press for the changeover, and (2) how to best arrange them. Up to then, every Fleet setup operator was expected to use his/her own set of tools. But the bald truth was that the required tools were never all on hand when they were needed, and lots and lots of time was spent hunting them down.

To remedy this situation, the team first developed a list of essential items. Then, using the $1,000 that Fleet management budgeted for the project at the outset, the team

8-5. New Changeover Cart.

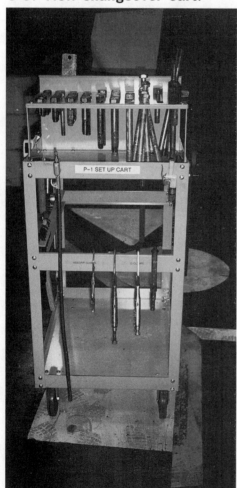

The Fleet team loaded up two crayon-yellow rolling carts with the tools and backups needed for a quick changeover—one complete cart for each side of its 500-ton stamping press.

purchased two complete tool sets and two crayon-yellow changeover carts (one for each side of the press) so tools would be positioned right next to the press. Each cart held an identical set of custom tools, plus wire brushes, a tape measure, paper toweling, T-handle Allen wrenches (for the roller conveyor system), ball peen hammers, hacksaws, pins for plate alignment, bolts, washers, and tie-down straps. In short, everything an associate needed to do the changeover—and lots of just-in-case items.

For another $200 or so, Fleet bought a label maker, which the QCO team used to complete the labeling of the dies, die rack, new tools, and the new QCO carts (Photo 8-5). (See the Resources section for details of label-making systems.)

At the same time, the team rehabilitated the stand-up desk in the vicinity of the press. First they cleaned it and changed its color from dingy gray to sparkling blue (to match the color coding for P-1 dies). Then they added a backboard to hold current work orders, hour-by-hour production, and information on upcoming changeovers. They also made sure the desk had all necessary information on prepping and doing P-1 changeovers. Compiling this information meant collecting and verifying lots of details, including size and location references on dies, belts, plates, feed lengths, stock, and oil mixtures. In this way, the desk became the nerve center for the P-1 area and is now in constant use (Photo 8-6).

At this stage, order began to emerge at a gallop in the P-1 area, and the five Fleet associates had grown into a fully functional team, now ready to tackle the QCO procedure systematically, beginning with step one!

8-6. Stand-Up Desk.

This stand-up desk is the nerve center of the P-1 area, full of critical information needed to make P-1 changeovers rapid and exact.

Use 5S + 1 to Build Trust and Confidence

The point of this story should be clear. Take stock of the process and developmental needs of your group before you undertake a project that requires you to share the load. If you and your associates don't feel ready to work cooperatively together, don't give up. Just look for ways to get ready.

And one of the best ways to get ready is to engage in a simple, concrete improvement process together. Implementing visual order is one such process. Its requirements are obvious and practically everyone can make a concrete contribution. As this happens, confidence in oneself and the group grows, even as small, visible improvements are made in your work area.

When that happens, other powerful changes begin to take root and you may start telling your own 5S stories from the shop floor that inform and inspire others.

What makes these four stories worth telling is the clear way in which associates with different objectives from different work settings applied the principles of visual order and made a tangible contribution to their company. These are stories that inspire and inform because they stand witness to the remarkable determination in each of us to improve.

Before we move on to Part Three of the book and learn about the + 1 portion of the 5S + 1 approach, let's take a short side trip into the offices that surround the shop floor and see what happens when visual order is implemented there.

One: The Big Picture		
1. Toward a Visual Workplace	2. Visual Systems in Context	3. The Five Start-Up Requirements
Two: 5S Method		
4. S1/Sort Through and Sort Out	5. S2–S4/ Scrub, Secure Safety, and Select Locations	6. S5/Set Locations: Borders
7. S5/Set Locations: Addresses	8. 5S Stories From the Shop Floor	9. 5S+1 and White-Collar Applications
Three: +1 Method			
10. People: What to Expect	11. +1: Building and Sustaining the 5S Habit	12. +1: Leading by Example	13. +1: Leading Through Standards
Four: Go!		
14. Showcase, Scope, and the System	15. Training and Education	16. The Hundredth Monkey

Chapter 9

5S+1 and White-Collar Applications

> Time is the inventory of the office.
> —Nick Vanderstoop
> GM of Canada Ltd.

Have you ever stood at the doorway of an empty office, baffled, confused, and uncertain? You know you are in the purchasing department (for example)—and that is *all* you know.

9-1. The Office Challenge.

If this office looks familiar, you know very well how hard it is to find anyone or anything in an area without location information.

The Search for Meaning

The entire office is empty of people. Not a soul in sight. You face a sea of desks without owners, each populated with uneven piles of reports, memos, computer readouts, and all other manner of paperwork (Photo 9-1). There is no one to point out the person you are looking for or tell you that she is at a meeting, home sick, on vacation, or no longer working there.

You take the hint and turn to leave, knowing that you'll come back later and unless you find a guide, the same thing may happen again. It doesn't surprise you. This is often what happens when you go to any of the company's nonproduction areas: accounting, customer service, field service, quality, human resources, data systems, drafting, engineering. If you can't find a fellow human to guide you through, you might as well turn back.

From a visual systems viewpoint, the most striking feature of most offices is how much you do *not* see of what goes on there. Not only is basic location information rarely in place but, unlike the shop floor, few clues are given about the process. The workplace is mute.

Visual order in nonproduction areas is as critical to a company's well-being and profitability as it is on the plant floor. In the opinion of many, it is more important because, in their view, the level of waste is even higher in offices than on the shop floor. When an enterprise undertakes 5S + 1 in the offices, you know the company is serious about running fast and lean.

The Secret Thief of Time

Seeing the truth behind white-collar activity requires us to change our mind-set about three things:

1. Information is the output of an office. Information is its product. That product can take many forms: reports, letters, memos, or some other manner of document, decisions, presentations, and the spoken word.

2. Motion is every bit as widespread and deeply rooted in nonproduction areas as on the factory floor. It expresses itself much the same way: as searching, walking, reaching, stretching, bending, questioning, interrupting, waiting, waiting, waiting, and waiting. Each one of these "activities" delays us that much longer from adding value to the task at hand. Motion in white-collar areas is so constant and random, it goes unnoticed and unnamed. Over time, it comes to be considered "normal." In truth, it is chronically abnormal. We just got used to it.

3. Time is the inventory of the office. When we run out of parts on the shop floor, work stops. When we run out of information in an office (a needed signature, a missing sales figure, etc.), we set that work aside and pick up a different job, document, file, drawing, letter, report. We find "something else" to do. We call it keeping busy.

Office Lead Time/Office Flow

Establishing the fastest possible flow of work in your office is directly linked to your ability to name your own outputs and notice when they stall (your so-called "backlog"). Identify each and every time this happens and *why it happens* and you will have taken the first steps toward vastly reduced lead times.

To appreciate the toll that motion takes on office productivity, train yourself to see piles of *time* on your desk, instead of paper. Then get into the habit of tracking the *item's* behavior (not yours). You can do this simply by marking any document or request that hits your desk with its arrival time. Note the date, hour, and minute. Then record the time it leaves your desk *for good*. Keep track of this on a graph. You may be amazed at what you learn.

The fact is this: The lead-time clock is still running on the report waiting for a signature, even though you pick up something new to work on in the meantime. The lead-time clock is still ticking on the first task. And it keeps on ticking until that task is complete and moves downstream to the next process or into the waiting hands of its customer. No matter what we may choose to do in the meantime, waiting is measured in absolute time.

Getting Started in Nonproduction Areas

Lead-time reduction in white-collar areas begins with visual order. As on the shop floor, so in the office: Begin with 5S + 1.

9-2. Roped-Off Area.

Here are the combined results of the first cycle of red-tagging in three nonproduction areas: finance, marketing, and sales. What a haul!

S1/Sort Through and Sort Out

Begin by separating the essential from the nonessential. Apply the 3-Tag technique and get rid of the junk.

Some office associates prefer to focus on what to keep, instead of what to toss. They use green tags exclusively and simply cart unwanted items to a central dumping area without bothering with red tags. They also may not find yellow tags relevant. So be it, as long as the clutter goes. Photo 9-2 shows you the red-tag items identified in the first cycle of S1 in a sales/marketing and finance office; the team had to rope off an entire corner of the floor to fit in all the debris.

S2/Scrub the Workplace

Clean it up, dust it off. Compared to shopfloor chips, grease, and grime, S2 in offices is typically a snap. Anyway, most office areas have daily cleaning done in-house or by an outside vendor. A clean workplace is usually not a difficult goal for white-collar settings.

S3/Secure Safety

Next, conduct a safety check and raise safety awareness in each nonproduction department. Common risk elements in offices include loose electrical and computer wiring, cords stretched across walkways, poorly conceived emergency exit routes, unplanned heavy lifting, sharp corners, and poor ergonomics. Look for ways to improve these through visual order.

S4/Select Locations

S4 can be a major doorway to an accelerated flow of paper and information in any office, especially in an office that houses multiple functions like procurement, customer service, field service, and accounting. Whether on the production floor or in an office, the goal of S4 is smart placement.

Smart placement means finding a physical layout that quickens the flow of work between functions. The procedure for doing this in an office is identical to the one on the shop floor. Working with your associates, document the current work flow on a What-Is Map. Then, develop a Could-Be Map and see how many physical roadblocks you can remove on paper by realigning the components of that area.

S5/Set Locations

In S5 for offices, we put location information in place to give everyone a fighting chance to find what they need—including your desk, whether or not you are at it.

As with visual order on the shop floor, setting locations in offices involves three acts:

1. Put a border around each item.
2. Put a home address on each border.
3. Put an ID label on each item.

Let's look first at the bordering process.

External Borders

In nonproduction areas, we make a distinction between external borders and internal borders. An external border is one you can see; it is out in the open, visible to anyone who walks by.

As before, outline nonmovable items, workways and walkways, and movable items. Use duct tape or plain masking tape first until placements are verified; then move to plastic tape or paint (sealants are likely not to be necessary). Use dots instead of a full boundary on high-use items like chairs and wastebaskets.

You already know why borders are important. They show the relationship logic within your work area and are great antiaccumulation devices. But don't be surprised if others do not share your enthusiasm for this first step in smart placement. They will probably give you any one—or all—of the following four reasons for not laying borders:

Four Reasons for Not Laying Borders in Offices

1. Most office items (small equipment, furniture, cabinets, files) are never moved. Therefore, borders are not needed.
2. There are few safety issues (such as traveling machine parts) that make borders necessary in a nonproduction area. Therefore, borders are not needed.

3. Our offices are nicely carpeted and borders would look out of place (read "ugly"). Therefore, borders are not wanted.
4. We often host special guests, customers, and other VIPs in our area and do not want it looking like a shop floor (read "ugly"). Therefore, borders are not wanted.

Those four points are enough to dampen anyone's enthusiasm about external borders, so don't be surprised if you find yourself backing off. Accept compromise here, but don't give an inch on internal borders.

Internal Borders

Internal borders are not visible to the casual observer. They are out of sight, inside cabinets, desks, and closets. When combined with home addresses and clear ID labels, they trigger instant item recognition and item recoil. They are also vital in preventing office stock-outs.

Put borders in place for all fixed and consumable supplies. Use the control dimension of lines to define minimum and maximum supply limits as well as the trigger points for reordering. Add a red line or a red sheet of paper as reorder signals. (If you use a sheet, write complete reorder information directly on it and/or contact data for the person inside the company who needs to be alerted.)

Here's another pointer on supply bordering. Put a border down as a visual control on each side of the supply limit and let these lines serve to both indicate the quantity-on-hand and differentiate between locations if items are out.

Home Addresses

When your internal borders are in place, address each location. Where consumable supplies are concerned, use the actual package label as the address. In that way, you will have complete reorder information at a glance.

Home addresses are crucial in offices, but they can be much more low-key than on the shop floor, since you will not need to recognize them from a moving forklift. Trans-matic Manufacturing, a precision deep-draw stamping company in Holland, Michigan, is making impressive strides in implementing visual order on the shop floor and in its offices. Go into the office of Rob Ptacek, director of operations, and you will find an array of home addresses in muted blue and white across his work surface and on top of desk-high filing cabinets. While nearly invisible to the casual observer, these addresses are handy to Trans-matic associates who need to access vital information. More than once these addresses have allowed others to locate crucial documents accurately and quickly while Rob was off-site or waiting expectantly on an airport telephone.

Front-office home addresses also serve the four associates who work next to Rob in customer service and production control, functions that have a high level of interaction with suppliers, customers, and production personnel. Folks from the shop floor are free to go to Mary Wiley in production control, for example, to check on the status of material and scheduling changes. Because Mary's area is a picture of visual order, people can find their way easily without her even being in the building. Life has become much easier at

Trans-matic since visual order was introduced, and the team still sees plenty of room for more visual information sharing.

Another point of interest: Rob has developed a modified 5S checklist that he calls the **PEEP Index,** which stands for "a **P**lace for **E**verything and **E**verything in its **P**lace." The Index is used in Trans-matic offices and on the production floor to point the way to further improvement. (See Chapter 11 for more on 5S checklists.)

ID Labels

Put an ID label on each office item and "hand tool": staplers, scissors, rulers, paper cutters, hole punches, and the like. Label all small equipment: copiers, shredders, computers, printers, scanners, and so forth. Make the ID information complete. Make it driver's license level. Mark the exact name of the computer as well as its specs (586, 100Mhz, graphic card, audio), and the software it runs. True, your systems person has that information back at his/her desk. How much handier it is for everyone to access it directly from the machine.

If you follow this route, make sure to date the ID label and schedule periodic updates so the information stays current. While you are at it, put in the name and contact information of the support person responsible for each machine and any other information that promotes 100 percent equipment availability.

The Principles of Visual Order as Applied in Office Settings

Home Addresses and Visual Controls

Combining visual indicators with visual controls can give a powerful boost to location information and item recoil. Photo 9-3 shows an excellent example of this: a wooden shelving unit for distributors' quotes binders and OEM quotes in the customer sales and service (CSS) department at United Electric Controls (UE).

Before this shelving unit was built, finding needed information was a struggle. Distributor quotes were kept in folders in a filing cabinet in one corner of the department and were often misfiled. Binders of OEM quotes could be found in a rickety bookcase in another corner. Each of the binders weighed nearly 10 pounds and got temporarily "lost" many times during a given workday.

When 5S + 1 came to the company, the CSS team took on the challenge of the quotes. First, the team did away with the file folder system. All quotes were put into uniform binders: red ones for distributor quotes and blue ones for OEM quotes. Each set of binders got its own name label and number in sequence. That was the visual-indicator part of the solution.

The visual-control part came when the wooden shelving unit was built to house the binders. Instead of open shelving, each shelf had a series of slots into which one (and only one) binder could fit. Each binder had its own home. The internal structure of the unit does not offer the choice of crowding more into the space; only one binder fits in each slot. That controls behavior.

9-3. Visual Order and Control Comes to the Bookshelf.

Ryta Mullen stands proudly by the excellent minisystem she and her co-workers created in UE's CSS department. Capitalizing on visual controls, the slotted bookshelf allows for one book per cubbyhole, and the book holder on the top ensures that you put the first binder away before you take out another one.

A second visual control device that the team came up with is the slanted wooden shelf on the top of the unit. It is only big enough to hold one binder at a time. That means you are forced to put one binder away before you can look at another one—even if someone else left it there. Look again at the photo.

This excellent office minisystem not only minimized motion for the CSS associates; it allowed people from other departments to be self-regulating. For example, before the unit was introduced, if someone from sales came to the CSS area to verify a quote, s/he would almost certainly have to find a CSS associate to help. Now a person could go directly to the shelving unit and get the needed information without disturbing anyone else.

The Drawer and the Monster

Early in the UE 5S+1 implementation, Debbie Martin (CSS manager) and the nine associates who worked there decided to take another big bite out of departmental motion. They standardized the use of the upper right-hand drawer of all the desks in the area. Each of these drawers was to be laid out exactly the same and have exactly the same things in it: a uniform set of pencils, pens, notepaper, and forms (purchase orders, change orders, advance notices, credit slips). In this way, if a CSS associate was on the phone with a customer but not at his desk, the associate could go to any nearby desk and have instant access to a standard set of CSS tools.

Similarly, CSS associates wanted everyone in the department to have easy access to all department procedures. A massive three-ring manual of these procedures was placed on the top of every desk. It was affectionately dubbed the "Monster." Again, if an associate was away from his own desk and needed procedural information quick, he could use a colleague's Monster.

The system seemed to be working well until it was discovered that the frequent updates that each associate was supposed to make in the manual in response to memos from Debbie were either incorrect, incomplete, or simply overlooked. The information was not reliable. The visual order part was working but the content itself was not.

This problem was entirely solved when CSS associate Ryta Mullen volunteered to make these changes in each Monster herself and in a timely manner. The Monster system has been working seamlessly ever since.

Personnel Addresses

Addresses for individual employees are a matter of enormous importance in nonproduction areas. No other visual device is more fundamental and so rarely provided. Those little wooden nameplates that peep out from under piles of paper simply do not cover the need.

When asked, I lay down the law on this one: *Each and every person in each and every office must have a visible, accurate, and complete address.* The minimum is the person's name and extension number in large, dark, bold letters. Photo 9-4 shows you a bare-bones approach, taped in place over the desk of Ms. Hurton, a project engineer at UE.

The personnel address in Photo 9-5 gives a bit more information by including a photograph of Brenda (Fitch) Ripley, senior quality assurance coordinator at UE. Not

9-4. Joan's Address.

A simple personnel address like this one is the first giant leap in visually sharing some of the most basic workplace information: Who works here and what does she do?

9-5. Brenda's Address.

Brenda added a picture of herself. Thank you. Now we can find her when she is not at her desk.

9-6. Cindy's Address.

This is a great example of what driver's-license-style information means in a personnel address.

just a nice touch, a photo can be a great help to those who do not know Mrs. Ripley by sight. This addition hints at the wide range of key information shopfloor associates would like to know and need to know about those mysterious people who work in offices.

To date, the ultimate in personnel addresses is shown in Photo 9-6: the address of Cindy Barter, senior commodity specialist in UE's Supplier Development Department. Notice the completeness of information, which is repeated in Exhibit 9-1 so you can see the logic of each line. This level of visual information sharing proved so helpful that the company is considering adopting Cindy's template companywide.

Putting It All Together at GM

One of the most creative and complete office implementations of visual order was developed by Nicholas Vanderstoop of General Motors of Canada in the late 1980s. At that time, Nick was head administrator of GM's North American Parts Distribution Center in Woodstock, Ontario. I was working with Nick's group on a combined visual order/ team problem-solving project.

As my work there was nearing completion, GM management decided to capitalize a complete overhaul of the front office space at the Woodstock facility. Nick was ready with a vision waiting to happen. Working with the front office team, Nick thoroughly redesigned the space for an up-front savings of $750,000 over the earlier plan. In the process, Nick created an entirely new approach to office productivity, one that dissolved one information bottleneck after another and brought into practical application the concepts of 5S + 1.

The first thing Nick and his team did was to relocate all office processes into the

Exhibit 9-1. Details: Cindy's Address.

Address Information	What It Means
Cindy Barter	Name
Buyer #6	Computer ID number. This tells us how Cindy is identified in the computer records. Note: Her name is not used.
Ext. 207	Cindy's phone extension.
Responsibilities Screw Machine Parts Sintered Metal Bar Stock Wire & Cable Motors Bellows	The products that Cindy is responsible for purchasing.
Alternate: Jon Birkett	Whom to contact if Cindy is not available. Jon is her backup.

same area, regrouping them into cross-functional clusters. In a heartbeat, communication between departments improved significantly.

Sharing the same physical space also facilitated knowledge transfer, one of the core outcomes of Nick's vision. In a brilliant move that married visual order with cell design, Nick asked each island of associates to identify its work outputs, work procedures, and standards of service and capture them in brightly colored files called "knowledge folders." These got color-coded by priority and kept within easy reach of everyone on a lazy Susan in the center of the desks. Once these knowledge folders were completed, people could cross-train each other and work-share.

The new physical layout took several years to optimize and was later formalized into elegant modules of office furniture. Mounted on easy-to-move casters, individual modules could be reconfigured at will. Always at the center were the brightly color-coded knowledge folders, mounted now on a two-tier daisy wheel to ensure easy access.

Nick's accomplishment was a brilliant white-collar adaptation of visual systems and cellular manufacturing. And it all began with optimizing the physical work flow by making it visible and alive in the layout of the workplace through visual order.

We now move to Part Three to learn about the +1 portion of the 5S + 1 approach: building and sustaining the 5S habit.

Three

The + 1 Method

One: The Big Picture		
1. Toward a Visual Workplace	2. Visual Systems in Context	3. The Five Start-Up Requirements
Two: 5S Method		
4. S1/Sort Through and Sort Out	5. S2–S4/ Scrub, Secure Safety, and Select Locations	6. S5/Set Locations: Borders
7. S5/Set Locations: Addresses	8. 5S Stories From the Shop Floor	9. 5S + 1 and White-Collar Applications
Three: +1 Method		
10. People: What to Expect	11. +1: Building and Sustaining the 5S Habit	12. +1: Leading by Example	13. +1: Leading Through Standards
Four: Go!		
14. Showcase, Scope, and the System	15. Training and Education	16. The Hundredth Monkey

Chapter 10

People: What to Expect

Habit is behavior, learned over time.

The principles of visual order cannot take root, let alone serve as a bridge to the next improvement level, if there are not enough people on board and participating in the effort. To achieve this, you must convince a number of people to adopt behaviors that may be largely unfamiliar to them. They must learn new habits.

Developing new habits is not easy. Usually it means not only learning new behaviors but unlearning old ones. And the old ones can hold on tight unless the mistaken beliefs that undergird them are also unlearned. These beliefs are linked to how we perceive ourselves and how we perceive others. Every day, we make choices and act based on beliefs that may not be true.

Unplugging these beliefs and adopting new ones can either be dull and uncomfortable—or exciting and uncomfortable. It depends on how you look at the situation, what your intent is, and how you approach it.

A Launch Scenario

Your company is two months into the 5S+1 implementation and five of the six principles of visual order are nearly in place. Most workplace items are ID'd and have a home address. People are beginning to do things differently. They are putting things back, and noticing when items don't come home on time. Their eyesight and insight are beginning to develop.

A small group of people seem very motivated. Enthusiastic, imaginative, full of energy and ideas, they act as if bringing yet more visual order to their area will "make their day." How can they get so excited about finding a new location for those coils? ("It's the *perfect* place," they croon.) In their spare time (and somehow they find plenty of it), they work on some new visual minisystem or other. John from the machine shop is figuring out a scrap separation system. Debbie (supplier development) and Cindy (customer service) have put together a visual display to help their two departments keep stock-outs to a minimum. And Bill (assembly) has come up with what he calls the *ultimate* workbench. They seem to eat, drink, and breathe 5S+1. When asked why, they will each give some variation of: "5S+1 is the answer to my prayers. Now I know how to make the workplace sing. Now I come to work and it makes sense!"

Other people are not so involved. Some are busy with other types of improvement efforts; they can't spare more time. Others wait on the sidelines. Mostly they watch. They watch John, Debbie, Cindy, and Bill bring order out of chaos—and they barely blink an eye. They do not mind 5S+1. "It's no skin off my nose," is a frequent comment from this group.

In some sense, they even like the changes. The packing minisystem that Bill created put an end to hunting for scissors and tape. They like the changes, but they just don't care to do anything themselves. Maybe someday, but not yet. They are watching. And they are waiting. Waiting to see if this thing called 5S+1 will last. Waiting to see if management keeps up its end of the bargain. Waiting to see if John or Debbie or Cindy or Bill get clobbered for their good efforts. Until all this is cleared up, they are not going to take the risk.

Then there are the people who are a breed apart. They simply don't have anything good to say about anything, least of all the latest new thing: 5S+1. They may be managers. They may be associates. In this company, there's a little of both. Their list of worries, complaints, and misgivings is long and familiar.

John, Debbie, Cindy, and Bill are convinced that visual order is very important for their departments, their company, and their own individual work. They feel upset that not everyone is on board. "Why don't they join in?" they ask. "Why is there such resistance?"

Resistance—or Inertia?

When we believe strongly in something and come to believe that it could be *the* answer that our department/company/world is waiting for, our eyesight can get a little cloudy.

Our tendency is to label as "resistance" everything and everybody that do not agree with us and embrace our idea. We see it as a lack of cooperation, not a preference.

Without a doubt, some of it is resistance. But there is another part—usually a larger part—that is the result of *inertia*. Let's be precise about both of these and define the difference between the two.

Resistance

The American Heritage Dictionary defines *resistance* as "any force that tends to oppose or retard." In medicine, the term *resistance* refers to the ability of a body to ward off disease, a part of its immune system. In electricity, it is used to describe the property that causes heat to be generated when an electric current passes through a channel. In air flight, resistance refers to the upward pushing force that is encountered by the exposed surface of an airplane wing.

In other words, resistance can fight disease, transform electricity into heat, and keep airplanes in the air. In these instances, resistance is not only not bad, it is natural and beneficial.

Inertia

The American Heritage Dictionary defines *inertia* as "the tendency of a body at rest to remain at rest, or [if] in motion to stay in motion in a straight line unless [acted upon] by an external force." In people terms, resistance might be interpreted as the decision to actively oppose or hinder something. Inertia, on the other hand, can occur when people are already involved in ongoing activity (whether another improvement effort or getting production out) and they simply keep moving in that direction.

Under inertia, people will keep doing the thing they are currently doing *until and unless* something comes along that causes them to change direction, that gets them to shift. They are not resisting. They are simply continuing to move in the direction in which they have been moving.

Inertia also applies to the tendency of a body (an object) to remain at rest if it is already at rest. You get a taste of this when people say they "just don't want to be bothered." We make a mistake if we call them "lazy" or "sluggish" or "difficult." Take them at their word: They are not resisting you; they just don't want to be bothered. Not right now, anyway. They are busy maintaining their current state of nonmovement.

You'll know inertia is "in the air" if you hear any or all of the following responses when you ask people to lend a hand or get on board:

> "We are doing fine just as we are."
> "We can't afford the disruption."
> "We tried that before."
> "Quality is more important."
> "Getting stuff out the door is more important."
> "We don't have time to improve—we can barely meet production as it is."
> "We are already doing all we can."

Recognize inertia for what it is and realize it can be harnessed in favor of the implementation. Bodies at rest tend to remain at rest, yes, but bodies in motion tend to continue moving in the same direction. The trick is to help people shift off zero (rest), begin moving in the direction of the implementation, and let the force of inertia start working in favor of maintaining that motion. This shift we are talking about is not a lifelong commitment to, for example, 5S + 1. It is simply an agreement to take a first small step. The emphasis here is on *small*. The need to shift the inertia is one of the important reasons for developing the improvement time policy discussed in Chapter 2. It is also a great argument in favor of starting small, as discussed in Chapter 14.

A Thousand Ways to Say No

Resistance is another matter. When resistance opens its mouth, you are looking "No!" right in the throat. There are countless ways to say it, but it is still "No!" Here are a few of the most popular variations on this theme, grouped in broad categories you probably recognize.

Corporate Culture

"It doesn't fit the way we do things."
"We don't see anyone else doing it."
"Our employees are too set in their ways."
"We have too many products."
"Our product is too simple."
"Our product is too complex."

Organization

"We're too big."
"We're too small."
"We're a union shop."
"We're a job shop."
"We're in the process industry."

Finance

"It can't be justified financially."
"It's not aligned with our current corporate measures."
"We don't have the money."
"We don't have the time."
"We don't have the people."
"We need to concentrate on sales and shipments."
"We have other, more pressing problems."

Fears

"It's just another scheme to squeeze more out of production employees!"
"Employees will take over!"
"Management will lose control!"

"Our employees don't care!"
"Our managers don't care!"
"Top management hasn't taken the lead!"
"We can't sustain the effort."

A Visual Workplace and 5S + 1

"This is a factory, not a hospital!"
"We're supposed to walk on these floors, not eat on them!"
"They didn't hire me/you/us to sweep floors/put down tape/make signs."
"This place looks like a department store, not a shop floor."
"Aren't there more important improvements we can make?"
"Why should we spend time and money to communicate the obvious?"
"Better communication? Isn't that what our new computer system is for?"
"If you want to improve communication, get people to clean out their ears."
"We don't have time to clean up! We barely have time to get our production out!"
"Our company looks a heck of a lot better than any other company around here!"

Pretty deadly, wouldn't you say? When you want to see visual order take root in your company and the forces of resistance and inertia are afoot, then it is a fair question to ask, "What can we reasonably expect from people? Will they ever get on board? If so, when?"

Putting Inertia and Resistance in Context: A Parable

The following parable illustrates some crucial information. For the bones of this story, my heartfelt thanks to Dr. Ryuji Fukuda, an extraordinary manufacturing improvement consultant and author of many books, including *Managerial Engineering* (Portland, Ore: Productivity Press, 1983), who shared this insightful tale with me so many years ago. It was much leaner then, but I have always found it rich in wisdom and meaning.

So there you are: You and your company are embarking on a great journey. You have decided to leave the Land of Waste, where so much time is spent searching, waiting, and wondering—and head out for a new world where clarity and self-order reign, the workforce is spirited and involved, and profits are better than you ever imagined. Your destination: a visual workplace.

To get there, you must cross a great ocean, the Ocean of Continuous Systematic Improvement. Your vessel is a rowboat called the *SS Visual Workplace*. And you are on that boat with a core team of employees like yourself. Each of you have a set of oars in hand, and together you are rowing vigorously in the direction of the distant shore. Your cheeks are red and your eyes, sparkling and steady. You breathe deeply and often. You are the Rowers—representing 25 percent of the workforce, at the very most (Exhibit 10-1).

Exhibit 10-1. The Boat and the Rowers.

There are others on the boat, a group larger than you and your fellow-rowers—and they are watching. That's it. They are watching you row. They are the Watchers.

For the purposes of our discussion, let's say there are four Rowers in the boat and eight Watchers. You and the three other Rowers make up 25 percent of the workforce, and the eight Watchers, 50 percent (Exhibit 10-2). Between the Rowers and the Watchers, 75 percent of the workforce is on the boat.

Exhibit 10-2. Rowers and Watchers: 75 Percent of the Workforce.

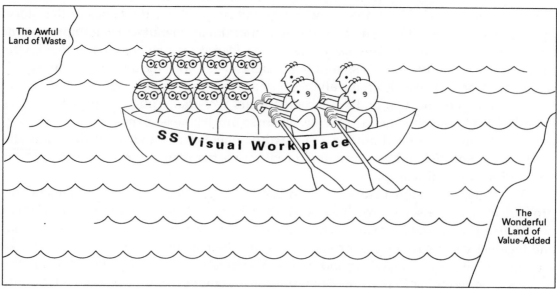

What about the other 25 percent? Where are the remaining employees?

You look around. You see some people on the shore you just left, sunning themselves amid the debris in the frightful Land of Waste, grumbling that they have been abandoned. Others are in the water, grumbling. They are the Grumblers (Exhibit 10-3.) Wherever they are, whatever they are doing, one thing is certain: The Grumblers are *not* on the boat.

Wait a minute! Two Grumblers are swimming toward your boat, with harpoons in hand, ready to do direct damage to your efforts. Better do something quick, Rowers! But what?

What Not *to Do*

What you, the Rowers, do next may well make the difference between getting to your destination or getting stuck in the doldrums, where the wreckage of countless other improvement initiatives can be found.

You may, for example, decide that you need to find out what is making the Grumblers so darned grumpy. You schedule one-on-one appointments with each one to talk things out. You are still in the dark. So you meet with the other Rowers to see if you can get some answers. Still no luck. Now you really start worrying. You know you won't get a good night's sleep until you find a way to get the Grumblers to cooperate.

Do this and you are making a very big mistake. It is exactly the wrong thing to do. Let me explain.

One of the main things to understand about Grumblers is this: They grumble. And for the most part—for whatever reason—they seem to enjoy it. When you run up against Grumblers on your journey, as you inevitably will, your next move is *not* to try to get them on board. Your next move is to continue doing what you are doing: rowing. Attempting to get the Grumblers to change their minds and get on board can have serious negative

Exhibit 10-3. The Grumblers.

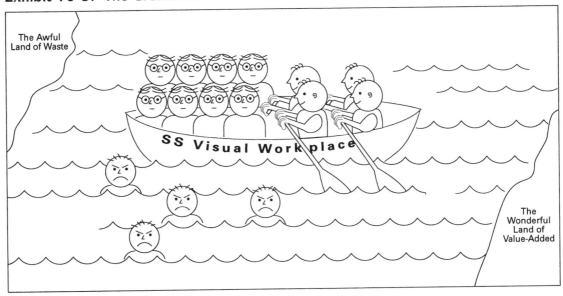

Exhibit 10-4. A Watcher Jumps Ship.

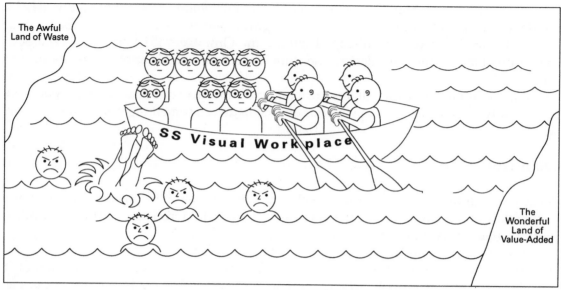

consequences for the entire implementation, unintended though they may be. Here's why.

Watchers watch. That is what they do at the start of anything. They watch the Rowers row. They watch the Grumblers grumble. And they also watch to see what the Rowers decide to do about the grumbling. They watch what the Rowers choose to pay attention to.

Watchers know about attention. They know it is energy. That is one of the reasons they do so much watching. It is their way of participating, of getting and giving. When Rowers focus their attention on the Grumblers, the Watchers know that the Rowers are hoping to get the Grumblers to change their minds and hearts and "get on board." The Watchers also know (from years of watching) that Grumblers are capable of eating up any and all energy that comes their way. They are like black holes in the universe. Grumblers can suck Rowers dry. And they often do. The Rowers get more and more exhausted and disheartened. Seeing that their well-intended efforts are not paying off, they become filled with self-doubt and anxiety. They begin to have misgivings about where they are going and how. They begin to doubt their own vision.

When the Watchers see this, they see the implementation going down the tubes and they do the only thing that makes sense to them. They jump ship, joining the Grumblers in the water (Exhibit 10-4). The Grumblers have won.

The Power of Attention

In the 1930s, the Hawthorne experiment[1] on the power of attention gave us a body of evidence, strengthened by the findings of hundreds of other studies that followed, that

1. For more, read Elton Mayo's *Human Problems of an Industrial Civilization* (New York: Macmillan Books, 1933).

what we pay attention to grows. Werner Heisenberg wrote about the same thing in his research on molecules and atomic structures: Pay attention to something and what is observed responds.[2]

Attention is energy. What it rests upon grows. It is a powerful force. When we pay attention to the Grumblers in an implementation, we do two things that don't help. First, we feed their basic pattern of resistance. Second, we send a clear message that resistance is more powerful in attracting our attention than the more neutral behavior of the Watchers.

The Rowers in our parable ended up paying more attention to the grumbling than to their rowing. When they did this, the tide began to turn against the implementation. The Watchers were already on the boat (on board) but felt overlooked. Indeed the Rowers did overlook the Watchers, even as they overlooked the fact that Grumblers change slowly and only when they choose to.

The Power of Choice

The pivotal issue in the parable and in your efforts to implement visual order is the right of the individual to choose. It is this act of choosing that puts the *pull* in the pull system called a visual workplace. And the power of choice can work for or against an implementation.

In the early stages of a visual workplace, information gets used only if an employee chooses to pull it into his awareness. If he does not, the information just sits there, powerless to benefit the employee or the company. In those early stages, the effectiveness of visual order hinges on individual choice.

At the outset, the Rowers in our parable made their choice: They decided to put their shoulders to the oar and row. We respect that. Watchers chose to wait. We respect that. And some people chose to grumble. We must respect that, too. There may indeed be negative consequences—and we must respect people's right to choose.

Grumblers choose not to participate in the implementation right now—and may never change their minds. Like Charley, they have their reasons. They let it be known that they wouldn't be caught dead pushing a broom and cannot be counted on to put things back. Some Grumblers can get noisy in their refusal to get on board. Some may even try to sabotage the effort.

Sooner or later, the organization must decide if it wants the extra baggage that Grumblers carry. And the Grumblers must decide if they are willing to meet the organization partway. Many Grumblers do. More than a few of the most steadfast 5S + 1 supporters I have had the honor and pleasure of working with over the years started out like Charley—grumbling.

To sum it up, Rowers have two main jobs: (1) to influence positive direction by doing their own work (modeling) and (2) to identify and pay attention to the people who are watching.

Here is another way for the parable to end.

2. Werner Heisenberg, *Physics and Philosophy* (New York: Harper & Row, 1962).

A Different Ending to the Parable

Even though the Rowers see the Grumblers doing nothing to help the effort, even though they see Grumblers swimming toward them with harpoons in hand, Rowers fix their eyes on the receding shoreline and keep rowing. Their oar strokes are strong and steady, and the boat pulls away. They keep rowing and as they do, the Watchers are captivated by the calm intent of the Rowers, who stay lighthearted now even as sweat pours down their brows into their blinking eyes. A Watcher shifts around a bit and puts on a crooked smile. A few moments later, she picks up some oars and starts to row, clumsily at first, and then more gracefully. A watching neighbor follows suit. And then another joins in, and another, and another.

Soon, the boat slips into a tailwind, and the crew raises a mast and sail. The sail puffs and fills. The Grumblers are barely visible on the receding shore. A dinghy hitched up to the back of the boat is sent back to pick up anyone new who wants to come on board. It comes back full.

Remember: What you give your attention to grows. It's universal law. And it can work for or against your goal. You choose.

What You Can Expect by Implementing 5S + 1

What level of involvement can you realistically expect in the first twelve months of implementing 5S + 1?

As suggested by the parable, a few people will get on board immediately, as soon as the initiative is announced. They instinctively grasp the importance of visual order and its potential benefits to lead time and the bottom line. Others will come on board during the first month, following the general awareness sessions and formal team training. At this point, your core group of Rowers is in place. They will represent from 10 to 15 percent of the population of the pilot areas. That's right, the number of Rowers is likely not to reach the 25 percent mark for another six to twelve weeks. And when it does, get ready to see mountains move. You have reached critical mass. Grumblers can hover around 10 percent for starters and rise as high as 30 to 40 percent in the very early part (the first month) of the implementation. If you keep true to the values and procedures described in this book, a good half of them will shift over to the Watcher group within two months. The remaining grumps are likely to stay pretty committed in their resistance, but their lower numbers (around 10 percent) will lessen their negative impact.

Similarly, the Watcher population typically starts at around 50 percent and swells to 60 or 70 percent in the first forty to sixty days, as Grumblers shift over. Don't forget: The Watcher group is ripe for conversion. Value them and help them implement their initial ideas. Some will quickly become Rowers, making room for more Grumblers to shift into the Watcher role. See Exhibit 10-5 for a summary of what you can expect.

The proportions you see in Exhibit 10-5 can slip and slide, depending on a variety of factors, the most potent of which are: (1) visible evidence of management's support or lack thereof, (2) the attitude of formal and informal leaders, and (3) the quality and length of the workforce's previous experience with improvement initiatives and team-

Exhibit 10-5. What You Can Expect in the First Year of a 5S + 1 Implementation.

Implementation Breakdown	Month 1	Month 3	Month 6	Month 9	Month 12
Rowers	10%	15%	20%	30%	35%
Watchers	50%	55%	55%	50%	50%
Grumblers	40%	30%	25%	20%	15%
Total	100%	100%	100%	100%	100%

based approaches. You can, however, expect many Watchers to become Rowers and some Grumblers to convert to Watching—or even Rowing!

☆　☆　☆　☆　☆

In this chapter we showed what you might encounter in terms of passionate commitment, inertia, and resistance. In the next chapter, you'll learn about a set of specific tools for actively and progressively building employee involvement so that visual order turns into a workplace habit.

One: The Big Picture		
1. Toward a Visual Workplace	2. Visual Systems in Context	3. The Five Start-Up Requirements
Two: 5S Method		
4. S1/Sort Through and Sort Out	5. S2–S4/ Scrub, Secure Safety, and Select Locations	6. S5/Set Locations: Borders
7. S5/Set Locations: Addresses	8. 5S Stories From the Shop Floor	9. 5S+1 and White-Collar Applications
Three: +1 Method		
10. People: What to Expect	11. +1: Building and Sustaining the 5S Habit	12. +1: Leading by Example	13. +1: Leading Through Standards
Four: Go!		
14. Showcase, Scope, and the System	15. Training and Education	16. The Hundredth Monkey

Chapter 11

+1: Building and Sustaining the 5S Habit

I hope this doesn't turn into another one of those flavor-of-the-month programs. I've seen so many of those come and go.

—Assembly Associate

Implementing the first five principles of visual order (S1–S5) is a straightforward process. We follow a set of simple steps until only needed items remain in the workplace, and they are clean, safe, and in their home locations. As a result, less and less time is being spent searching, wondering, wandering, and waiting. Microsupervision is beginning to disappear as the workplace becomes more self-explaining every day and, as a result, more self-regulating.

To ensure continued progress, you must now turn these new principles into a *habit*.

Turning visual order into a habit is precisely the purpose of the sixth and final principle. It is called **+1/Sustain the 5S Habit** (**+1** for short), and it is the glue that holds the other five together. The means for doing this is a set of nine sustaining tools that inspire, focus, monitor, and motivate associates and managers to get and stay involved. This is the technology of getting people to participate in a process of systematic change.

The tools you are going to read about are the result of nearly a decade of watching companies succeed and fail in their improvement efforts. You have the option of not adopting them, in the belief that your workforce has what it takes to keep on the true and steady. If you choose this option, do not be surprised when your initial gains evaporate within six months and the workplace returns to its previous condition. We have all seen this happen in dozen of companies: The waters close over, and the process (in this case 5S+1) joins the legions of other improvement efforts that once burned brightly and then vanished. Without the +1 tools of 5S+1, the gains will not hold.

Not putting these tools in place is the fastest way for initial efforts in visual order to bite the dust. Management may fault "sluggish" associates if this happens. Associates will say management failed to support the process. The associates will be correct.

The Nine Sustaining Tools: Overview

Here is a summary of the nine sustaining tools:

1. *Visual workplace code of conduct.* The standards of behavior that spell out the values and practices needed, from the outset, to create an environment favorable to achieving a visual workplace.
2. *The 5S corner.* The supplies that individuals and teams need on hand to rapidly create and implement their own visual solutions.
3. *5S checklist.* A list of specific tasks that area associates agree need to be done regularly so that visual order in the area is maintained and improved.
4. *5S patrol.* A small rotating team of area associates charged with applying the checklists in their area and sharing the results.
5. *Visual workplace steering team.* A group of area volunteers charged with coordinating, monitoring, and leading the implementation.
6. *Visual minisystems.* A cluster of visual devices that work together to promote a specific performance outcome.
7. *Visual workplace coordinator.* The person responsible for providing administrative and logistical support to the implementation and for coordinating its various activities.
8. *Management champion.* A manager or executive with high credibility who is respon-

sible for visibly supporting the 5S + 1 process, providing it with regular top management feedback, and going to bat for it, if needed.

9. *Management watch.* The regularly scheduled time slot when the management champion tours the work areas under 5S + 1 improvement in order to visibly and concretely recognize and influence the effort through the use of watch cards.

These tools are designed to work together. Taken as a set, they create a synergy of intent and function that guarantees the forward movement of the process over time. Exhibit 11-1 gives an overview of all nine tools within the context of the five practices in 5S + 1. In this chapter, we will concentrate on the first four tools.

The Visual Workplace Code of Conduct

The standards of behavior that spell out the values and practices needed, from the outset, to create an environment favorable to achieving a visual workplace.

Values govern behavior. They represent what we prize, what we hold as true, and what we believe about ourselves and others. Values underlie every decision we make and action we do, even if we cannot say exactly what those values are. They guide us and they reflect us. People can tell a lot about what you value by the way you respond to everyday life.

In implementing visual order (or any continuous improvement process, for that matter), we are asked to interact with dozens of people and systems. Sometimes we are at a loss on how to respond. "How do I handle this?" we ask. "What should I say? What should I do? What shouldn't I do?"

The visual workplace code of conduct is a set of seven standards of conduct to help you align your choices with values that support 5S + 1 outcomes. This code of conduct is designed to help you decide how to respond. Read the seven standards in Exhibit 11-2 before you go on and think about what they mean.

Can you see how these values could help as you implement visual order in your area and help others get involved? Let's look at a few examples. For instance, remember the story about Charley and his old table in Chapter 4. That was a case when Standard III (get permission) was ignored and, as a result, some people lost interest in the implementation. Standard IV (don't vote) is a reminder to avoid polarizing your group with a vote. For example, if your area is in the process of 3-Tagging and an item has eight red tags on it and only one green tag, the item stays. Majority does *not* rule. The code provides you with practical guidance in these and many other real-life situations.

Let's look at Standards V and VI more closely.

Standard V: *True Consensus*

One of life's everyday challenges is knowing when to push, when to pull, and when to hold still. Standard V speaks to this in suggesting that we work for consensus—true

Exhibit 11-1. 5S + 1 (read from the bottom up).

5S Handle	Description
+1 Sustain the 5S Habit	**Tool 9—Management Watch:** The regularly scheduled time slot when the management champion tours the work areas under 5S + 1 improvement in order to visibly and concretely recognize and influence the effort through the use of watch cards.
	↑ **Tool 8—Management Champion:** The manager/executive with high credibility, responsible for visibly supporting the 5S + 1 process, providing it with regular top-management feedback, and going to bat for it, if needed.
	↑ **Tool 7—Visual Workplace Coordinator:** The person responsible for providing administrative and logistical support to the implementation and for coordinating its various activities.
	↑ **Tool 6—Visual Minisystems:** A cluster of visual devices that work together to promote a single performance outcome.
	↑ **Tool 5—Visual Workplace Steering Team:** A group of area volunteers, charged with coordinating, monitoring, and leading the implementation.
	↑ **Tool 4—5S Patrol:** A small, rotating team of area associates, charged with applying checklists in their area and sharing the results.
	↑ **Tool 3—5S Checklist:** A list of specific tasks that area associates agree need to be done regularly so that visual order in the area is maintained and improves.
	↑ **Tool 2—5S Corner:** The supplies that individuals and teams need on hand to rapidly create and implement their own visual solutions.
	↑ **Tool 1—Visual Workplace Code of Conduct:** The standards of behavior that spell out the values and practices needed, from the outset, to create an environment favorable to achieving a visual workplace.

Exhibit 11-1. ***Continued.***

5S Handle	Description
S5 Set Locations	Make a home for each item in the work area with a border, home address, and item ID. *A place for everything and everything in its place.*
S4 Select Locations	Locate each remaining item in a spot that supports an accelerated flow of work and information. *Get rid of the waste of motion.*
S3 Secure Safety	Make all items in the area safe and promote greater safety awareness.
S2 Scrub the Workplace	Remove grit, grime, and grease from all items. Paint as needed. Promote dirt prevention. *Cleaning is inspection—Cleaning is ownership.*
S1 Sort Through and Sort Out	Clear out the clutter; remove all non required items. Keep only what's needed. *Get rid of the junk.*

Remember: The first *S* is for spirit!

Exhibit 11-2. The Visual Workplace Code of Conduct.

The Visual Workplace Code of Conduct	
Standard I	Remember that the *first* S is for Spirit.
Standard II	Ask *first*—then listen.
Standard III	Get permission *before* moving or removing items in the area of another.
Standard IV	Resist responding to conflict with a vote.
Standard V	Work for true consensus in the face of conflict.
Standard VI	Influence positive direction by doing your *own* work.
Standard VII	Remember to use the strengths of the steering team.

consensus—in the face of conflict. What exactly does "true" consensus mean, and how is it different from false consensus?

Many people (managers and associates alike) believe that reaching consensus either means (1) having your own way by getting the other person to say yes or (2) caving in and going along with others, against your better judgment. Wrong! Neither one is consensus. That's just politics as usual.

True consensus requires two things of us. First, it requires an active search for disagreement. That means we make special efforts to find out what the objections of others are. We dig out the differences and surface the opposition in detail. When these are known, understood, and appreciated, we move on to the second requirement: Find areas of agreement until there is enough agreement to move forward. We look for common ground. In a sentence, true consensus is:

> The active search for disagreement until enough agreement is reached for people to move forward together.

For more on the team process, see Appendix B.

Standard VI: *Modeling*

If you are reading this book, you are probably a Rower. You really believe in the power of visual order and would like to see it take root in your company as soon as possible. Standard VI—influence positive direction by doing your own work—is written especially for you.

There is one word that captures the intent of this standard: *modeling*. **Modeling** refers to your decision to help people do the right thing by doing it yourself. You demonstrate through your own behavior the behavior you want (and hope) others will adopt.

No matter what others are doing around you, you stay the course. In the face of resistance, inertia, and the halting process of consensus, you elect to do what you know is right and good. This is the code of the Rowers. They lead through their own example. Sometimes they do it quietly. Sometimes they do it with great force. They keep true to the process by keeping true to themselves. They do not let the choices of others cancel out their choice. They do their own thing—and respect the right of others to do the same. They respect the spirit of the workplace.

You'll come to appreciate much more about Standard VI in the next chapter when we talk about the visual workplace steering team and visual minisystems.

The 5S Corner

> The supplies that individuals and teams need to have on hand to rapidly create and implement their own visual solutions.

Most visual devices are low-cost, low-tech solutions, designed and implemented by associates. To be able to do this, people need ready access to some basic supplies. These supplies make up the 5S corner.

A 5S corner can be a simple cardboard box, a drawer, a tabletop, a corner of a room—or an entire room. It can be any of these places as long as people can get the supplies they need *when and as* they need them. To some, the notion of a 5S corner seems too simple to matter. It does matter. Far too many excellent ideas never leave a person's imagination because a 5S corner is not in place. Mildred's latest visual solution is a case in point.

Mildred stopped by the machine shop on her way back from lunch to say hi to Doug. He proudly showed her a new minisystem he came up with last week for his tools. Millie was impressed and decided to put one together for her tools. When she got back to her area, Millie walked over to the 5S corner (a pull-out shelf near the packing table) and picked out some card stock, markers, and tape. Ten minutes later, the new minisystem was completed and fifteen seconds were eliminated every time Mildred reached for a tool. Lucky thing the corner was well stocked. If it hadn't been, she might have put off the minisystem for another day, and another, and another.

How to Qualify as a 5S Corner

1. Associates must know where it is located.
2. It must be nearby.
3. Associates must have easy access to it *at all times*.
4. It must be supplied with the basic materials for making visual devices (see below).
5. It must contain or be near a large, clear surface to work on.

Basic 5S Corner Supplies

- Scissors
- Rulers
- Yardstick
- Measuring tape
- Removable square/rectangular white labels
- Removable round labels (assorted colors)
- Magic Markers (assorted colors)
- Poster paper (white and assorted colors)
- String
- Thumbtacks/pushpins
- Scotch tape
- Glue or paste
- Clothespins (push and spring-loaded)
- Masking tape
- Duct or plastic tape
- Green, red, and yellow tags or stickers

Keep your 5S corner well stocked. This job is usually the responsibility of the steering team representative in your area or the company's visual workplace coordinator. Photo

11-1. 5S Corner at Lee Industries.

Here is the 5S corner at Lee Industries. Simple and easy to use, this 5S corner gives everyone in this small company quick access to the supplies that the local steering team rep keeps well stocked.

11-1 shows you the 5S corner at Lee Industries, sister company to Fleet Engineers. Notice its visual order: borders, home addresses, and ID labels.

The 5S Checklist

> A list of specific tasks that area associates agree need to be done on a regular basis so that visual order in the area is maintained and improves.

A 5S checklist is a simple way to make sure that things everyone agreed to do, get done. Unfortunately, many people's first encounter with a checklist was more like having a sharp finger pointing out what was not done (or not done well enough), with a rating or score carried out to five decimal places to register the extreme extent of your failure. This is a good example of using a checklist as a weapon, a form of attack based on someone else's notion of what you should do.

When it is over, you may be left with an acute sense of disappointment but rarely any clue on how to correct the situation or prepare for the next time. As a result, you either forget about the incident or brace yourself. This is not the spirit of a 5S+1 checklist (5S for short).

A 5S checklist is designed to be easy to use, relevant, specific, friendly, and a way to promote further improvement. It differs from the "punishment" checklist described above in at least four ways.

What a 5S Checklist Is

1. *It is area-specific.* You and your associates select the type of checklist you want to use (see below) and decide on checklist items (which actions or outcomes it will cover).
2. *It is empowering.* Not only do you and your associates develop your checklist; you also administer it. It is a self-report.
3. *It supports improvement.* A 5S checklist is designed to provide feedback on current improvement efforts and point the way to further ones.
4. *It evolves over time.* The 5S checklist that was useful in month three of the implementation, gets upgraded in month four, and again in month five.

Checklists are used throughout an implementation as both a learning and motivational tool. Through checklists, associates acquire the habit of identifying and maintaining a level of visual order that is acceptable to them. Just as importantly, checklists give area associates a chance to recognize and celebrate their victories along the way, even as they look for ways to move the process forward.

Two Types of 5S Checklists

5S checklists come in a number of shapes and sizes that can be sorted into two main types: (1) wall chart checklists and (2) clipboard checklists.

The Wall Chart Checklist

A **wall chart checklist** is a large chart (3 by 5 feet is not uncommon) that lists five to ten action items that area associates agree to do on a regular basis (usually daily). It can be made of paper, laminated, and/or covered with Plexiglas. When ready, the checklist is posted where it can be easily seen by the associates who work in the area.

Wall chart checklists are simple, straightforward, and purposeful. They help area associates maintain their work area at a preset level of visual order and develop the habit of routine daily cleanup. The wall chart checklist is particularly effective when people are checklist-shy (as in *gun-shy*) due to a prior bad personal experience or their feeling of being watched or judged if other types of checklists are used.

Exhibit 11-3 shows the action items that associates in the stamping area chose for their first 5S wall chart checklist (in a three-shift, twenty-four-hour factory). Determining which items to include is the first step of every 5S checklist process.

Exhibit 11-4 shows you the next step in the process. Associates added three columns for names, one column for each shift. These names were written in by hand because jobs rotated through the shifts on a monthly basis. Three extra columns were added so each person could check off tasks as completed and write down comments or questions they wanted to pass along. (In this area five associates work on first shift, and they divided the seven tasks between them. The three people on second shift did the same, as did the two associates on graveyard.) The wall chart checklist can be used alone or in conjunction with a clipboard checklist, as described in the next section.

Exhibit 11-3. Stamping Area Checklist Items.

---

1. Sweep and degrease floor.

2. Wipe down Press 3 and check lube points.

3. Wipe down Press 4 and check lube points.

4. Empty and rinse all chip bins.

5. Put all dies and fixtures back in home locations.

6. Put all hand tools and gauges back in home locations.

7. Organize and file paperwork.

The Clipboard Checklist

Named after the board it is usually clamped on, the **clipboard checklist** is a self-report and self-diagnosis tool. Where a wall chart checklist will help associates maintain and stabilize a certain level of visual order, a clipboard checklist is designed to drive those levels higher and higher. For this reason, *wait until at least four months into the implementation before starting to use a clipboard checklist in your area.* The wall chart checklist reminds us of what needs to get done. The clipboard variety asks and answers the question, "How well did we do it?"

How to Develop Your First Set of Clipboard Items. To help associates name clipboard items, give teams a template or worksheet with lots of blank lines and the first five principles of visual order as headings (Exhibit 11-5). Under each heading, ask people to write specific actions that make their area a "clear, clean, safe, and orderly workplace." Let them connect with what *they* really want to see improve. This first list will act as a stepping-stone to the next level.

Teams are rarely short of item ideas. Lists of twenty to twenty-five items are not uncommon. In the next step, each team pares down its lists to eight to twelve priority items. Don't worry if the number of items under the various headings is uneven. You don't need a uniform number. People focus on what's important to them and what they can see. Exhibit 11-6 shows one start-up list of clipboard items. Notice their detail and precision compared with the more general items of the wall chart checklist in Exhibit 11-4.

The 5S clipboard checklist differs from the wall chart–type in two important ways: (1) Items evolve and (2) items are scored, not just checked off.

Exhibit 11-4. Stamping Area Items in a Wall Chart Format.

Action Items (15 minutes before end of shift)	Person			Check When Done (add comments)		
	1st	2nd	3rd	1st	2nd	3rd
1. Sweep floor and degrease walkways.						
2. Wipe down Press 3 and check lube points.						
3. Wipe down Press 4 and check lube points.						
4. Empty and rinse all chip bins.						
5. Put all dies and fixtures in home locations.						
6. Put all hand tools and gauges in home locations.						
7. File and organize paperwork.						

1. *Items evolve.* Unlike wall chart checklists, the items on clipboard checklists change frequently. An item that may start as "Are the floors clean?" a month later can read, "Is every square foot of the floor shining clean and free of grease?" Or, the checklist item that six weeks ago asked, "Are all the chips swept up?" now reads, "Are all chip guards in place so chips drop directly into chip containers?" It is an evolution of practice.

2. *Items are scored, not checked off.* The wall chart checklist reminds us of what to do. The clipboard variety asks "to what extent were they done?" Accordingly, clipboard items are not just checked off, they are scored. Each item is individually rated. That means that some manner of scoring mechanism is built into each clipboard checklist.

You can develop a clipboard checklist that requires a simple yes/no response (Exhibit 11-7). But the true power of this type checklist is most evident when a scoring scale is

Exhibit 11-5. Action Item Worksheet.

5S CHECKLIST—Creating a Clear, Clean, Safe, and Orderly Workplace
CLEAR (S1)—Keep only what is needed.
CLEAN (S2)—Observe/prevent problems by keeping things clean.
SAFE (S3)—Zero accidents/zero injuries.
ORDERLY (S4/S5)—No more searching.

used. The six-point format in Exhibit 11-8 is a popular scale, similar to the clean scale presented in Chapter 5.

Like other clipboard elements, scoring values and their meaning evolve over time to keep pace with your area's changing needs. Resist any move to standardize these scoring scales across departments for as long as you can (until at least eight to twelve months after the launch). Exhibit 11-9 shows you a clipboard checklist with the six-point scoring device included.

Two Final Checklist Elements

Two more elements and your checklist will be a true engine of change: (1) a header (with scoreboard) and (2) room-for-improvement comments.

Exhibit 11-6. Start-Up Clipboard Checklist.

5S CHECKLIST—Creating a Clear, Clean, Safe, and Orderly Workplace
CLEAR (S1)—Keep only what is needed.
1. Have all extra U-containers been returned to stores?
CLEAN (S2)—Observe/prevent problems by keeping things clean.
2. Is the floor free of grinder dust, with no danger of slipping?
3. Are chips cleaned out of Press 3 on a regularly scheduled basis?
4. Are the scrap and trash containers emptied on a regular basis?
SAFE (S3)—Zero accidents/zero injuries.
5. Is the zebra-line tape near the Sundstrand visible and unbroken?
6. Are all safety guards on Press 3 in place?
ORDERLY (S4/S5)—No more searching.
7. Are large fans and extra pallets in their addressed locations?
8. Are supplies on the POUS shelf in their addressed locations?
9. Are aluminum and brass scraps separated into their proper barrels?
10. Are the parts templates stored in their addressed locations?
11. Is today's machining WIP in the kanban square near CNC 4000?

Header

A **checklist header** puts a lot of useful material at your fingertips.

• The name of work area the checklist is for
• The names of the people applying the checklist (see 5S patrol below)
• The checklist score from the last time
• The score on this checklist
• The difference (+/-) between the two scores

See Exhibit 11-10 for a sample checklist header.

Room-for-Improvement Comments

Each item on the checklist shown in Exhibit 11-9 requires a score—and nothing more. And that's a problem. Checklist results would have far greater impact if each score were

Exhibit 11-7. "Yes/No" Clipboard Checklist.

5S CHECKLIST—Creating a Clear, Clean, Safe, and Orderly Workplace	Yes	No
CLEAR (S1)—Keep only what is needed.		
1. Have all extra U-containers been returned to stores?		
CLEAN (S2)—Observe/prevent problems by keeping things clean.		
2. Is the floor free of grinder dust, with no danger of slipping?		
3. Are chips cleaned out of Press 3 on a regularly scheduled basis?		
4. Are the scrap and trash containers emptied on a regular basis?		
SAFE (S3)—Zero accidents/zero injuries.		
5. Is the zebra-line tape near the Sundstrand visible and unbroken?		
6. Are all safety guards on Press 3 in place?		
ORDERLY (S4/S5)—No more searching.		
7. Are large fans and extra pallets in their addressed locations?		
8. Are supplies on the POUS shelf in their addressed locations?		
9. Are aluminum and brass scraps separated into their proper barrels?		
10. Are the parts templates stored in their addressed locations?		
11. Is today's machining WIP in the kanban square near CNC 4000?		

Exhibit 11-8. Sample Six-Point Scoring Scale.

0 = Zero Result	**1** = Slight Effort	**2** = Squeaks By	**3** = Satisfactory Results	**4** = Above-Average Results	**5** = Outstanding Results

supported by some remarks on what was wrong or right. So add some lines for comments. Add a line after each item (as shown in Exhibit 11-11) or a section of lines below the items. As you will see in the next section, leaving room for comments adds a powerful dimension to the work of the 5S patrol, the team responsible for conducting the checklist. It calls upon patrol members to take the lead and share their perspective on the progress of the implementation in their area.

Exhibit 11-11 shows you a completed clipboard checklist, with header, scoring mechanism, start-up items, and space under each for improvement comments. See how these elements work with each other. Notice how the written comments support *and* go beyond items and their scores.

Now let's link up the clipboard checklist with how it is applied: the 5S patrol.

Exhibit 11-9. Clipboard Checklist With Six-Point Scoring Mechanism.

0 = Zero Result	**1** = Slight Effort	**2** = Squeaks By	**3** = Satisfactory Results	**4** = Above-Average Results	**5** = Outstanding Results

5S CHECKLIST—Creating a Clear, Clean, Safe, and Orderly Workplace	0	1	2	3	4	5
CLEAR (S1)—Keep only what is needed.						
1. Have all extra U-containers been returned to stores?						
CLEAN (S2)—Observe/prevent problems by keeping things clean.						
2. Is the floor free of grinder dust, with no danger of slipping?						
3. Are chips cleaned out of Press 3 on a regularly scheduled basis?						
4. Are the scrap and trash containers emptied on a regular basis?						
SAFE (S3)—Zero accidents/zero injuries.						
5. Is the zebra-line tape near the Sundstrand visible and unbroken?						
6. Are all safety guards on Press 3 in place?						
ORDERLY (S4/S5)—A place for everything and everything in its place.						
7. Are aluminum and brass scraps separated into their proper barrels?						
8. Are supplies on the POUS shelf in their addressed locations?						
9. Are large fans and extra pallets in their addressed locations?						
10. Are the parts templates stored in their addressed locations?						
11. Is today's machining WIP in the kanban square near CNC 4000?						
TOTALS						

Exhibit 11-10. Checklist Header.

Work Area	5S Patrol Team	Today's Date	Last Score	This Score	+/−

The 5S Patrol

> A small, rotating team of area associates, charged with applying checklists in their area and sharing the results.

The 5S patrol is a small team of people responsible for applying clipboard checklists in their own area and sharing the findings with the rest of their associates. As a rule of thumb, two people at a time serve on the patrol.

Timing

At the beginning, a 5S patrol usually happens on a weekly basis and takes about twenty-five to thirty-five minutes. As the implementation matures, that can shift to twice a month (or even monthly) and only takes about fifteen minutes to conduct. What is key is for the patrol to make its rounds at a preset time (e.g., Thursday mornings) so no one is surprised.

Membership

5S patrols are most effective when everybody in the area gets a chance to serve on a patrol on a regular, reoccurring, and rotating basis. Exhibit 11-12 shows how this works across five rotations, with two associates per patrol.

The first time, one member is rotated off after only one turn. After that, the rotation is staggered: Each patrol member serves two consecutive turns and then rotates off. In this way, the repeat patrol member can bring the new person up to speed on what the patrol saw the time before and the extent to which things did or didn't improve since then. Continuity is assured. As Exhibit 11-12 illustrates, Bill serves with Adam, fills Carol in when she arrives, and then rotates off to make room for David, who is briefed by Carol. The next week, Carol moves off and David updates Esme.

There are several benefits to patrol rotation. Not only does it let many associates get involved, it also builds personal confidence and skill in leading. It is an excellent people development tool.

Some companies let a team of associates from outside an area assess that area's level of visual order, using a checklist based on preset standards. While a case could be made that the area would benefit from a different set of eyes, this outsider approach can be problematic, especially if introduced too early in the process. If you must experiment with it, wait six to eight months after the self-report approach described above has been in use. By then, area teams will be better equipped to benefit from the outside feedback of peers.

One other point. Based on what I have seen in a number of companies, avoid management-led checklist patrols.

Exhibit 11-11. Completed Checklist.

Work Area	5S Patrol Team	Today's Date	Last Score	This Score	+/−1
Blades	Millie/Joe	2/18/96	29/55	33/55	+4

0 = Zero Result!	**1** = Slight Effort	**2** = Squeaks By	**3** = Satisfactory Results	**4** = Above Average Results	**5** = Outstanding Results		

5S CHECKLIST—A Clear, Clean, Safe, and Orderly Workplace	0	1	2	3	4	5
1. Have all extra U-containers been returned to the store?		1				
Three containers were found stacked by the Sundstrand.						
②. Is the floor free of grinder dust, with no danger of slipping?			2			
Much improved since last week, but we found oil! Where did it come from?						
3. Are chips cleaned out of Press 3 on a regularly scheduled basis?						5
Great work!						
4. Are the scrap and trash containers emptied on a regular basis?						5
Looking swell.						
5. Is the zebra-line tape near the Sundstrand visible and unbroken?		1				
The tape is still all torn up. This was one of the focus items from last week's patrol!?!						
6. Are all safety guards on Press 3 in place?						5
They're working just fine. Let's get rid of this checklist item. We don't need it anymore.						
⑦. Are large fans and extra pallets in their addressed locations?		1				
Millie nearly tripped on a pallet that was leaning up against the CNC.						
8. Are supplies on the POUS shelf in their addressed locations?				3		
Shelves look much better—but some of the IDs are still missing.						
9. Are aluminum and brass scraps separated into proper barrels?						5
Great job. John's new minisystem is really working.						
10. Are the parts templates stored in their addressed locations?						5
We found these in perfect order <u>again</u>. Is it time to take this item off too?						
⑪. Is today's machining WIP in the kanban square near CNC 4000?	0					
We found WIP in five different places in the area. Can we talk?						
TOTALS	0	3	2	3	0	25

Exhibit 11-12. Rotating Patrol Membership: For Continuity and Learning.

Rotation 1 (AB)	Rotation 2 (BC)	Rotation 3 (CD)	Rotation 4 (DE)	Rotation 5 (EF)	Rotation 6 (FG)
Adam/Bill	Bill/Carol	Carol/Dave	Dave/Esme	Esme/Fern	Fern/Joe

The Winning Combination: The 5S Patrol and the 5S Checklist

Combining the clipboard checklist with a 5S patrol can give a terrific boost to an implementation, especially if the checklist has a scoring mechanism. When this happens, clipboard checklists become engines for self-improvement. They keep area teams focused, diligent, and energized. Managers and supervisors stand back!

Take care, however, that the considerable strengths of the checklist/patrol combination do not turn into burdens. Scoring the items, for example, can demotivate instead of promote if it is done with the sting of judgment. In addition, valuable feedback from patrol members can get neglected if specific steps are not taken to make sure it is shared. Third, associates as well as patrol members can begin to feel overwhelmed if too many low-scoring items are tagged for improvement between patrols.

To reduce the likelihood of any of these happening, consider the following.

Getting the Most From the Checklist/Patrol Combo

1. Emphasize gradual progress. Make sure checklist results are presented in a positive, progressive manner. Emphasize that the process is developmental, not static. Improvement will and should happen gradually. Make sure associates know that low scores do not necessarily mean the process is failing—or some person or the area is not making an effort. Remind associates that lower scores simply point the way to further improvement.

2. Less is better (a repeat). The detailed items of a clipboard checklist can be an enormous help when area associates want to improve and need direction. But people can lose their way if too many items are on the list. They can feel overwhelmed. Remember to keep the number of items between five and twelve. Then people can see that what needs to be done, can be done. Because the focus of an area checklist shifts as the effort matures, there will rarely be a time when there is not more to do.

3. Narrow the focus. Responding to the call to improve eight to twelve items every week is far too strenuous for most areas to undertake. Avoid this and keep the momentum going by asking the members of each patrol to circle the two or three items they would *most like to see improved* by the next patrol. If the six-point scale is used, this usually means items with scores of two or less. These become the focus for improvement before the next patrol and where the new patrol look for evidence of progress.

Look back to the checklist in Exhibit 11-11. The three items you see circled there are the ones that Millie and Tom (members of the current 5S patrol) are asking associates to

Exhibit 11-13. Color-Dot Checklist Scoring Mechanism.

Color	Meaning
Red	Time to get started—we have a long way to go!
Yellow	We are moving in the right direction. Let's not stop now!
Green	We have arrived. Now let's sustain it!

improve by the next patrol. Again, this simple task of patrol members selecting what they consider to be the most important areas for improvement adds another dimension of personal empowerment.

Clipboard Variation: The Color-Dot Checklist

Before we leave the matter of checklists, let's look at a variation on the theme: the color-dot checklist.

This checklist uses colors for scoring, instead of numbers. The color-dot checklist has gotten terrific results in the early stages of an implementation, or later on if people grow weary of number scores (above). Instead of a number, stick a color dot in the scoring column (found in most office supply stores). Exhibit 11-13 shows you a sample scale. Notice that each color is defined in positive language. The color-dot approach is very user-friendly. Do not, however, expect this checklist to fuel improvement the way that number scores can. That's not its purpose.

Color-Dot Scoring

There are lots of ins-and-outs in using the color-dot approach, many of which you can discover on your own with a little experimentation. How the total score is calculated is not so obvious so I'll explain it now.

The total score on the color-dot approach always goes to the lowest color, with red as the lowest. For example, if all the dots are yellow except for one red dot, the total score is red. If all dots are green, except for one red, the total score for that checklist is red. If all are green with only one yellow, the total checklist score is yellow. It's as simple as that.

☆   ☆   ☆   ☆   ☆

This completes our examination of the first four of the nine +1 tools. In the next chapter, we see how the next two tools help to build the 5S habit: the visual workplace steering team and visual minisystems.

One: The Big Picture		
1. Toward a Visual Workplace	2. Visual Systems in Context	3. The Five Start-Up Requirements
Two: 5S Method		
4. S1/Sort Through and Sort Out	5. S2–S4/ Scrub, Secure Safety, and Select Locations	6. S5/Set Locations: Borders
7. S5/Set Locations: Addresses	8. 5S Stories From the Shop Floor	9. 5S+1 and White-Collar Applications
Three: +1 Method		
10. People: What to Expect	11. +1: Building and Sustaining the 5S Habit	12. +1: Leading by Example	13. +1: Leading Through Standards
Four: Go!		
14. Showcase, Scope, and the System	15. Training and Education	16. The Hundredth Monkey

Chapter 12

+1: Leading by Example

Fill up the room with grandfather clocks, their pendulums swinging in different rhythms and, in less than an hour, they'll start swinging together. In the same rhythm. Left to left. Right to right. As if they are physically joined, they swing in perfect unison. They do this on their own. We don't touch them.

—Charles Addison Ditmas III
The Keeper of the Clocks at Harvard College

The link between the five principles of visual order and the nine +1 supporting tools is similar to that which exists between learning the basics of basketball and mastering the game. At the outset, you spend a lot of time shooting, passing, and dribbling. That's a beginning—but it is just a beginning. Playing a forty-eight-minute game is still a long time off, and putting in a winning season, farther still.

Mastering a sport is a good metaphor for what it takes to make visual order a way of life in a company. Like mastering the piano or a martial art, the journey begins with learning the basic techniques: the scales on the piano, the forms in a martial art. Then through practice and coaching, these behaviors are internalized. They become second nature—a habit. Only then can you reach true proficiency.

At the outset of implementing visual order, you take pains to put the first five principles in place, and develop your skills. Over time, your eyesight improves and you get a feel for what you are after. Then it's practice, practice, practice, and the new procedures become customary and usual. Mastery emerges from that.

The practice part of the equation is the job of the +1 tools. Dozens of companies have already experienced how these tools work together and sink deep roots. One such company is United Electric Controls Company (UE), the case example we'll use to share details of how +1 works.

In this chapter you will learn about the visual workplace steering team and visual minisystems, the next two +1 tools.

UE: Company Background

UE is a manufacturer of temperature and pressure switches and controls for the process and original equipment markets. Privately owned since 1948, UE is located in Watertown, Massachusetts, with some 250 employees on its payroll.

The year 1987 was a turning point year at UE. Among other things, that was the year UE began its conversion from traditional to lean manufacturing, under the leadership of Dave Reis, UE president, and Bruce Hamilton, VP of operations. The company began a process of self-education, searching out methods and techniques that explained the change that needed to happen and how to do it.

Book study groups were started for managers and associates alike, along with action centers (team-based, problem-solving projects). A range of innovative tools was implemented in rapid succession: quick machine changeover, mistake-proofing systems, variety effectiveness process (see *Smart Simple Design* in the Suggested Readings), and policy deployment, to name a few. UE's Resource Center (a part of human resources) became the support center for the improvement process and for getting people involved. In 1990, UE won the Shigeo Shingo Prize for Manufacturing Excellence, a national award for companies of exceptional performance based on systematic methods (for more information, contact Utah State University). In the spring of 1992, UE contacted me to help in making the workplace visual. We began with 5S + 1.

During the first three months, eight shopfloor teams were trained in 5S + 1, participating in six half-day learning sessions. Each session or learning module concluded with an action assignment for teams to complete before the next session. In this way, the shop floor improved while people learned. In the third session, the group learned about the need for a visual workplace steering team and a call went out for volunteers: one shopfloor associate from each of the eight participating work areas.

The Visual Workplace Steering Team

A group of area volunteers, charged with coordinating, monitoring, and leading the implementation.

Steering Team Members

Implementing visual order is most effective when led by the shop floor. Members of the visual workplace (VW) steering team, therefore, are area associates, not managers and not supervisors. Members are peers and equals.

Managers and supervisors may be invited to attend a steering team session in order to assist on a specific task (as may technical staff, customers, suppliers, etc.). Or they may be invited to sit in and observe and make comment. The purpose here is not to exclude anyone from the process, least of all key decision-makers. Management has a definite role in the implementation, described in Chapter 13—but it is not as a steering team member. The purpose of an all-associate team is to develop and maximize the benefit of the in-depth involvement of the value-adding sector of the enterprise.

The VW steering team is not a project-based group, responsible for successfully completing a short-term project, for example, of some three to six months. The VW steering team shares responsibility for a long-term process of companywide change, with a visual workplace as its ultimate goal.

If your company is new to a companywide change process, there may be a strong temptation to put a manager is charge, precisely because the process is on-going and because the steering team may not yet exhibit a fully developed set of meeting and leadership skills. But note: the steering team is not in charge of the 5S + 1 implementation. The management champion is, but that work is behind the scenes (details in next chapter). Resist getting a manager directly involved in the steering team. If the team needs development, assign, instead, a skilled facilitator to show the team the ropes. This is precisely what Annie Yu, UE's visual workplace coordinator, did; you'll read more about this role and Annie's simple but invaluable contribution in Chapter 13.

Exactly what is the work of a VW steering team? Let's get to the details.

The Steering Team Process

The success of the VW steering team depends on two things: (1) the *tasks* team members perform and (2) the *process* by which they do them. In other words, the *what* and the *how*.

Tasks can keep a steering team busy from dawn until dusk: checking the 5S corner for supplies, helping associates lay borders, making sure people understand how to develop a checklist, coaching patrol members, stirring up enthusiasm in areas that are dragging, writing up 5S + 1 announcements, making a place to post them, preparing the agenda for the weekly session and modeling—keeping the momentum going. The list is endless. The key is finding the right balance between task and process.

Exhibit 12-1A. Task-Process Pyramid.

Exhibit 12-1B. When Process Comes First.

Exhibit 12-1C. Then It's Time for Tasks.

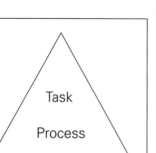

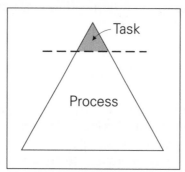

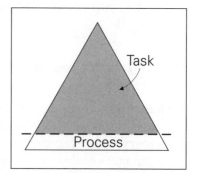

Every meeting is a blend of process and content—how the meeting is run plus which specific tasks need to be completed. That blend shifts, based on the needs of the group.

Sometimes a group needs to focus more on process, especially early on as people are getting to know each other and learning the ropes.

As the group gets settled and trust grows, the focus is more on content and less on process—getting tasks done.

Balancing Tasks and Process

Look at the triangle in Exhibit 12-1A. It represents what goes on in steering team meetings, a mixture of task and process. Exhibit 12-1B shows a bar at the top of the triangle, separating task from process. This is a snapshot of a particular team meeting where the focus was more on process (how things get done) than on task (what gets done). In Exhibit 12-1C, the bar has moved; it's now near the bottom of the triangle. That means that the focus of the meeting has shifted: Tasks dominate the meeting. The balance has tipped in favor of getting things done.

That is the way it goes. From meeting to meeting, the balance point is always shifting. Even within a given meeting, one agenda item may look at task and the next at process. The focus continues to shift. At the outset of an implementation, these shifts are governed by the needs of the team. The first main issue is process: how members will conduct themselves and team business (see norms below); then what needs to get accomplished. Later issues shift to how the implementation will proceed and through what tasks.

Every successful team-based implementation is a story of this shifting balance. The bar between task and process moves up and down. Consider this as you assess how things are going and what needs to happen next. Set your team agenda accordingly. If you and the team don't see the way clearly, set an agenda item to answer just that question: How are we doing? Where are we going? Are we progressing? Are we stuck?

As an added help, use the tool of the triangle and bar to learn about your own team process. Let each team member draw an individual triangle, placing the bar where they think it is now. Then ask each person to place the bar where they think it ought to go. Poll the group and let the results guide the discussion.

Team Norms

A steering team is smart to determine a set of norms. Setting norms is a process by which teams decide how they want to conduct business and themselves: How do we want to work together to fulfill our joint purpose?

> "When do we meet? Where? For how long? Do we get started when half the group has shown up, or wait for everyone? How long should a regular meeting last? What happens if a member continually misses a meeting or is always late? How should we make decisions? How do we change our minds? What about confidentiality?"

These are important questions that deserve clear answers. For this reason, norms are best set as soon as the team forms—at the very first meeting. By the end of that first session, team members have not only had the chance to hear each other out; they have learned the basics of effective meetings. See Appendix C for a complete norms worksheet that your team can use for setting norms. Exhibit 12-2 provides additional detail on the meeting process.

Agendas, Decisions, Action Items

A second steering team tool is a one-page meeting worksheet. On one side, there is space for team objectives and for the agenda. The reverse side is used for tracking decisions, questions, and the all-important *action items*.

Action items are the lifeblood of the steering team. They are the bite-size tasks spelling out exactly what the team has decided to do before their next meeting to move the process forward—and who will do it. A due-by date is also assigned, indicating when the person pledges to complete the task. Another terrific support, a copy of this worksheet can be found in Appendix D.

Statement of Purpose

Developing a statement of purpose (or mission statement) is not required but it can help. Think about what the team is for and about; then put it into your own words.

The UE steering team, for example, felt strongly that they should not police the implementation. They wanted others to see them as colearners, coparticipants, and helpers—as indeed they were. Their statement of purpose in Exhibit 12-3 reflects this.

UE: The Tasks—What to Do First

Members of visual workplace steering teams typically are somewhere between enthusiastic and wildly enthusiastic when it comes to visual order. To many, 5S + 1 is the answer to the prayer "Please, dear Lord, let me work with dignity and be productive."

The UE steering team was no exception. They saw the possibilities of a real change

Exhibit 12-2. Suggested Team Norms and Meeting Guidelines.

Some Team Meeting Guidelines

1. Meeting Time. Generally, a steering team meets once a week, every week, at the same designated time, for a minimum of forty-five minutes and a maximum of ninety minutes.

2. Action Items. An action item is a short but specific task that usually gets completed before the next session. Taken in their sum, these items move the process forward. Without them, a steering team stalls.

3. Agenda. Effective meetings require an item-by-item agenda developed in advance. Make sure each agenda item is a specific person's responsibility and assign the time in which it is to be covered (advice: the team leader covers an agenda item *only if* no one else will or can). Open the session by reading aloud that day's agenda. Close by reading all new action items.

4. Team Roles. Many steering teams choose to rotate team roles on a regular basis. This gives everyone a chance to experience and learn what each role is all about. Consider rotating roles not less than every three months. If the implementation gets rocky, consider designating one strong team leader for six to nine months or until things stabilize; keep the other roles constant as well.

5. Confidentiality. Most people need to feel emotionally safe before they share their true feelings. While strict confidentiality is not a requirement, the team needs to agree about the extent to which they are willing to let the content and process of team sessions be shared with others.

---

and wanted to get going. Like clockwork, however, members of the team would come to the weekly session complaining about the seeming lack of involvement of the rest of the workforce. The Grumblers were grumbling, and the Watchers were watching—and the Rowers (the steering team) felt alone and unsupported.

Individual team members would vent and get support. Given their pledge of confidentiality (see above), they felt safe. With their own grievances off their chests, individual members could earnestly encourage their teammates to continue: "Keep your eyes and ears open for what you *can* do and for opportunities to get others involved (even one other person). Our goal is to move the process forward, even a little." Photo 12-1 shows you the UE steering team, past and present.

Bulletin Board. The UE steering team's first team project was to set up a bulletin board. While a bulletin board is not a 5S+1 requirement, it can do a lot to bring people together and recognize the gains. For UE, this was truly the case. The team posted the statement of purpose you read in Exhibit 12-3, then the 5S+1 principles, and above it all a huge computer-generated "5S Bulletin Board" banner. Photo 12-2 shows you the bulletin board about three months into the implementation.

Exhibit 12-3. Statement of Purpose: UE Steering Team.

PURPOSE STATEMENT

- *We have representatives from each department in operations.*

- *Our role is to get people involved, to inform, promote, and sustain 5S + 1.*

- *We will continue to learn more about 5S + 1 and teach others.*

- *We are the eyes and ears of UE. We will listen and bring to the steering team your recommendations, concerns, and problems regarding 5S + 1.*

- *If you need help implementing 5S + 1 in your area, you can ask one of us for assistance.*

- *We are the link between operations and management.*

- *We will help develop standards necessary to sustain 5S + 1.*

- *We will not police people to clean up their areas or badger people to follow 5S + 1.*

Beverly Scibilia	Michael Holmes	John Pacheco
Bill Antunes	Mildred Williams	Randy Campbell
	Luis Catatao	

12-1. UE Steering Team.

This is a combined shot of UE's first VS steering team, when 5S + 1 was launched in 1993, and its current members. From left to right, seated: *Beverly Scibilia, Annie Yu,* and *Mildred Williams.* Standing: *Regina Santos, Luis Catatao, Bill Antunes, John Pacheco, Michael Holmes, Doug Kuntz,* and *Maria Helena Cabral. (Randy Campbell not shown.)*

12-2. 5S Bulletin Board.

The bulletin board at UE took time to develop and keep updated—and lots of people were interested. Notice the regular features plus an area-by-area scoreboard on 5S checklists.

The team also looked for ways to make positive statements and fill up the space (10 feet by 4 feet). What they developed sparkled with innovation. We'll look at two: the *5S highlight of the week* and the *5S question of the week*.

1. *5S highlight of the week.* The highlight of the week is a photograph (Polaroid or otherwise) of a recent visual order device or minisystem, plus the story behind it *as told by* the people who developed it. To cut down on lead time and paperwork, that person simply goes to UE's Resource Center and dictates the story to any available person at a computer. Five minutes later, the story is printed out, the photo glued on it, and the completed highlight posted on the board. Photo 12-3 shows you how it looks on the bulletin board, and Exhibit 12-4 gives you the exact wording.

2. *5S question of the week.* Steering team members regularly interviewed associates on visual order issues. This might be another shopfloor associate, a supervisor—or UE's president, Dave Reis. Again, the person to be interviewed showed up at the Resource Center, sat at a computer with the steering team member, and responded to a question. Five minutes later the interview was printed out and on the bulletin board. Exhibit 12-5 shows you the interview between steering team member Michael Holmes and Bruce Hamilton, UE's management champion.

During all this, steering team members continued their work on the grassroots level, helping a person here, another person there; and, as individuals, they continued to develop their own visual devices and visual minisystems in their areas.

12-3. 5S Highlight of the Week.

These highlights changed often as UE associates came up with new visual devices. And any associate who wanted to got his or her ideas posted.

Visual Minisystems

A cluster of visual devices that work together to promote a single performance outcome.

Balancing action and patience is a continuing challenge for many steering team members. They are, after all, Rowers, and extra eager to see lots of improvement happen. While the big picture may not be transforming fast enough for them, it may be exactly on schedule.

In times like these, encourage people to develop visual minisystems. A **visual minisystem** is a group of visual devices that work together to bring visual order to a specific part of the process or corner of the work area. Minisystems usually develop randomly in the first few months of the 5S + 1 process and often from the efforts of individuals as compared to groups.

Exhibit 12-4. 5S Highlight of the Week.

5S Highlight of the Week

Problem Area

Our problem area is the 650 final Assembly Area. There are four benches back to back. We are having trouble deciding how the work should flow across the benches.

5S Implementation

I've begun by implementing the first of the 5Ss—Sort Through/Sort Out: **eliminate all unnecessary items.** I've sorted through all my fixtures, kept only the ones needed for the 650 order. I got rid of the ones I no longer use. Next I implemented the second S: SCRUB. I scrubbed all my shelves and hung up signs for the kanban, the *incoming* work, and the *outgoing* work.

Benefits of the 5S Implementation

When the bench, shelves, and floor around you are clean, it not only looks better but you feel better about your work area, and I think you work better too. Having signs in the different sections makes it easier to find the area you're looking for. Also it makes it easier to find the parts you need.

Opportunity for Improvement

The next project should be the 800 area. Stay tuned.

UE is a case in point. The speed and quality with which minisystems developed at UE is a story by itself. Two members lead the charge—Bill Antunes and John Pacheco.

The Minisystem Artistry of Bill Antunes

One of UE's first minisystems was the handiwork of Bill Antunes, a production technician who joined the company in 1987. (The term *technician* replaced *hourly employee* when all UE employees became salaried employees in 1987.) Hardworking, energetic, and inventive, Bill was working in UE's sensor department when he got trained in 5S+1.

In no time, every problem Bill encountered seemed to call out for visual order through a minisystem—and life in sensors was never the same. In the ensuing months, Bill developed over a dozen visual minisystems. Here are some of them:

1. Shipping station minisystem
2. Workbench minisystem
3. Stock-out minisystem
4. Coil storage minisystem

Exhibit 12-5. 5S Question of the Week.

> ### 5S Question of the Week
>
> MIKE H.: What do you have to say about someone who thinks 5S is just a pass-over?
>
> BRUCE H.: I am a patient person, sometimes too patient. I think communicating is a two way street. My first thought is if someone feels that 5S is a pass-over, it might be partly because many past efforts for improvements have fallen by the wayside for lack of support.
>
> Secondly, it may be because I haven't adequately communicated to those people that 5S is not a passing thing. 5S is a basic improvement and the start of all improvements. And we have been slow in getting started. I'm going to take that approach for a couple of months because I think it's tough communicating a new idea. After that, I'm going to assume that people do know that IT IS IMPORTANT AND EVERYBODY NEEDS TO PARTICIPATE!!

5. Order delivery minisystem
6. Brazing tips minisystem

We'll look at the first three.

The Shipping Station Minisystem. The shipping area in sensors had always been a thorn in Bill's side—a huge table, covered with cardboard boxes of all description, constantly spilling onto the floor. And under the table was a rat's nest of more boxes, with scissors, tape, stapler, staples, and string mixed in. The hammer could never be found.

By the third training module, Bill knew what he had to do— and did it. In less than twenty-four hours, he transformed the table into a model of visual order. Everything had a place. Each place was addressed. All items (including the hammer) had an ID label and were within easy reach, available at a glance. All the tools and materials needed to pack a shipment were in one place. And people loved it. Bill's first visual minisystem was a huge success and, as this book goes to press, is still fully operational (Photo 12-4).

The Ultimate Workbench. Bill's reputation as a visual order impresario went entirely off the map when he turned his attention to his own workbench. The conversion of his bench from a disorderly accumulation of tools, WIP, and work orders (see Photo 12-5) into visual order perfection exceeded my wildest dreams. This was art. (See Photos 12-6 through 12-10.)

Bill's bench became a model for the rest of the department. Although no one achieved

12-4. The Shipping Station: Bill's First Minisystem.

The simple and powerful work that Bill Antunes did to put location information in place on the shipping table eliminated a ton of motion. Instead of having to search for everything, from scissors to packing tape, it is all at your fingertips.

12-5. Bill's Bench: Before.

This early Polaroid gives you a sense of what Bill's workbench looked like before 5S + 1. Notice the disarray, the haphazard way that tools and supplies cover the work surface, and the complete absence of visual order.

12-6. Bill's Bench: After.

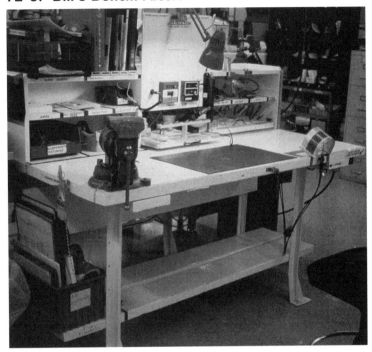

This is a long shot of Bill's bench, after it was transformed. The fresh coat of white paint was only the beginning of the change. Let's take a tour.

12-7. Bill's Bench: Left Side.

On the left side of his bench, Bill organized various papers, binders, tapes, and support items. Notice the clear borders between items and home addresses on everything.

12-8. Bill's Bench: Center.

The center of the bench is for actual value-adding work: soldering. The solder platform is on a pull-out shelf, making it easy to clear the work surface at a touch. All the support switches and items are centralized around it. The door that covers the pull-out doubles as a work order bulletin board.

12-9. Bill's Bench: Right Side.

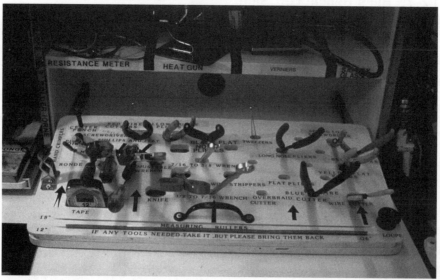

On the right side of the bench is another pull-out shelf, where Bill stores all his hand tools, with a cutout as home for each implement—and the address label tells you which one. Notice the ruler that is built into this handy shelf along with Bill's generous invitation to "help yourself." Of course you will return everything. The level of visual order on this bench leaves you no choice.

12-10. Night Closedown.

When Bill goes home, he is sure that when he gets back, his bench will be just as he left it—a Plexiglas pull-down plate plus padlock ensures it, and still lets us admire this splendid minisystem.

the depth of detail Bill had built in to his bench, the surrounding workstations noticeably improved along 5S + 1 lines—and have stayed that way.

Bill always found time for minisystems, and people's initial and vocal skepticism turned into quiet respect. Although no one in sensors was as eager and ready as Bill, nearly everyone was willing to lend a hand, share an idea, or give some feedback. People were beginning to think visually.

The Stock-Out Minisystem. Strictly speaking, Bill Antune's stock-out minisystem is a visual display board and not a visual order solution; nevertheless it is worth the look. A stock-out happens when material or parts run out before the job is completed. As a result, that work order is put on hold until the missing parts are received.

As a job shop, UE could process thousands of *different* work orders in any given production period, so stock-outs of any kind had serious consequences for lead time and delivery, not to mention the stress they put on people. Besides that, a stock-out (however small) forces you to stop work on the current order, clear it off your bench and/or out of your machine, find a place to store that WIP, and then set up for a new order.

Two UE groups were responsible for making sure that stock-outs did not happen in Bill's department: assembly associates and purchasing associates. Assembly associates needed to notice when stock was running low and report it to purchasing. Purchasers, in their turn, needed to react quickly to secure an urgent shipment from the supplier.

Previous to Bill's solution, communication on stock-outs was done on slips of paper. The associate sent a paper slip to alert the purchaser; the purchaser responded with a paper slip when the order had been made and a delivery date set. As you can imagine, this approach was highly unreliable, with paper slips continuously missent, misplaced, or simply lost. Tensions ran high and no one really knew where things stood for certain. The result was lots of finger pointing, and stock-outs continued unabated.

Bill answered the stock-out challenge simply and powerfully: with a white board, divided into two columns, and two Magic Markers. Here's how it worked. First, if a part is getting low, the associate writes the part number in the column marked LOW-ON-PARTS. If the part runs out, the associate writes the part number in the column marked STOCK-IS-OUT. A purchaser checks the board regularly, circling any new alerts and thereby letting assembly associates know their message has been received. Purchasing returns when a delivery date is secured to mark that date next to its part number. And when the part actually arrives in-house, the purchaser erases the item from the board as a signal to assembly that the part is now available. All the information both parties need is on the board, available at a glance (see Photo 12-11).

12-11. Stock-Out Minisystem.

The colors of this minisystem are red on the left for stock-outs, and blue on the right for low-on-stock. The date when the purchaser was promised delivery is circled next to the part number in question. A simple and highly effective visual display.

This simple yet highly effective system put an end to parts chasing in the sensors area and continues to function flawlessly at the writing of this book, nearly three years after it was developed.

The Minisystem Artistry of John Pacheco

John Pacheco has been at UE for thirteen years and works in UE's machining area. Like Bill, John experienced the principles of visual order as a bolt of lightning. And like Bill, he started simply.

A Modest Beginning. John's first minisystem was in the tube cutting area: a simple container for holding the water basket, a place for any stainless-steel (S/S) scrap, and a home for his coffee cup (Photo 12-12). That was it. That got John started and then there was no stopping him.

12-12. John's First Minisystem.

A container with "water" labels all over it, a scrap bucket for stainless steel with ID label and address, plus a home address for a coffee cup, were the elements of John Pacheco's first minisystem.

Stop in the Name of Safety! Over the next several months, John looked for the visual solution whenever he found himself—or anyone else—in motion or struggling with a job.

One day, John's supervisor, Paul Plant, challenged John to find a visual solution for getting people to put on safety glasses when they entered the machine shop. That was a hard one. People simply seemed to ignore the SAFETY GLASSES REQUIRED sign that hung down from the area's 12-foot ceilings (Photo 12-13). "Small wonder," reasoned John. "How many people look up while they are walking?"

The minisystem he devised literally stops you in your tracks and then practically puts safety glasses on your face (Photo 12-14). One of these STOP-stands is positioned at each of the area's two entrances. They really work.

A Parade of Resourcefulness. John Pacheco was just warming up. Over the months, John came up with dozens of visual devices and minisystems. Nothing was exempt from his scrutiny, and there seemed to be no end to his visual creativity. Here are five of the others:

1. Cutoff saw minisystem
2. Scrap-separator minisystem

12-13. EYE PROTECTION REQUIRED—Ceiling Sign.

John Pacheco and his supervisor, Paul Plant, noticed that not many people, when they enter a hazardous area, bother to look up to notice a WEAR YOUR SAFETY GLASSES sign like this one hanging down from the 15-foot ceiling in UE's machining area.

12-14. Stop Sign.

John's brilliant visual solution stopped people in their tracks and made it easy to comply with UE's safety glasses requirement.

3. Work-order minisystem
4. Variable-volume minisystem
5. Dust-collector minisystem

You have already seen the before/after of the cutoff saw minisystem in Photos 1-1 and 1-2 (Chapter 1). Photo 12-15 gives you a wide shot of John's Scrap Separator Minisystem, which prominently displays an ID label for each barrel, thereby putting an end to scrap mix-ups. His work order minisystem was also a winner, going in steps from good to great (see Photos 12-16 to 12-18).

Bill Antunes, John Pacheco, and other UE employees got bitten by the visual minisystem bug and their enthusiasm infected others. No one who witnessed minisystems in action could deny their effectiveness in taking the struggle out of a job and helping people do work that makes sense.

12-15. Scrap Separator.

Although associates were supposed to separate different kinds of scrap (aluminum, brass, stainless steel, etc.), this did not always happen. So John had some simple computer-generated indicators made for the barrels, put them on a cardboard backing, and attached them to the barrels with big black binder clips. The problem disappeared.

12-16. Paperwork Mess.

This is how the desk where John and his associates did their paperwork used to look.

12-17. Wooden Pull-Out Shelf.

John's first step was to throw out all the nonessentials (S1) and find a home for the essential ones (S4). After removing a shelf from a nearby metal storage rack, he installed a wooden pull-out shelf and put things in order.

12-18. Perfect White Shelf.

A few weeks later, John improved on the good and made it great, with a fresh coat of white paint, clear home addresses, and ID labels. Red plastic tape signals priority work, and a lock (unseen) on the rollout shelf ensures its stability. Splendid!

The Power of Resonance

As I was informed by Charles Ditmas, Keeper of the Clocks at Harvard College (and quoted at the opening of this chapter), if you put a collection of pendulum clocks in the same room, within a short period of time the differing sweeps of their pendulums will become uniform, in exact unison with *the rhythm of the clock with the most powerful swing*. The phenomenon is called "resonance," and it is one of the hidden benefits of visual minisystems.

Steering team members do a lot of joint work to support 5S + 1, putting up a bulletin board and doing other things that you will read about in the next chapter. And when team members work individually, creating visual devices and minisystems, they are putting the law of resonance to work: Simply *do your own work, fully and sincerely, and others will line up with that effort in their own time.*

This is precisely the intent of Standard V of the Code of Conduct you read about in the last chapter: Influence positive direction by doing your *own* work. John, Bill, and other Rowers influence the direction of the implementation by personally engaging in the behaviors they wish others to adopt. Whether you call it leading by example, modeling, or resonance, it can have a powerful positive effect on the implementation process.

Resonance is how the 5S + 1 process touches people who have not participated directly in any formal training. In many instances, this makes a more compelling case in favor of visual order than any amount of talking or instruction. This is exactly what happened in Manny's Miracle.

Manny's Miracle

There is a bright-yellow door just off UE's Machine Shop. Always locked, this is the door to the toxins room. Behind it, you can find barrels of chemicals, used and otherwise. The person with the key to the door is Manny Sousa, facilities manager at UE.

Manny has worked at UE for eighteen years. Like Bill Antunes, John Pacheco, and so many UE employees, he is fiercely proud of working for UE. And his work is impeccable, just as he is—looking great in a starched white shirt and ready smile, cool as a cucumber, and capable (see Photo 12-19).

Two months into 5S + 1, I was hanging up my coat in the Resource Center when Maureen Hamilton, the Center's coordinator, pulled me aside and whispered, "Did you see it? Did you see what Manny did?" I was blank. "Wait, I'll get the key," she said. Five minutes later, Maureen was back with a key and led me to the toxins room. I had been in that room only once before, and my mind flashed back on that memory (see Photo 12-20).

Now I stood before a newly painted door of bright yellow. Maureen unlocked the door and we stepped inside.

The room was spotless! A dazzle of order! Clean. Shining. I stood amazed. The barrels of chemicals that had been grimly in their racks were clearly labeled and carefully stacked on a freshly painted red rack. Under the spigot of each barrel was a bright yellow drip bucket, and under each bucket was a bright-red dot, marking its home location on the freshly scrubbed floor (Photos 12-21 and 12-22).

12-19. Manny.

Manny Sousa, UE facilities manager, in front of the famous yellow door of his magnificent visual mini-system.

12-20. Toxins Room: Before.

Here is what the toxins room looked like before Manny performed his 5S + 1 magic.

12-21. Yellow Buckets.

Instead of letting drips from the barrel collect on the floor, Manny bought these simple heavy plastic pails—bright yellow to match the door. Later, they were replaced by OSHA-approved metal drip buckets.

12-22. Red Dots.

Bright-red dots were all the address the drip buckets needed.

12-23. Strange-Can Address.

This toxin can had such a strange shape it was easy to give it a home address that required no location label. (See also Photo 12-24.)

12-24. Strange Can at Home.

12-25. Hand Truck Shadow.

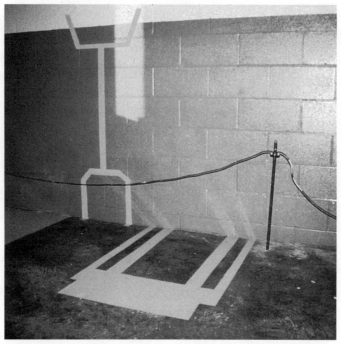

Again, this silhouette home address is distinctive. Everyone knows what belongs there.

12-26. Hand Truck at Home.

Here are the occupants of the address shown in the previous photo.

12-27. Shovel Address.   **12-28. Shovel at Home.**

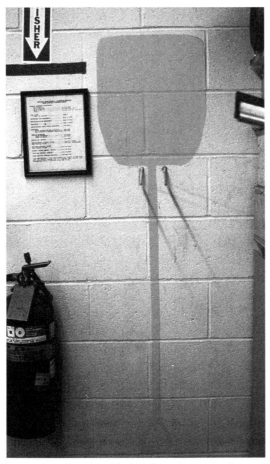

The same goes for this bright-yellow shadow address outside the toxins room. What belongs there is no mystery. (See also Photo 12-28.)

A strangely shaped can was also at home in a location that needed no address (Photos 12-23 and 12-24). Likewise, the hand truck and barrel lifter; their address silhouettes were painted directly on the wall (Photos 12-25 and 12-26).

The detail of the change was thorough and impressive. As we left the room, Maureen pointed out the yellow "shadow" home for the toxin-room shovel, just to the right of the yellow door (see Photos 12-27 and 12-28). Perfect!

The fact is, Manny had never gone to a single day of the formal 5S+1 training. He attended a two-hour awareness session, sat through 150 slides, saw what other UE employees were up to—and "got" it.

☆ ☆ ☆ ☆ ☆

Implementing visual order is not rocket science. You see it: You get it. That is one of the powers of the 5S+1 approach, and it spreads through many avenues in addition to good training. Two of the most influential tools are the steering team and visual mini-systems—and the resonance they create.

In this chapter you saw that individual behavior and group behavior can—separately and collectively—exert a powerful influence on the direction and speed of an implementation. These are the linchpins of success. It is called *leading through example*. In the next chapter you will learn about another success factor: the strategic partnership between management and the steering team that is called *leading through standards*.

Chapter 13

+ 1: Leading Through Standards

When the plant manager of a stamping factory heard that a steering team made up of hourly associates was to lead the way to visual order, he said:

> "Lead! How are they gonna lead? My shopfloor crew is smart and tough but they're gonna need more than bulletin boards, minisystems, and resonance if they are supposed to lead this process!"

Perhaps you can imagine your own manager with similar misgivings. Maybe you have them yourself.

It's true. By themselves, a bulletin board, minisystems, and resonance cannot ensure the effectiveness of your steering team. If these were your only supports, you would be justified in fearing that your implementation would not get far. But there is another mechanism in the steering team toolbox—a secret weapon.

In this chapter we revisit the steering team function to learn about that secret and about the three remaining +1 tools: the visual workplace coordinator, management champion, and management watch.

Standards: The Steering Team's Secret Weapon

Up to this point, if associates were reluctant to get on board with 5S+1, that was their choice. Steering team members led through example, attempting to influence positive direction by modeling the values and behaviors they wanted others to adopt.

Now a second leadership approach is added: leading through standards. (We'll discuss the timing of this shortly.) **Leading through standards** means that certain practices that support 5S+1 are specifically established. Adherence is no longer a matter of personal preference; these practices become standard, required, and uniformly applied in all work areas participating in the implementation. They become company policy.

In sports, standards are the rules that determine how the game is played. In the workplace, standards tell us what is supposed to happen—exactly what must be done, how, how often, how much, and by whom. 5S+1 standards describe what is supposed to happen related to implementing and sustaining visual order. 5S+1 standards are specific, relevant, and observable and, taken as a sum, form the baseline for results. Here are some common 5S+1 standards.

Common 5S+1 Standards

1. All areas participating in the implementation will red-tag during the first week of each month.
2. All areas will use the official red-tag removal form (see Exhibit 4-2) when disposing of capital assets.
3. All areas will use a 5S checklist (either wall chart, clipboard or both) on not less than a weekly basis.
4. All nonmovable floor items will have a taped or painted border.
5. Nothing is to be stored directly on the surface of the production floor.
6. The doors of all cabinets and shelving, along with all locks, are to be removed.

Leading through standards links the success of individual work areas with the whole. While the emphasis is still on individual creativity and contribution, standards extend their scope. Photos 13-1 through 13-3 show you a visual order device developed in one department that became standard throughout the factory. Photo 13-3 shows the level of cleanliness and order that is acceptable on the grinding bench.

13-1. Big John at His Bench.

John Christian, a highly respected veteran grinder in Hamilton Standards Blade Company, gave his calm, firm support for the 5S + 1 improvement activity in his area.

13-2. 5S Standard at the Bench.

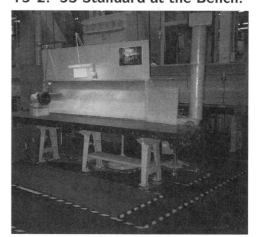

A Hamilton Standards team came up with an outstanding tool for sustaining visual order at the grinding bench. They took a photo of the bench when it sparkled, then posted the photo directly on the bench. No one needed to ask what had to be done at the end of the shift. They just made it look like the photo.

13-3. Close-Up of Standard.

A close-up of the 5S + 1 photographic standard for the grinding bench.

Timing Is Everything

At the beginning, setting 5S + 1 standards is not just a question of what but when. It is a question of timing. Start setting 5S + 1 standards too early, and you risk choking off individual and group creativity. Start setting them too late, and existing patterns of inertia and resistance may have become too deep to reverse.

In 5S + 1, setting standards is not done cookie-cutter fashion. Rather than importing another company's standards into your own, let your standards evolve as a customized, home-grown process. At its best, this process is a joint effort between the steering team and management that is based on the actual needs of your implementation, with the steering team leading the way. As the UE team put it in the purpose statement you read in Chapter 12:

> We are the eyes and ears of UE. We will listen and bring to the steering team your recommendations, concerns, and problems regarding 5S + 1.

How to Set 5S + 1 Standards

People trained in 5S + 1 know that their company's first 5S + 1 standard could relate to just about anything. It all depends on what turns up as a priority. The need leads.

Like all 5S + 1 standards, your first one will be linked to an actual workplace condition. Here's how to start.

How to Determine the Need for Standards

1. Look at how the implementation is going: What is working? What is not?
2. Listen to what associates are saying: What are they complaining about? What do they like?
3. Share what you see and hear with the others on the steering team.
4. Stay alert to the emergence of a theme, usually of complaints: That theme will lead you to your first 5S + 1 standard (and the next and the next).

Let's look at how this happened at UE.

Too Many Colors: A Need for a Standard

In about the third month of the UE implementation, steering team members began to hear repeatedly one comment around the shop floor. It went something like this: "Our work area is starting to look like a circus. . . ."

Departments were using colored paper to show the difference between operational locations: one color for incoming material, another for outgoing, a third color for inspection, a fourth for rework, and so on. Each department picked its own colors and, in a playful way, tried to top each other's color choice. Green went to bright green to phosphorescent green. Pink, yellow, and blue followed the same escalation. Besides a carnival-like shopfloor look, mix-ups happened because, for example, green would mean incoming in one department and nonconforming material next door. On top of this, UE's health office reported an upswing in eyestrain complaints.

The steering team saw an opportunity to *recommend* its first 5S+1 standard: Standardize colors for shopfloor locations. (Notice the word *recommend*. We'll return to it in a moment.) First, they decided the operational categories that needed specific locations: test, inspection, calibration, WIP, rework, scrap, nonconforming material, packing, kanban, assembly, incoming material, and outgoing material. Then, they assigned a color to each. That was it.

And what was their next step? If you think it was to announce the new standard, you are wrong. Here's why.

If, as its next step, the UE steering team had announced the procedure they had just drafted as a new 5S+1 standard, they would have run up against two blockbuster problems. First, the team members would have been acting on their own authority—and they had none. Steering team members are associates, not managers. Therefore, the steering team has *no* official authority. (Except in the case of self-directed teams, few shopfloor teams can establish company policy.)

Second (and closely linked to the first), steering team members are shopfloor associates, the peers of all other shopfloor associates—and must remain so. If the team was allowed to establish a company standard on their own, their co-workers might see them as "bosses" and not as colleagues. Trust would erode, along with people's willingness to freely share their personal comments and complaints. (That is why the UE steering team made that special point in its purpose statement: *We will not police people to clean up their areas or badger people to follow the 5S+1.*)

Here is the six-step process for setting 5S+1 standards that are sustainable. After each step is a note about the way it happened at UE.

Setting Standards: Step by Step

1. *Steering team drafts the new standard.* The steering team identifies the need for a 5S+1 standard and then drafts it.

The UE steering team developed the SOP for standardized color-coded locations (discussed above).

2. *Steering team proposes the new standard to management.* When the draft is complete, the team submits it to management for approval—usually to the management champion.

The UE steering team showed the draft to Bruce Hamilton (UE management champion) and asked him to approve it.

3. *Management approves the new standard.* Or, management reviews the proposed standard and either supports it or comes up with an alternative procedure to address the need.

Bruce reviewed the proposed standard and approved it.

4. *Management announces the new standard.* Management announces the new standard to the workforce, establishing it as official company policy. This can be done at a company meeting and/or through a signed memo that goes to all employees or to all supervisors for sharing.

13-4. New Standard Posted on the 5S Bulletin Board.

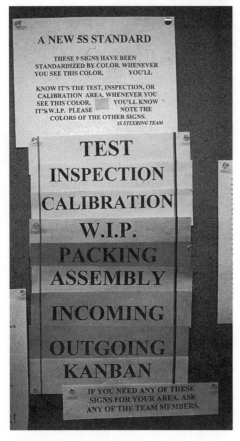

These are the nine color-coded location categories standardized by UE's steering team.

Bruce wrote a memo announcing the new standard and distributed it to all UE shopfloor supervisors. Dave Reis, UE president, also announced the new standard at a companywide meeting and gave it, and 5S + 1, his personal support.

5. *Steering team supports the new standard.* The team takes steps to facilitate the new standard.

The team posted Bruce's memo on the 5S + 1 bulletin board, along with the colors of the new standard (Photo 13-4). The team placed stacks of preprinted color-coded location sheets in the Resource Center so associates could help themselves. And each steering team member brought a set of sheets to his/her work area and helped to install them.

6. *Steering team monitors adherence and strengthens as needed.* The steering team monitors the extent to which the new standard is practiced. If adherence is weak, team members track compliance on a chart (called a visual scoreboard) and implement other visual devices that help people more fully comply.

UE team members observed no adherence problems related to the new 5S + 1 standard. The support they gave (described above in step 5) was sufficient to ensure 100 percent adherence.

However, this does not mean that the steering team can resolve every visual order issue with a new standard, as the following example illustrates.

Inventory Location: A Really Big Problem

UE is a job shop, with literally thousands of orders for differently configured products flowing through its departments each month. At the point of this story in UE's growth, simply locating the inventory you needed for a given work order could be the first and seemingly insurmountable challenge. For example, on your search for a specific subassembly, you might be directed to look for it "under the third workbench to your left as you enter the OEM department from the outside hallway." Or, "Go over to the model shop and look behind that big black box with the red letters next to John's desk. You'll see a rack. I'll bet you find what you need on one of those shelves. If you don't, come find me again" This is the language of motion.

As 5S + 1 took root at UE, people became less willing to search for inventory. Complaints grew into a groundswell of protest. Associates wanted an end to the motion they had silently accepted in the past. They asked the steering team for a solution.

Members of the steering team lived the problem every day, along with everyone else. They wanted to help but knew it would be a huge job—a global one—that could eat up the team's time and resources. So they asked the Resource Center to form an action center (a UE project team), with a steering team member on it. The group was called the *Global Inventory Location* action center—and the solution they developed was brilliant.

Inventory Location Action Center

The action center met once a week for an hour. Slowly and surely the solution began to evolve. By month three, it was ready to implement, with full backing from the steering team. Instead of trying to clear up the confusion department by department, they created an inventory grid system for the entire shop floor that designated home locations for UE's entire inventory.

Details: Grid Pattern. Establishing a grid system like UE's is a two-step process. First, establish the grid pattern, then assign each cell in that pattern a specific inventory address. At UE, the pattern was tied to the physical layout of the production floor, keyed into the I-beams (steel pillars) that support the building at 30-foot intervals. This created the first level of the grid: an array of 30- × 30-foot squares, the 900 square feet of floor space formed within each four-pillar cluster.

Each 30- × 30-foot square then got a letter—from *A* to *L*—and a number—from 1 to 8 (for the eight rows of I-beams supporting the ceiling). Each square was then subdivided into 100 squares of 3 × 3 feet each, numbered from 1 through 100. The number starting point and positioning were standardized and designated "00." When finished, the grid pattern covered every inch of UE's shop floor in a checkerboard fashion. See Photo 13-5.

Details: Grid Addresses. With the grid established, large visual indicators (signs) were put on each I-beam, corresponding to its location on the grid (Photo 13-6). The 00

13-5. Inventory Grid.

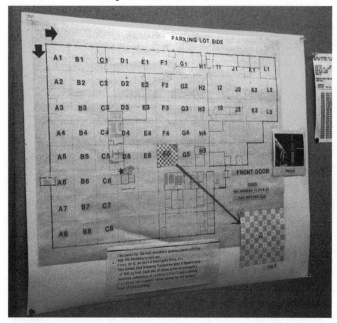

UE's inventory grid was a checkerboard map of precise location information, keyed on the facility's I-beam structure.

location of the subsquares was also clearly marked. Inventory addresses were then derived from the corresponding grid address, starting with the subsquare location.

Let's say, for example, that part number 6256-222 was located at F586B. The first two digits (F5) tell us that the inventory can be found in the 30- × 30-foot square located on the 5 side of the F girder. The next two digits (86) tell us that the inventory is stored in the 86th square within the F5 checkerboard. All we need now is the elevation (height) at which the inventory can be found. Is the inventory on the floor? In a bin? On a shelf? Or a workbench? And if on a workbench, then where—on top of it or underneath? Shelf location is designated by letters: *A, B, C, D, E*, etc., starting from the ground-level shelf and moving up. The final element of our sample address is *B*, indicating that the part is located on shelf B, second from the bottom.

This exceptional visual solution to accurate inventory location took a big bite out of day-to-day shopfloor motion at UE. It also saved large chunks of time during UE's annual physical inventory, with some UE associates claiming time reductions of over 50 percent.

The message of UE's grid success is twofold: First, there are powerful opportunities for applying the principles of visual order in your company—so be on the lookout. Second, as stated at the opening of this chapter, the steering team has a crucial role to play in leading 5S+1 in your company. This is not just one of personal example and behind-the-scenes support, but one of up-front leadership, setting the direction and the pace of the implementation. Leading through standards plays a big part in this.

The team also gains strength from the final three +1 tools: the visual workplace coordinator, management champion, and management watch. Let's look at these now.

13-6. I-Beam Address/Inventory Grid.

The I-beam to the right makes accurate UE inventory information handy and available at a glance: grid location F5 and grid location F6.

The Visual Workplace Coordinator

The visual workplace coordinator is responsible for providing administrative and logistical support to the implementation and for coordinating its various activities. Not a glamorous position but a critical one, the job of **visual workplace coordinator (VW coordinator)** means organizing the activities of the entire implementation and providing the glue that holds it all together. Here are some typical duties.

Typical Duties of the VW Coordinator
- Making sure that work areas slated for the implementation are prepared and scheduled for training
- Coordinating the logistical and material needs of in-house and external coaching
- Checking/ordering/restocking 5S corner supplies
- Staying available to the steering team; clarifying information and procedures; and providing coaching, feedback, and support as needed
- Keeping a thumb on the pulse of the implementation
- Bridging with management and advocating to management when additional resources (funds, time, support) are needed
- Learning how to be an in-house 5S + 1 coach by shadowing the visual workplace consultant when she is on-site

To succeed, a coordinator must be thoroughly and formally trained in the 5S + 1 process, have enthusiasm for and belief in visual order, be willing to model and support the values of the code of conduct, and must have enough time. This last point is crucial.

VW coordinators are usually (but by no means always) management (from training managers to human resources VPs). If your candidate is loaded with other duties, do her and the implementation a favor: Find someone else for the job or off-load some existing duties. Be realistic: The coordinator must have enough time (this is the improvement time versus production time issue again)—*time to do the job*. A rough weekly estimate for performing the duties listed above is two to three hours after the first month. Add an hour if the coordinator sits in on regular steering team sessions.

The coordinator can also be a powerful force in helping shopfloor associates develop their personal and leadership skills. Let's look again at the UE scenario.

UE: Developing People

Recall that Annie Yu filled UE's coordinator spot. She did a remarkable job—and her work with the steering team was a highlight.

As mentioned earlier, project-oriented teams (action centers) were common at UE and ongoing change teams, like the VW steering team, were not. Leading and supporting an ongoing process of change means the team must identify and complete specific tasks *while* promoting a process consistent with the values of the code of conduct. As we have read, the balance between task and process frequently shifts. Finding the right balance point often calls for a level of skill and discretion that few shopfloor people have had a chance to develop. By contrast, the VW coordinator usually has a strong cluster of such skills. Using these skills too directly can hamper the team from developing skills of their own.

One of the most important ways that Annie helped the implementation was in her application of what I call "leading through questions"—shorthand for using an indirect approach to skill building.

When, for example, the UE team got stuck and did not seem to know what to do next, Annie asked a series of questions to help the team discover for themselves what was preventing a forward movement. To illustrate, here is a short exchange at one of the team's early meetings when I sat in as an observer.

Annie:	What is your objective for today? What do you want to accomplish before the end of the meeting?
Team:	[*Silence.*]
Annie:	What kinds of things do you see happening in your own areas that you want to talk about here?
Team:	[*Lively discussion.*]

It took Annie only two short questions to get team members focused and on track. Using a round-robin approach, the team let each member talk in the order in which they were seated around the table (those who did not wish to speak, simply said "pass"). Ten minutes later, the team got stuck again.

Annie simply asked, "Any ideas of what might happen next to get the implementation to the next step?" Bingo! More round-robin discussion. Gradually, week by week, the team began to pick up on Annie's quiet approach and began to guide themselves, unprompted. They moved away from round robin and into spontaneous discussion. Soon they were using this new learning in their interactions with co-workers in their own areas. They had acquired new skills, confidence, and understanding and began to pass these along to others.

The positive impact of this simple people-development process on an implementation cannot be underestimated. It is the very essence of what is meant by *empowerment*. A company with empowered teams can get off to a flying start. If your company is still making its way toward this, the role of the VS coordinator can be a major leverage point for helping associates learn how to lead by using personal skill, not power.

In this and so many other ways, Annie's support of the implementation at UE played a big part in its stunning success. And when UE decided to become self-sufficient and sought a license (see the Resources section) for teaching the 5S + 1 methodology internally, she was in a perfect position to be the in-house trainer and coach.

The Management Champion

The **managment champion** is a manager or an executive with high credibility, responsible for visibly supporting the 5S + 1 process, providing it with regular top-management feedback, and going to bat for it, if needed. He or she is often the person who made the initial decision to go ahead with the implementation. In some cases, the champion is recruited after the implementation gets launched, but not usually.

The important thing is that this champion be willing and on a senior level. Not every high-ranking manager is "qualified" to be the champion. Though the time commitment is relatively modest (one to two hours a week), it is *regular*—every week. Some executives are too busy to commit. Other may not like the limelight of this high-profile role. One president, for example, supported astonishing operational improvements in his organization but wanted no part of the glory. He simply refused. His support remains strong but without personal visibility. He would not be the right person for the role of management champion—and he knows it.

The management champion is a friend of the implementation, ready to go to bat for it, if and as needed. To qualify, a candidate must be: (1) enthusiastic about visual order, (2) thoroughly trained in its principles, concepts, and methods, and (3) willing to model, through his own behavior, the values of the visual workplace code of conduct.

> *Tip*   If yours is a union shop, ask your company and union management to consider forming a joint management champion position.

The main tool by which the champion supports the implementation is called the **management watch** (the ninth and final +1 tool). Using it, the champion shows the company's commitment to visual order by his/her own physical and regular presence in the workplace. Before we discuss the watch, which in my experience is an indispensable sustaining tool, here's another way to build a functional relationship between management and the shop floor related to 5S + 1. This one is not required, but in many companies, it is exceedingly useful.

Schedule the steering team to make a formal presentation to management on a regular basis. Sometimes called the Quality Council or Lead Group, this is management's time to appreciate the 5S + 1 progress and suggest new directions, and the team's time to speak to management about wider issues of support and strategy. In addition, steering teams have often used the format of a formal presentation to their advantage by inviting other associates to present both their solutions and their struggles.

The Management Watch

The **management watch** is the regularly scheduled time slot when the management champion tours the work areas under 5S + 1 improvement in order to visibly and concretely recognize and influence the effort through the use of watch cards.

The management champion is responsible for conducting the management watch on a regular and scheduled basis. At the outset, this generally means once a week. Later (after a year or so), this may be reduced to once a month. But happen it must.

During a management watch, the champion tours each area participating in the implementation and looks for two things: (1) evidence of improvement and (2) opportunities for further improvement.

The Recognition Watch Card

When the champion sees concrete signs of improvement, the champion writes up a Recognition Card, the first of the two cards used in the watch process (the process works best when the two cards are different colors; for example, blue for recognition and yellow for the other). Each type card has words printed on it, is laminated, and has a hole-punch at top. You will see why in a moment.

When the champion sees a condition, device or minisystem he appreciates, he writes words of praise on the card in erasable marker, and then hangs it (by elastic or string) at/on/near that improvement. Photo 13-7 shows you a recognition card hanging on a newly decluttered supply cart. Exhibit 13-1 gives you that card's standard wording; the blank spaces are for comments. Feel free to modify the language you find to suit your company. Just be sure it recognizes people's 5S + 1 improvement activity.

Opportunity Watch Cards

If the champion sees the need for improvement, an Opportunity Watch Card is used. Photo 13-8 shows one hanging on a wooden storage rack, questioning the number of bins that are cluttering the area; it's yellow. Exhibit 13-2 shows you the template for the Opportunity Watch Card.

Both cards stay in place until the next watch. During that time, area associates get a chance to read them and, where necessary, respond to them. On the next watch, the champion reads any carryovers related to recognition cards, and looks for the changes

13-7. Blue Watch Card (Hanging).

This Recognition Card (blue) is hung exactly where the improvement happened—a big change from the clutter and debris the management champion saw when he came by the week before.

requested on opportunity cards. If these changes are satisfactory, the champion writes "Done and thank you!" or words to that effect. If more improvement is needed, that gets written on the same card, and the card stays in place so that it can be rechecked the next time. When either kind of card is removed, it is photocopied for the record and then wiped clean for use on another watch.

> *Tip*   Make sure you use a heavy-gauge laminate to make watch cards stiff. Or you can back them with cardboard before you laminate.

Associate Response

Without exception, the response of associates to the management watch has been positive. People seem to really appreciate the time that the champion is willing to commit to this process (Photo 13-9) and the specific, regularized feedback they get on their efforts. They seem to especially appreciate the involvement of otherwise rarely seen managers. This alone can give an implementation a big boost.

Just remember: The watch is and must continue to be regularly scheduled. That

Exhibit 13-1. Template: Recognition Watch Card (Blue).

• **Your Company** • **Your Town, U.S.A.** • *—Recognition Watch Card—*	
Area Name	*Date*

Our Goal

A Visual Workplace: A work area that is self-explaining, self-ordering, self-regulating, and self-improving, where what is *supposed* to happen *does* happen, on time, every time, night or day. The foundation of this level of excellence is a visual order/5S+1: a clear, clean, safe, and orderly workplace.

Instructions on the Use of the Recognition Watch Card

1. The purpose of this card is for you to call attention to any improvement and/or visual device you consider noteworthy in this area that supports visual order (one improvement per card please).

2. In the space below, describe what you observe and why you appreciate it. Please be as specific and concrete as possible and use full phrases or sentences.

3. If you think the improvement could be used in other areas, indicate this in the space provided below. The steering team rep in this area will coordinate this and update you below on any results.

4. Please write *thank you* and sign the card. Then fasten it on or near the improvement. *Thanks.*

Your Remarks & Recommendations	**Signed By**
	_____
	_____
	_____
	The steering team shared this idea with the area(s) you named with the following results:
This device might also apply in the following area(s): _____. Please share it with associates there.	_____ _____ _____

13-8. Yellow Watch Card (Hanging).

The management champion used this Opportunity Watch Card (yellow) to ask area associates why there were so many carts in their location. And he hung it precisely where the clutter was the thickest.

means people know the manager will show up within a certain frame of time—say, every Thursday. They also know they will get feedback in a clear and standardized form and that it will be improvement oriented.

Feedback Guidelines for Watch Cards

The main guideline for watch card success is to make sure that the intent of each type of card is met. A well-phrased recognition card can instill pride and trigger further improvement. A well-worded opportunity card can prompt a flurry of focused improvement activity.

The only time the impact of the watch gets shaky is when the champion has not yet mastered the art of giving specific feedback. This can be corrected with thirty minutes of effective coaching.

Most problematic watch card feedback is simply too general. "Great work! Thanks!" on a recognition card is about as flat and unusable as "This needs to improve!" on an opportunity card. Follow these three guidelines for improved watch card comments:

Watch Card Comment Guidelines

1. Be concrete and specific. Give details.
2. Use full phrases or sentences—not just a string of adjectives.
3. Make your feedback legible. If people can't read it, they can't use it.

Exhibit 13-3 gives you some examples of not so useful and very useful feedback.

Exhibit 13-2. Template: Opportunity Watch Card (Yellow).

· **Your Company** · **Your Town, U.S.A.** ·		
—Opportunity Watch Card—		
Area Name	*Sub-Area*	*Date*

Our Goal

A Visual Workplace: A work area that is self-explaining, self-ordering, self-regulating, and self-improving, where what is *supposed* to happen *does* happen, on time, every time, night or day. The foundation of this level of excellence is a visual order/5S + 1: a clear, clean, safe, and orderly workplace.

Instructions on the Use of the Opportunity Watch Card

1. The purpose of this card is to call attention to any condition you observe in this work area that could be improved through an application of the 5S + 1 (visual order). Write your observations in the space provided below (one per card please). Feel free to make specific improvement recommendations.

2. Please be as concrete and detailed as possible. Use full phrases and sentences. Avoid shorthand or code.

3. When you are done, sign the card and fasten it on or near what you observed.

4. On your next *watch,* check to see what improvement has occurred. If you're satisfied, write *done* and *thank you* on the card (plus any other comments). Then leave the card where it is. If you are not satisfied, add today's date and your comments and leave the card where it is. *Thanks.*

Your Observations & Recommendations	**Signed By**
· **Cluttered** · **Not Clean** · **Not Safe** · **Not Orderly** (circle all that apply)	_____ _____ _____

13-9. Bruce Filling Out a Card.

Bruce Hamilton, UE's vice president of operations and management champion, is often on the shop floor interacting with and supporting improvement teams. Here he is filling out watch cards during his weekly management watch.

Exhibit 13-3. Examples of Watch Card Feedback.

Feedback Quality	Recognition	Opportunity
Not So Useful Feedback	Great improvement. Thanks!	What a mess!
More Useful Feedback	Fixtures are neatly arranged and labeled. Great work! Keep it up and thanks.	Please get rid of the clutter in this area. How can you know what you need? And what are these sneakers doing here?
Not So Useful Feedback	Things are really looking better in this area! Thanks!	This needs to get better.
More Useful Feedback	Yellow borders and fire extinguisher ID really help keep things in order. Great touch. Thanks. Can you do the same in the P-1 area?	The floor looks cleaner but it still has a long way to go. I nearly broke my neck on the oil spill near the CNC. Please make eliminating the source of that spill a priority this week.

Exhibit 13-4. The Blueprint.

Leaving the Subbasement

At this point in your implementation, the nine sustaining tools are in place, and visual order is at a showcase level in your company.

With that, the first level of the blueprint for a visual workplace is complete in those areas participating in the implementation (see Exhibit 13-4). Your organization is now ready to extend 5S+1 companywide.

But before you do that, read the third and final portion of this book to learn about the key implementation issues.

Four

Go!

One: The Big Picture		
1. Toward a Visual Workplace	2. Visual Systems in Context	3. The Five Start-Up Requirements
Two: 5S Method		
4. S1/Sort Through and Sort Out	5. S2–S4/ Scrub, Secure Safety, and Select Locations	6. S5/Set Locations: Borders
7. S5/Set Locations: Addresses	8. 5S Stories From the Shop Floor	9. 5S+1 and White-Collar Applications
Three: +1 Method				
10. People: What to Expect	11. +1: Building and Sustaining the 5S Habit	12. +1: Leading by Example	13. +1: Leading Through Standards
Four: Go!		
14. Showcase, Scope, and the System	15. Training and Education	16. The Hundredth Monkey

Chapter 14

Showcase, Scope, and the System

You want three things out of your first cycle of 5S+1. You want to observe how the 5S+1 methodology works in your company. You want measurable results. And you want a 5S+1 showcase that reveals to others the vision, practices, and benefits of visual order, the first step toward a visual workplace.

Your 5S+1 Showcase

Creating a 5S+1 showcase means you have produced a living demonstration of what visual order means in at least one work area. Once you have one showcase, the standard has been set and it can spread from there. People can go to that area and see how 5S + 1 functions and behaves. Not only is the place clutter-free, clean, safe, and orderly, the people who work there have the habit of visual order. A range of +1 sustaining tools are in place. Day after day after day, the same high level of order is maintained, with a constant stream of new and surprising additions. The place shines with awareness, and value is added as a matter of course.

That work area is ready to go beyond self-explaining and self-ordering and become a work area that is self-regulating and then self-improving. It is ready to move to the next stage in the blueprint you read about in Chapter 2.

There is no way to overestimate the importance of a showcase in bolstering your implementation and pointing the way to the future. Your showcase area is the baseline. It has set the standard for further improvement, only this time as a catalyst for a companywide application.

As you grapple with a certain and predictable unevenness in the rate with which different work areas get on board with 5S + 1, know that your real goal is to get *only one* of them to do it right and do it thoroughly. Your goal is to support just one of those areas sufficiently so that showcase is achieved. Chrysler Corporation calls this their learning line. That's a good way to think of it. Just as Disney World may have served as your vision place to get started, so your showcase serves as your on-site vision place.

This is the place people will come to to be informed, to be inspired, to see how it is done in your company, to learn how to get from point A to point B, and to find out what point B will look like when they arrive.

Scope

Your showcase will be one of the work areas you have targeted to take part in 5S + 1. Depending on the circumstances of your own company, that may be the one area out of the eight that hits the jackpot first—or it may be the one area that is the focus of your entire implementation. That is, you may start small, pouring all your efforts into a single work area, or you may implement companywide, launching 5S + 1 in six to eight areas simultaneously. Deciding on the scope of your implementation (where to begin and how many different work areas should participate) is a decision that must come early in your 5S + 1 planning process.

Basically, you have two choices. You can start with a very small, narrow focus, or you can launch in multiple areas.

Starting Very Small: Choice 1

It is perfectly acceptable to start on a limited scale, implementing 5S + 1 in just a few work areas or even just one. Starting very small is the wise choice when some or all of the following conditions prevail in your company:

• *Otherwise occupied.* Your company is on the verge of its annual physical inventory and you cannot spare the resources. Or the entire company is in the throes of converting to a new MIS system, going after ISO certification, or installing a gain-sharing program. Perhaps the shop floor is ramping up for a new product line or occupied in applying quick changeover and/or cell design techniques. Yet another companywide improvement initiative may well sink the corporate boat.

In other words, your company may simply be stretched too thin to launch a companywide implementation of visual order. Instead, you can elect to: (1)combine 5S + 1 with an existing improvement process (remember the Chapter 8 story about the quick changeover initiative at Fleet Engineers) or (2) make a modest launch only, work out the bugs, create a showcase, demonstrate results, and prepare for a more intensive application later, when the timing is right. You don't want to postpone the introduction of visual order, since its principles and practices are central to *all* other improvement work. But you do want to wait to do it comprehensively, and so you decide to implement now on a very limited scale.

• *Flavor of the month.* Perhaps your company has been subjected to an endless parade of improvement programs over the past several years. Each started with fanfare and speeches from top management, but not one of these programs ever stuck around long enough to become a process and make a difference in the way things were done. They were like triple-dip ice cream cones on a hot summer's day. They looked yummy but melted away before you could get them in your belly.

If this sounds like your company, you can be sure that most people will put 5S + 1 in the same category: just another flavor-of-the-month, a great idea that is going to go nowhere. Don't risk it. Start small and without fanfare. If need be, don't even call the effort 5S + 1. Don't call it anything. Don't promote it. Don't make promises. Just pick out one or two work areas where success is likely (supervisor and associates express interest) and just do it—systematically. Keep it low-key. Let it spread through a grassroots approach.

• *Improvement fatigue.* Many American companies have done an awful lot of improving over the past ten years. They have practically turned themselves inside out to change (for the better) the way they do business. The majority of these organizations want to keep on growing. Better than most, they understand that a growing company is a competitive company. Still, from time to time, a company needs a collective rest. It may be suffering from improvement fatigue.

If your own company fits this description, start very small. You may be raring to go, but others may not be. Expect to be disappointed (then you won't be) as you look for willing candidates. And don't get on anyone else's case if they don't want to get on board even for a try.

You may have to settle for doing the work by yourself. Quietly, modestly, steadily. Do your own good work and they will find you. The pull of excellence—the success of your own efforts—is irresistible. You will be ready with your own small showcase just about the time they become ready to give your original offer some serious consideration.

• *Limited training resources.* 5S + 1 is simple but it is not easy. Its success depends on three types of training:

1. Training area associates in the 5S + 1 methodology
2. Reinforcing the learning
3. On-the-spot coaching

You can bring in outside expert training resources or you can attempt to train on your own.

If you decide to introduce 5S + 1 on your own, start small. Take just one or two work areas for starters. That will allow you a learning curve as well as the time to work out the logistics of training, refine your instructional approach, and figure out how the methodology links. Starting very small can be the right choice for you and your organization. See Chapter 15 for much more on the training function.

One final point. In our discussion of inertia (Chapter 10), we talked about inertia as an issue of mass (in this case, a certain critical number of people). The objective is to convert a mass that is inert and at rest (the Watchers) into a mass that is in motion (the Rowers). This can happen more readily, and often more quickly, when you start small. You are likely to achieve that critical mass much sooner than if you were to begin with a broader implementation.

If any—or all—of the above applies to your company, by all means start very small: (1)Implement in one to two areas only, (2) focus on getting tangible results, and (3) make that showcase shine.

Starting very small can mean starting in one cell. This was the choice made by Alpha Industries, a semiconductor manufacturer in Woburn, Massachusetts.

Starting Very Small at Alpha

Alpha, which had more than doubled its market in 1994, knew that bringing visual order to the facility was part of the answer to coping with and maximizing the growth. Another part was getting a new MIS system in place.

In 1995, Alpha opted to do both and on two separate timelines. The MIS conversion would proceed comprehensively and at full force. Visual order would proceed modestly at the outset. The target 5S + 1 site was a semiconductor manufacturing cell which we'll call the SCM Cell. The SCM Cell (some 1,500 square feet) and its nineteen associates are under the leadership of Ken Bushmich, a man of vision and knowledge. Four months before 5S + 1 came to Alpha, Kenny's area was not a cell at all but merely a section of plant floor where production got carried out along strictly traditional lines.

Kenny changed all that by reorganizing the production schedule based on the principles of one-piece flow. After computing the batch size and other scheduling requirements, Kenny had all extra inventory removed (S1). As he once said, "There was so much WIP out there, you couldn't tell what was happening!" Then he put a kanban board (a powerful visual device) in place and explained how it worked to SCM associates. Cellular manufacturing had begun at Alpha.

About five weeks into the kanban process, 5S + 1 was launched. Four cell members became a kind of modified steering team. For the next five months, Ellen Babson, Russ McGibbon, Earl Scranton, and Sau Tran met two to three times a week, along with George Cassello (on loan from the maintenance department), to work through the tasks of a 5S + 1 Action List that just seemed to get longer.

Working with other SCM associates, the team cleared out the clutter and went after motion in each part of the process with a dogged determination. In semiconductor manufacturing, value-adding work is done under a microscope, in an area no bigger than the size of a large postage stamp. A steady and intense focus is an operational imperative. Every interruption is a distraction that costs precious processing time and can cause quality losses.

The SCM Cell steering team, with the complete cooperation of other cell associates, first concentrated on identifying and eliminating the grosser forms of motion: where associates went when they left the cell and why. When the team had visually solved that motion, they went after the reasons associates left their chairs. Once they had nailed the causes, team members realigned the physical flow (S4) and put new location information in place to minimize motion further.

As part of this: (1) All workplace items and supplies were put out onto open surfaces for easy access, (2) several cabinet doors were removed, (3) borders were put into place, and (4) all items were labeled and given a home address.

In addition, after motion in each individual operation was minimized, a new job slot, called Setup, was created and assigned as much non-value-adding activity as possible. Bernice Pereira, a thirteen-year Alpha associate, volunteered for the job. Based on the kanban trigger, Bernice prepared all work orders in advance, sorting the paperwork, and cleaning and preparing material. As a result, the other associates could simply pick up their orders and begin value-adding work. Designating a setup person proved a major timesaving breakthrough for the cell.

Once the grosser forms of motion were eliminated, the team went after the less noticeable kinds—reaching, stretching, bending, twisting, turning, looking. This was motion that occurs while an operator is in the chair and at the workbench. The team began with the first operation in the SCM process (the Bonding Bench), and designed a new prototype bench that was based on the actual work flow (S4) and had specific, bordered locations for everything used there (S5).

In addition, instead of asking operators to share tools as in the past, each bench had a complete set of tools as well as a set of spare parts, such as thermal couples and light bulbs. As a result, bonding operators were able to work steadily and rhythmically, with a tight and constant focus. Once the prototype bench was tested and perfected, a similar bench was made for each other bonder in the cell, with individual adjustments as needed (left-handed versus right-handed).

Starting small at Alpha paid off for the SCM Cell. Five months into the process, value-adding activity had increased from 33 to 51 percent. Average cycle time dropped from eight days to two days. Throughput had risen by 53 percent. The SCM work area used to keep 30,000 diodes of WIP (work-in-process) per day for a variable output of 1,000 to 8,000 diodes per day. The new cell enjoyed a predictable output of 6,000 to 7,000 diodes per day, with only 12,000 to 15,000 diodes of WIP. Not only did output increase but inventory costs plummeted.

Yes, there is still a long way to go in the SCM cell, and the growth spurt at Alpha has not yet settled down. Alpha knows that many conditions that prevent cycle time from dropping further in the SCM Cell are linked to areas in the company where visual order is still a stranger. Starting very small was the right choice for Alpha in 1995. It is now time for the next step—spreading the benefit companywide.

The Companywide Launch: Choice 2

It is never advisable to launch 5S + 1 throughout an entire facility at once. That is not what is meant by *companywide*.

A companywide launch means to implement visual order in a series of areas that are functionally linked along the value-adding stream. If Machining wants to get on the 5S + 1 bandwagon, try to get fabrication involved as well. If Assembly is interested, invite a subassembly area to join in. Invite Shipping/Receiving and Material Handling as well as Maintenance and the Tool Room. In other words, line up functions that are naturally connected. In this way, the operational chain on your shop floor is represented, clearing the way to explore how visual order can link up and strengthen the flow of function along that chain.

A workable guideline for a large-scale implementation is six to eight work areas. Have teams of two to four associates from each area attend the formal training for a class size of between thirty and forty people—and include some managers and supervisors as well as your management champion (of course). Any training group larger than forty or so can become unwieldy for your initial implementation cycle. (See the discussion in Chapter 15 on education and training.)

Once the implementation gets rolling, you will be amazed at how quickly news of your efforts and your early victories will run through the facility. This is especially true with a companywide launch. When the improvement imbedded in the 5S + 1 methodology begins to unfold, the common concern of many companies is how to handle the other areas that are clamoring to get on board, learn the methodology themselves, and transform their own areas. The question could then well become, "How much success can our organization handle?" Some dilemma.

The Companywide Launch at UE

We have already discussed several core aspects of the 5S + 1 implementation at UE in Watertown, Massachusetts. Its approach was classic. By 1989, the interest of UE's management in visual systems was sufficiently piqued to send two UE employees to a public seminar I conducted in the Boston area.

How did it go for them? Let me put it this way: Luis Catatao (production technician) and Dan Fleming (production manager) came, saw, and conquered! They took to the learning like ducks to water, bears to honey, eagles to high places. Get the picture? I was at the UE facility quite regularly over the next two years and, at each visit, I would see new iterations of what was triggered during that day-and-a-half seminar. Brilliant visual devices were springing up in unexpected places.

While the applications that Luis and Dan developed were shining, UE had started too small to reap any measurable benefit. A call from Bruce Hamilton, VP of operations at UE, in 1993 changed all that. He wanted a plantwide implementation of visual order in eight operational areas—and he wanted it as soon as possible. We began.

As you may recall from an earlier discussion, eight teams went through six 4.5-hour learning modules and associated action assignments. Some forty employees were trained, including Annie Yu, the coordinator, and Bruce, the champion. This was an exciting period of growth and innovation at UE—and a challenging one. The shop floor began to change, and all the struggles and victories described in the early chapters came into play.

By the middle of 1994, UE had decided to go for a license in the methodology, with Annie Yu as the lead instructor. Licensing was the right move for UE because the company wanted to spread visual order throughout its Watertown facility and to other UE plants in other states.

UE took about twelve months to cycle through 5S + 1, and several areas wanted to get trained in the other levels of the Blueprint for a Visual Workplace (visual standard sharing, scoreboarding, etc.). UE management saw wisdom in waiting in order to let the new practices of visual order root more deeply. We had another reason for waiting: UE was about to take on the challenge of ISO 9000.

As ISO fever took hold and UE began to march to a new drumbeat, the 5S + 1 gains held. In fact, they tangibly assisted UE in its quest for ISO certification. As Bruce Hamilton explained, it laid the groundwork.

The 5S + 1 story at UE doesn't end there. UE got ISO-certified a year later and immediately took on an aggressive schedule for converting the entire shop floor to one-piece flow and cells. I stopped by for a quick look-see several months later as the heat of summer descended over New England. The shop floor was—how can I put this delicately?—a wreck.

While remnants of visual order were still observable, the shop floor was a clutter of cells in the making. UE, in its never-ending march toward excellence, had undertaken to convert its entire plant floor to cells in a nine-month time frame. Not two days went by without one work area or another getting rearranged, condensed, reconfigured or moved. Like Dr. Lothario emerging from the eighth dimension, cells were coming and going at mind-bending speed as UE began to find an accelerated production flow.

I'll never forget the day I stopped by and saw two 10-foot workbenches that had been exquisitely ordered and bordered in the heyday of 5S + 1. They were literally on their way out the door, their taped addresses empty but still visible on each surface. The replacements, benches not more than 3 feet long, were waiting in the wings. A few quick photos to commemorate their long years of service—and the 10-footers were gone.

What was happening at UE and where had 5S + 1 gone? Two months later, the answer was clear. It had gone deeper, only to resurface again, clearer and stronger than ever. By the fall, 5S + 1 was back with a vengeance, only this time it was integrated into cell design and one-piece flow. UE's understanding of visual order was so strong and deep that it could let go of it, push through the next cell cycle, and then weave that order back in. This is what you want—and can expect—when you launch 5S + 1 methodology companywide and stay the course. The workforce begins to think visually and, once started, there is no going back.

So that's what a companywide implementation can look like. But the question of exactly where to begin still remains.

Choosing the Pilot Areas: The Laminated Map

Based on what management decides in reference to scope and with a written improvement time policy in hand, your 5S + 1 implementation begins where you and other key stakeholders decide it should begin. And it does not spread into others areas, unless and until you decide it should. The work areas that are involved in 5S+1 are the result of a conscious, specific, and controllable plan.

This is no easy task, you may say. Ordinarily, I would agree with you. But there is yet another tool in the 5S+1 tool kit that makes this decision doable. The tool is called **the laminated map.**

Dazzling in its simplicity and effectiveness, the laminated map is the secret tool behind your successful implementation. Use it. You will be amazed at its power.

The laminated map is merely a print out of the layout of your facility. Once laminated, it is used in two specific ways. First, you use this map to decide which work areas will be involved in the implementation, marking them off on the map (the lamination allows you to write directly on it—and make adjustments). Second (as you'll read later in this chapter), you use the laminated map to track the 5S+1 progress in each area as well as the overall progress of the entire implementation.

Here are the five steps for using the map in its first application: to help you decide which areas to involve in the implementation.

Using the Map to Choose Pilot Areas

1. *Get a map of your company's floor plan and laminate it.* When you are ready to decide where to begin, get your hands on a paper map of your physical plant. Then have it laminated. Photo 14-1 shows you a plain laminated map, before work has begun on it.

14-1. Start-Off Laminated Map.

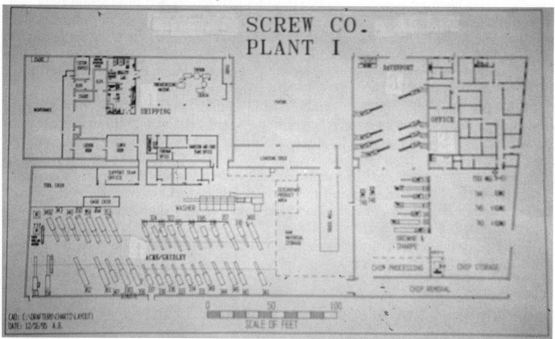

Working together, a group will now divide up the company into its natural work areas and mark them on the map.

14-2. Laminated Map: Natural Work Areas Outlined.

The first step is done: The natural work areas, in this case, seventeen, have been identified.

If you do not have such a map, get one made on CAD or professionally prepared. I have seen some companies succeed with a hand-drawn map of the layout. Precision and exact dimensioning is not a critical issue. This map does not need a high level of detail, such as electrical outlets, plumbing, coolant systems, and other elements of the physical infrastructure. By the same token, if your map already has that information, so be it. (Later on, you may find that extra information useful, for example, in S4/Select Locations as you work out an improved flow.)

2. *Divide the floor plan into its natural work areas.* Working with your colleagues and using a dark, nonpermanent marker, divide the floor plan into natural work areas, using your marker to draw a complete boundary around the area (even where there are walls) (Photo 14-2).

Natural divisions may be based on product types, function, customer, or some combination of these. In FM Company, an automotive stamping plant, the team first defined *natural* according to operational functions: stamping press, shipping/receiving, quality test, paint, and die storage. Other areas were designated based on product types: fenders, mud flaps, and doors. Still others were identified by customer name: Ford, Chrysler, and GM. All of these were perfectly acceptable because they made sense to that company.

Make sure every square foot of your map is assigned to a work area (even if you are absolutely certain an area will not be participating in the first implementation cycle. Include all walkways, hallways, cafeteria, closets, rest rooms, entranceways, and the like. Every square foot of the floor plan gets designated and outlined on your map. This is because, in 5S + 1, every square foot of the physical work environment will eventually be "owned" by a specific work area or team.

14-3. Laminated Map: Blue Dots in All Areas.

With a blue dot in each area, the group is now ready to consider where to begin the implementation.

If nonproduction areas in your company are participating in the implementation, mark these work areas as well: engineering, drafting, purchasing, customer service, finance, marketing, sales, for example. If not, draw a single border around the administrative section as a collective.

3. *Put a blue-dot label on each area.* Put a removable blue-dot label on every area on your map. In Photo 14-2, team members identified seventeen natural work areas; they went on to put one blue dot in each area (Photo 14-3). The blue dot signifies: *The area is not an implementation focus—yet.*

You are now ready to decide where to begin.

4. *Select your start-up areas—and put a red dot on each.* Working with other associates and the management champion, select the area or areas where you would like to begin the implementation. These will be areas that qualify as useful proving grounds for the 5S + 1 process. Put a red dot on each. A red dot for this tool means: *Let's get started!* Photo 14-4 shows that the team targeted five start-up areas, red-dotting each one of them.

As with all improvement processes, red-dotting is done best when everyone has a say in which areas get started. You and your colleagues may decide what looks possible, but before you finalize your choices, check with the people who actually work there—plus the supervisor. Here are some cautions.

- Avoid any area in the process of setting up a new product line and/or with an excessively heavy production schedule.
- Avoid any area whose supervisor has a known "allergy" to improvement. Don't take the chance of putting a group of well-meaning, hardworking associates in

14-4. Laminated Map: Red-Dotted Start-Up Areas.

Five start-up areas have been selected, each marked with a red dot. The darker dots are the red ones.

the middle of this potential battleground—unless your VP specifically asks you to do so and is ready to ride out the storm with you and the others.

- More work areas may clamor to participate than the company has resources to support. It becomes management's job, then, to say yes to some and "later" to others. These areas will still be able to participate in the general awareness sessions that will be held in the first few months of implementation. You may be surprised at how much they are able to accomplish on their own, based on that two- to three-hour educational session (see Chapter 15 for more).

5. *Finalize the selection.* Finalize your selection by returning to a blue-dot status any area that cannot be included in the first round of implementation.

With your red dots in place and your laminated map in hand, you are now ready to begin the implementation.

Collecting Baseline Metrics

In Chapters 2 and 3, we discussed the importance of collecting a set of baseline metrics at the start of an implementation and what those metrics might be. Whichever you choose, make sure to collect baseline data on motion with lead time versus conversion time as the central metric. Every area in the implementation should be required to do a value-adding analysis. The choice of which other measures to compile can vary from area to area. For example, distance may be an exciting performance measure for your material handling team but not have much relevance to machining. They might prefer to track the number and duration of interruptions (Exhibit 14-1).

As soon as each area selects its set of metrics, it is time to gather the data. Teams are then trained (Chapter 15), and implementation of the first five principles of visual order begins, the details of which were already presented in the 5S Method portion of this book (Chapters 4 through 7). The next and second use of the laminated map will help you move through them as well as the +1 portion of the methodology.

The Laminated Map Revisited: Planning and Tracking

The laminated map has two broad purposes. The first is to help you identify where to begin your implementation. The second is to help you measure 5S+1 progress. This refers to progress that each individual work area is making as well as the overall progress of the initiative. In this sense, the map serves as a scoreboard that helps you track and even calibrate the rate of 5S+1 change within and across the entire implementation. We'll talk about the individual application first.

The Map as Individual Planning Tool

The procedure for turning the laminated map into a planning tool for your own area is simple. Acquire a submap of your area, either by enlarging your area as it appears on the large plantwide map or through CAD. (The concept here is similar to the relationship of directories and subdirectories in computers.) Laminate the submap.

Now, working with your colleagues, section off the enlarged map of your work area into its natural subareas. The thinking here is the same as it was for the larger map discussed earlier. If you work in a stamping press department, for example, natural subareas might include: (1) the press itself, (2) coil storage, (3) the dies crib, (4) WIP storage, (5) the belt storage, and (6) bin storage. Draw boundaries around each of these six areas in nonpermanent marker (so you can make adjustments easily). As before make sure each square foot of your area is bounded. No no-man's-lands, please.

Put a blue dot in each subarea. Then decide where to begin. Will you first do S1 (Sort Through and Sort Out) in coil storage? In the area closest to the press? In belt storage? My advice to you is to select a specific bounded starting point, especially if your area is large. Once you get the hang of the process, you can widen the effort. The tendency in most improvement activity is to lose focus and get scattered. The laminated map is an effective tool in the other direction. So pick a focus with your team and exchange the blue dot for a red one.

The Map as an Individual Scoreboard

Now you have your plan in hand. The dots tell you where to begin and where you will wait to begin.

Exhibit 14-1. Interruptions as a Baseline Metric: Checksheet Example.

Your Name	Today's Date	
How to use this checksheet: Please put a check mark (√) or hatch mark (/) next to the right item each time you had to do it today. Then do a daily tally and total before you go home and leave this sheet with Cindy.		**Daily Tally**
1. The number of times I was interrupted—even for a moment—for any reason.		
2. The number of times I had to look/search for something—while still sitting at my work.		
3. The number of times I had to look/search for something or someone—and had to get up from my work.		
4. The number of times I had to wait for something or someone—even for a moment.		
5. Other forms of motion that kept you from your work (please specify) _____ _____ _____		
6. Other forms of motion that kept you from your work (please specify) _____ _____ _____		
	Grand Total	

You are now ready to use the map to track 5S + 1 progress in your area. To do this, we introduce two new dot colors: (1) yellow to represent a midway level of progress and (2) green to represent completion. As improvement progresses, the color of the dot in each subarea changes from red to yellow to green. Each color change signifies that a certain level of achievement has been reached in that subarea. See Exhibit 14-2 for each dot's general meaning.

Exhibit 14-2. General Meaning of Each Dot Color.

Dot Color	General Meaning
Blue Dot	Relax! This is not yet an area designated for 5S + 1 improvement.
Red Dot	Get busy! This is an area designated for 5S + 1 improvement. You've a long way to go!
Yellow Dot	You're on your way! Keep going!
Green Dot	You've arrived! Now sustain it!

Finer Tracking

If it serves your purposes, this dot approach can be used with even greater precision by tying each color shift to an exact set of criteria. The color changes if and only if those conditions are reached. In this way you scoreboard or measure 5S + 1 improvement level by level. Exhibit 14-3 spells out the criteria for each shift and for each level.

Post your color-dot laminated map at the entrance of your area for all to see. One of the beauties of this map is that it speaks for itself, sharing information boldly and at a glance. Add another dimension to your map by marking an expected target date for each shift on the dot itself. This scoreboarding approach can be highly effective in keeping teams focused and engaged, with "going to green" the culminating experience. Visit an area the day after it "went to green" and you are likely to see a group of associates glowing with the quiet, pleasing knowledge that says "We made it!"

The Map as a Companywide Scoreboard

The laminated map can be an invaluable tool for helping individual work areas as well as the entire company discover the pace of improvement that is right for them, one of the most challenging aspects of any change process. If the pace is too slow, the momentum can't build nor the benefits spread. If too fast, pressure and stress may result, two things most companies have more than their quota of, especially companies already on a growth path.

☆ ☆ ☆ ☆ ☆

We just discussed how an individual work area uses the laminated map in as a scoreboard. Three other entities can also use the map: (1) the steering team, (2) the visual workplace coordinator, and (3) the management champion.

The Map and the Steering Team

The visual workplace steering team keeps a large companywide laminated map close at hand. This map provides the team with an overview of the implementation and helps team members keep track of emerging pockets of challenge and excellence. This map is the official scoreboard of the implementation. The team posts the map so everyone can

Exhibit 14-3. Precise Criteria for Shifts in Dot Color.

Code	Color Shifts	Precise Criteria
Blue		This is not yet an area designated for 5S + 1 improvement.
Going to Red	From a blue to red dot.	Associates in this area have made a commitment to implementing 5S + 1 here. They want to be held accountable for their progress.
Going to Yellow	From a red to a yellow dot.	The following steps are fully implemented: S1: Sort Through and Sort Out (with on-going red tagging at least monthly) S2: Scrub the Workplace S3: Secure Safety (securing safety through visual order is in the process of being applied) S4: Select Locations (what-is and could-be maps have been used in the selection process) S5: Set Locations (includes ample use of borders, plus a complete application of home addresses and ID labels—for the area, all processes, operations, machines, workbenches, tools, shelving, personnel, storage, WIP, etc.)
Going to Green	From a yellow to a green dot.	The following has been fully implemented: S3: Secure Safety (completed) +1: At least one type of 5S checklist, plus a weekly management watch is in practice in this area

keep their eyes on the big picture and supervisors can see the plan, its schedule, its victories, and its challenges. The team carries it to meetings with the coordinator and the management champion. The message of the steering team is clear:

> Here is our battle plan. You can hold our feet to the fire on the areas with red/yellow/green dots. Progress will be made and you will see it first in those areas.

Dates can often be seen on the dots of the steering team's map as their way to target the shifts. Some teams keep two maps with target dates as a diagnostic tool—one map with the planned pace of change and the other reflecting the actual pace. By keeping both maps up-to-date, the team can notice the lack of a color shift, a signal that things may be slowing down and some coaching may be needed.

The Map and the Visual Workplace Coordinator

The coordinator will have a map that replicates that of the steering team. Besides the obvious benefit of seeing the status of the entire implementation on one sheet of paper, the coordinator can, for example, use the map to track (1) which areas want to come on board next, (2) which areas need formal training, and (3) where 5S corner supplies need restocking.

As with the steering team, the coordinator brings the map to discussions with the champion and other managers who want an update on the investment.

The Map and the Management Champion

The laminated map is an essential tool for the management champion. Besides all the secondary applications named above, the champion uses the map as the primary scoreboard and guide for the management watch.

The watch, you may remember, is restricted to work areas that have a red, yellow, or green dot. Blue-dot areas are off-limits—generally. I say "generally" because, as you might expect, to a manager, *off-limits* is more of an invitation to enter than a warning to stay away.

This is exactly what happened in one organization implementing 5S + 1. The champion, who was also the company owner, took to his management watch duties with enthusiasm. He developed a special fondness for yellow opportunity cards. It must have been something about their promise of a speedy and specific response to his recommendations that hooked him.

In doing his rounds one Thursday in the red-dot (and above) areas, he spied something in a blue-dot area that he didn't particularly like—a mess around the drawing compound vat. He entered the area and expressed his displeasure through a series of yellow watch cards. Yes, he knew the "rules"—he knew he was not supposed to do the watch in a blue-dot area. He also owned the place. What are you gonna do?

The associates said nothing, studied the yellow cards, and implemented the boss's recommendations. As it turned out, their response was a brilliant new visual minisystem, one of the best in the plant up to then.

The steering team, however, was in a state of alarm. Worries about "loose cannons" and "loss of control" could be heard. When I got an emergency call, we caucused over the phone and came up with the following compromise which the team was to present to the champion:

- The champion can go wherever he likes in the plant.
- If he sees something positive in an "off-limits" area, he may write up a blue recognition card.
- If he sees something he wants improved in an "off-limits" area, he puts his comments on a card of some color other than yellow—say orange or violet or pink or some other easy-to-see color (any color but green).

The intention was to send a clear signal that the president knew the area he was commenting on was off-limits and though he could make comment freely, the workforce knew he knew it was off the beaten path. The integrity of the 5S + 1 process was thereby protected—and people felt safe.

"Just as long as he doesn't use a green card," I remember repeating. "Green watch cards are used later in the implementation: As standards begin to get shared visually, the champion will use green cards to point out opportunities for making standards visual. Agreed?" "Agreed," the team replied. "We'll tell the boss to use any color but green." Click. End of conversation.

This *ad hoc* solution worked beautifully in conjunction with the laminated map procedure—except the champion decided to use green cards. What are you gonna do?

How the 5S + 1 Process Works

The watch card story is amusing, and it also confirms one of the main points of this book: Be systematic in your approach. At the top of this chapter, I mentioned three things that you want from the first cycle of visual order in your company: a showcase, measurable results, and an experience with how the 5S + 1 methodology works.

The 5S + 1 process is a systematic, step-by-step methodology. The elements are sequential and closely linked. Change or skip one element and you impact all of them. Therefore, you are advised to adopt a scientific attitude when you implement 5S + 1. Observe what works and what doesn't. Then use what you discover to identify the patterns in your organization that need to be adjusted in order to maximize the 5S + 1 approach.

The temptation will be great to skip certain steps or substitute your own method for the one described in this book. Under some circumstances, I would encourage this. But your first implementation is a research project. Resist the temptation to change the methodology. Implement the 5S + 1 process as presented in this book *without deviation* the first time through. And look at the results. If they are not satisfactory, then you can consider an adjustment but not before you have completed the experiment.

The value system expressed in the visual workplace code of conduct, for example, is central. The entire approach is rooted in that. Do not expect to get great results if you ignore these. The order of the steps is also critical. If you implement home addresses before you 3-tag, your failure is guaranteed. If you put checklists in place before reaching a standard level of cleanliness, people will get confused and even hostile. If you set locations without first doing What-Is and Could-Be Maps, you miss an exceptional opportunity to realign the logic of production and accelerate the work flow, and will probably rob people of an understanding of smart placement.

The 5S + 1 methodology works because it is simple, practical, systematic, incremental, and actionable. Each step is grounded in hands-on tools that empower area associates to make changes that are relevant and important to them. Yes, adaptations to the methodology can be made—but only after you have identified and understood the trade-offs. Stay particularly alert to alterations that support ancient patterns of confusion, ever-widening complexity, hierarchy, and false convenience.

Exhibit 14-4 spells out the thirteen essential and indispensable steps required for success. Notice that implementing the first five principles of visual order (item 8) is just one of these.

Exhibit 14-4. Thirteen Success Essentials.

1. Explore the possibility of implementing visual order in your company.	Read this book for a book study group, go to 5S + 1 public seminar, visit a 5S + 1 company, schedule a management briefing on-site for your key decision makers (if a union shop, make sure union leadership is invited).
2. Decide to commit—or not to.	Make this a clear step.
3. Select your implementation leaders.	Identify your management champion and visual workplace coordinator.
4. Draft an improvement time policy for your company.	Remember: Drafting the policy is only the first step. It must then be operationalized, tested, and modified as needed.
5. Decide on the scope of your implementation.	Using a laminated map, target the work areas that will participate in the first implementation cycle. If starting small, look for strong success factors. If companywide, focus on linked functions. Sketch out an implementation timeline.
6. Select and gather baseline metrics.	Which measures will the company want to see improve in order to justify its investment in the implementation? Let each target area perform a value-adding analysis and collect data on other selected measures.
7. Get teams trained.	Teams must be thoroughly trained in the 5S + 1 process if they are to succeed. Make sure the champion and coordinator attend. Begin general awareness sessions now or below, as a part of your + 1 efforts. See next chapter for details.
8. Implement S1 through S5.	Implement the first five principles of visual order, systematically and in order. Set up your 5S corner at the outset.
9. Begin to implement + 1 tools.	Call for volunteers and form the steering team. Make sure it starts meeting weekly right off the bat.
10. Start 5S checklists.	Each area chooses at least one type of checklist; if the clipboard, then start a 5S patrol.
11. Launch management watch.	Launch your management watch three to four weeks after checklists get started.
12. Keep going until showcase.	Use the laminated maps to help each area ''go to green.''
13. Go back to step 5 (above) and expand implementation.	As soon as you have your first showcase, you are free to bring new work areas officially into the implementation. Follow the same procedure as you did in the first cycle, beginning with step 5 in this exhibit.

The System *Is* Empowerment

An early mentor of mine, Dr. Ryuji Fukuda, often used to say:

> Managing improvement means getting people to do ordinary things extraordinarily well.

As human beings, we make mistakes. Even in the best of conditions and with the best of intentions, we forget. For a company to achieve extraordinary results that are also repeatable, a system is needed. The same is true for an improvement process like 5S+1: It must be systematic if it is to assist people in achieving exceptional levels of visual order.

In my experience the structure that every system provides is the central ingredient for true empowerment. Empowerment is never an issue of just permitting people to do what they think is best. The core issue of empowerment is to establish a system that allows people to know with certainty the right thing to do—*and how to do it*. Without a system, people are empowered in name only.

The process of strategic, companywide improvement begins and ends with a systematic approach—standard procedures that structure the key steps of the change into the process of change itself. In 5S+1, that structure is created by following *in order* the five principles of visual order and then applying the nine +1 tools. This structure is the result of a decade of research and experimentation on the shop floors of literally dozens of American companies. Following this standardized system of values and tasks allows each step to build on the previous one and produce a chain of predictable results.

The use of a systematic improvement approach is what differentiates ordinary from extraordinary companies. But exactly why is this so? It is so because only a system can eliminate the core problem faced by so many companies undertaking transforming change. That is the problem of individual discretion, human choice. This may at first look like a contradiction in terms, considering our lengthy discussions on the importance of the individual.

While respect for the individual remains key to the entire process, without a system of clear principles and practices, people get bogged down in microdecisions that make it difficult to identify even the smallest next step. If that happens too often, the individual and therefore the company will never get on with the task of the change itself. This is the crux of a huge misunderstanding about empowerment.

How do we empower people? We empower people by providing them with absolutely predictable ways of producing excellent results every single time. We call these standards! We empower them by creating systems that work. We do not empower people by abdicating our own accountability for what they do and how they do it. Instead we focus squarely on developing standardized processes that ensure the results we expect and need. This is why I urge you to follow 5S+1 as a system—a model that you follow with precision in order to get the outcomes that are imbedded in the process.

Ray Kroc Meets 5S + 1

Ray Kroc and the story of McDonald's is a great case in point.[1] Ray Kroc originally stopped by the McDonald brothers' hamburger stand in California to sell them a mixer. Before he left that day, he asked to franchise their business. The brothers agreed. They had nothing to lose, since they already knew their business would not succeed as a franchise—they had tried and failed to do that very thing twice before.

On his first day on the job, Kroc did not go to work *in* the hamburger stand: He did not make a hamburger; he did not make a single french fry. On his first day on the job at McDonald's, he went to work *on* the hamburger stand. He began developing the McDonald's system. He began to standardize the process, identifying all the essential elements of success. He made a standardized operational prototype of the business that included the range of procedures that needed to be accomplished to run and maintain the business and sell product. He also began to develop what would become a vast array of visual devices and minisystems to ensure that those procedures were followed to the letter. He knew that 100 percent adherence was crucial, so he developed a perfect turnkey operation.

As Ray Kroc saw it, his customer was not the person who wanted to eat a hamburger. His customer was the person who wanted to buy a business opportunity: the franchisee. To land franchisees, Kroc had to develop a system that ran like a top. Today, any employee in any of the 11,000 franchised sites in the United States alone knows exactly how to do the ordinary tasks extraordinarily well: flipping a hamburger, making french fries, making a malted, replenishing the cash drawer, tallying receipts, reporting the numbers. All of these procedures were included in Kroc's system of indispensable steps—remarkable results that were predictable as well as repeatable. Quite a feat when you consider that the average rate of personnel turnover at McDonald's is 300 percent and the workforce is made up almost entirely of teenagers working for minimum wage!

The system is the answer. It is the solution. The 5S + 1 system presented in this book is a series of standard procedures that have been tested and proofed on the shop floors of America's best companies. It is the lever by which an ordinary workplace is transformed into a visual one. That's the point. Follow the 5S + 1 system and you will get predictable, remarkable, and repeatable results every single time.

Let's move on to the next chapter and look at ways to get your workforce trained in the 5S + 1 methodology.

---

1. Many thanks to Michael E. Gerber for his rendition of and insights into the Ray Kroc story. For more, read Michael E. Gerber, *The E-Myth Revisited: Why Most Businesses Don't Work and What to Do About It* (New York: HarperCollins, 1995), and/or listen to the tape set, *Taking Charge of Your Business* (Niles, Ill.: Nightingale-Conant Corporation). And a thank-you to my brother, Gary L. Galsworth, for introducing me to Gerber's work.

One: The Big Picture		
1. Toward a Visual Workplace	2. Visual Systems in Context	3. The Five Start-Up Requirements
Two: 5S Method		
4. S1/Sort Through and Sort Out	5. S2–S4/ Scrub, Secure Safety, and Select Locations	6. S5/Set Locations: Borders
7. S5/Set Locations: Addresses	8. 5S Stories From the Shop Floor	9. 5S+1 and White-Collar Applications
Three: +1 Method		
10. People: What to Expect	11. +1: Building and Sustaining the 5S Habit	12. +1: Leading by Example	13. +1: Leading Through Standards
Four: Go!		
14. Showcase, Scope, and the System	15. Training and Education	16. The Hundredth Monkey

Chapter 15

Training and Education

Give me a fulcrum and a lever long enough and I will move the earth.
—Archimedes

The groundwork for a successful implementation is in place. You know where you are going to begin and why. Key decision makers are committed, and you know how you are going to measure your progress. Now it is just a question of putting one foot in front of the other—and the first footstep is training and education.

There are two instructional components to every successful 5S + 1 implementation. The first is Awareness Education, and the second is Team Implementation Training. Let's go through them in order.

Awareness Education

You cannot identify which work areas are better suited for the first implementation cycle than others, you cannot use the laminated map to your advantage, you cannot help understand which metrics will provide useful feedback—you cannot do any of these things *until and unless* you and your colleagues understand enough about 5S + 1 and visual order to make informed decisions. Every improvement journey begins with awareness.

You can gain that awareness in several ways:

1. Read this book and start a study group.
2. Attend a public seminar on 5S + 1 and the visual workplace.
3. Invite an outside resource into your company to conduct a 5S + 1 Awareness Session or Management Briefing.
4. Design an Awareness Session of your own for your company.

You are already reading this book, so that takes care of option 1. If options 2 and 3 interest you specifically, read the Resources Section in the back of this book. And if option 4 appeals to you, read on.

Creating Your Own Awareness Session

First, if you are going to develop your own awareness session, you need to understand how the 5S + 1 model works. This takes us back to the first three options: Read this book thoroughly and start a study group on the book, attend a public seminar, or arrange for an on-site briefing.

Collect Material

Next, develop the material you'll need for your awareness session. This is easier than it may sound. You need material that can help your associates understand the basic principles and concepts of visual order and 5S + 1. Develop a library of instructional materials that make it easy for others to learn what you know.

You can buy the slides and videos that support this book (see the Resources section). You can also capture your own real-life examples of visual order on videotape and/or 35mm slides. Your sources for this material are close to home. Go to the post office, the mall, supermarkets and department stores, and other public places and take footage and photos. Roads and highways are teeming with excellent examples of visual location information. When you do this, follow all safety precautions and be prepared to pull over often (carefully and safely) to photograph examples. Many places will not object.

Some will, including some toll roads and parkways. If they do, be prepared with your thanks, bow out gracefully, and seek examples elsewhere.

Whenever you or one of your associates goes to someplace like Disney World, a sports stadium, a county fair, or an airport, stay on the lookout for great visual system examples, and take some slides. Slides are more flexible to use than photographs: You can pause at any point when you show them to elaborate on a point or deal with questions, and they can be arranged and rearranged easily. Substituting one slide for another is also easy when better examples are found. And your collection will grow as other people contribute examples.

In addition to documenting community devices, keep your ears and eyes open for nearby companies known for best practices in visual order and visual systems. Ask to take slides. Take slides and videos of your own shop floor in its *before* condition. When the time comes, you'll be asked to track the *after* condition as well. But more about that later.

Also consider dividing some of your examples into the four types of visual devices, as discussed in Chapter 2: visual indicators, visual signals, visual controls, and visual guarantees.

The point is, you can find plenty of excellent examples close to home that will help people see at a glance what visual systems are and their importance to everyday life. The jump between that and their importance to everyday work is a short one. (See the Resources section for tips on film.)

State the Benefits

The next step in developing your teaching material is to identify the benefits in a language your company can understand. Why would visual order be important in your area? What would it do for the work flow, for all the searching and waiting that seems to be so much a part of every workday? Identify these areas and prepare to talk about them in your own words.

Talking about the positive impact of visual order is a topic about which associates and managers will have much to say. Get a well-respected hourly spokesperson who is enthusiastic about visual order to talk to the workforce for five to ten minutes. Combine that talk with a few words from the management champion on the corporate perspective.

You might also want to include a short talk on resistance and inertia so that everyone knows that you know what they know. Many people have found the parable of the Rowers an effective way to head off the idea that either everyone wants to or must support the implementation. Also consider introducing the laminated map early so people can see that the process of 5S + 1 in your facility will have a defined and controlled focus, even though the target areas are yet to be chosen.

Your homegrown awareness session could take anywhere from forty-five minutes to two and a half hours, depending on how much you want to cover. However long or short it is, make sure to end the session with a call to action. You and/or the management champion, for example, might say:

"We are looking for a few good work areas to get on board by the end of the month, in time for the training. So if you like what you heard and saw here today, talk things over with your supervisor [or team leader]. We want you to get involved to the extent that you are interested.

"You can row. You can watch. Or you can grumble. But this change is going to happen in our company. And sooner or later, we are going to want to have you on board. Thanks!"

A Word About Awareness Logistics

In case you and management decide that you want to raise everyone's awareness about visual order within the same short period of time, plan ahead. If your workforce numbers 300 employees, for example, you can either schedule a large off-site gathering or four or five smaller repeat sessions on-site, with 50 to 60 employees in each.

Please note: There is nothing in the 5S + 1 methodology that requires a large companywide awareness session. In many circumstances (for instance, when you start small), it might be better to forgo companywide anything and stay low-key, concentrating instead on awareness education for associates in the target area(s) only.

Team Implementation Training

If you are launching an implementation of a limited scope (one to three work areas), your team training will likewise be limited. With two to four employees per work area, a typical class size could range between ten and twenty, with a handful of supervisors and managers thrown in to round out attendance. Given that you follow the other guidelines discussed in this section, the likelihood of successful learning is high. Just remember the proof of the 5S + 1 pudding is in the results and the eventual spread of the process companywide.

By the same token, your company may want to bring in outside resources to assist in the transfer of knowledge and skill. Outside experts can provide a caliber of coaching and consulting that many organizations do not possess inside their walls. If you elect to do this, you have the capability of launching the implementation companywide. Six to eight work areas simultaneously is the rule of thumb (see the Resources section). As important as the issue of who trains is the question of what type of transfer approach to use: How do you intend that people will learn?

Say No to a Blitz

The blitz approach to visual order is an attempt to put a whole new set of principles, values, and practices in place in the span of four to five days. It is an approach that has gained some popularity of late. While it can from time to time be useful to loosen some serious logjams in thinking and application, it has never been known to create long-lasting, sustainable improvement.

In fact, experience suggests an absolute bias *against* the blitz approach when implementing visual order and/or the other steps on the way to a visual workplace. In Chapter 3, we read about the negative impact the blitz approach had on ABC Company. A true story and a sad one. While a blitz can result in some before/after conditions that can be dramatic, these results rarely last. There is very little evidence that the improvement initiative will grow and spread.

The reverse is too often true: Employees who may at first be excited by the prospect of workplace organization can soon become discouraged and even disgruntled as they see their gains erode. In a blitz, no one has time to learn or to acquire new habits. In fact, the workforce can be turned off to all future improvement attempts.

Some blitz efforts bring in outsiders—strangers—to "do the transformation" while the greater part of the actual workforce is asked to get out of the way. The impact of this can be disastrous, especially in union environments. However well-meaning and skilled these outsiders may be, they are first and foremost outsiders. Some of them have never set foot in a plant before, and most are new to the critical change factors of the host plant—its history, culture, process, and customers. The mere presence of these strangers can (and often does) cut out of the picture the very people who have a stake in improving the process—and the experience and ingenuity to do it and do it right. What happens after the outsiders leave is often not pretty.

The short of it is this: The blitz approach is all too often a hit-and-run recipe that creates zero ownership for the people who have to live with the change after the event is over.

Are there any circumstances under which a so-called 5S blitz might make sense? Yes. When the host company has already completed at least one full cycle of 5S + 1—that's about twelve months in real time. Such a company would already have at least one (if not several) 5S + 1 showcases up and running. Its steering team would be fully operational, working smoothly with area teams and with the coordinator and champion. And the general workforce would already have a high level of understanding relative to the vision, intent, and process of bringing about visual order to the shop floor, even if they had not all engaged in it directly.

Such a situation could be fertile ground for rapid improvement. In such a case, a blitz approach with outside participants could offer the host company the added people-power it needs to push for the next level—and offer the outsiders a quality learning experience with shopfloor people as tutors.

Another word of caution: Never allow an outside blitz group to implement S1/Sort Through and Sort Out on behalf of one of your work areas. S1 is far too fundamental, personal, and sensitive a process to turn over to an outside force.

So if you are considering the merits of a blitz approach to assist in your company, proceed with both eyes open. The possibility of an "overnight" transformation makes great brochure copy but rarely delivers. The blitz approach is all too often a showy start with a dismal finish.

Say Yes to Incremental Hands-On Learning

Better, long-lasting changes result when learning is bite-sized and combined with action. Called **incremental hands-on learning**, this instructional approach lets teams learn a series of new concepts and tools in small segments, asking them to apply new learning immediately in their own work areas. The result is a steady, visible improvement of how the shop floor looks and runs as new practices get established, then deepen and spread.

Time and again, incremental hands-on learning has proven itself the method of choice in implementing 5S + 1 in the United States. Here are some keys to effective incremental hands-on learning.

1. *Modularize the learning.* The first key is to present the learning in short modules of four to four and a half hours each over a several-week period. Let the sequence of the 5S + 1 approach be the guide. For example, S1 plus the 3-Tag technique can be taught the first week, along with the basic principles of visual systems and the four types of visual devices.

2. *Close each module with an action assignment.* The second key is to close each learning module with an action assignment that requires teams to apply what they just learned. An obvious first assignment is S1/3-Tagging.

3. *Make sharing results a learning tool.* The third key is to make the sharing of actual results a part of every learning session. My favorite way for teams to do this is through videotape. As part of their action assignment, each area team makes a short video of the *before* conditions (2–3 minutes) and the *after* conditions (2–3 minutes) in its area to show what things looked like before they implemented 5S + 1 and what they look like after improvement. This is called a Video Report Card. Exhibit 15-1 shows you some sample white pages (with instructions on the bottom) for the first documentation cycle, which teams use to give their videos a more "professional" look.

Another simple technique for documenting 5S + 1 progress is called "one-point" or "fixed-point" photography. Here's how it works.

Pick a spot on the floor of your work area and take a photograph/slide from that location. Mark the spot carefully with a plastic dot or square of paint and return to that spot a week later and take another photo/slide of exactly the same view. Return again a week later and take another shot, and then the following week, another shot. By fixing

Exhibit 15-1. Sample Video Sheets.

Welcome to the

_____

of

_____

in

_____

[This is your opening shot. Fill in the name of your work area and company, and the location of your facility. Hold the shot close up for five to six seconds.]

1

Exhibit 15-1. ***Continued.***

Three Conditions We Want to Improve

as of _____, 1996

• _____

• _____

• _____

[This is your second shot—the before part of your video (before any improvements). Fill in the date of the taping and the conditions you/your team want to improve. Follow this by three to four minutes of tape that show your area as it currently is. No cleanup or improvements before taping, please.]

2

Our Overall Goal Is to Achieve:

A VISUAL WORKPLACE:

A Self-Explaining, Self-Ordering, Self-Regulating,

Self-Improving Workplace

Where What Is *Supposed* to Happen *Does* Happen—

On Time—Every Time—Day or Night

[This shot follows the tape of your area before any improvement. Hold seven seconds. Follow directly with next page.]

3

Exhibit 15-1. *Continued.*

5S + 1
—PRINCIPLES OF VISUAL ORDER—

Our Improvement Results

as of

————————————————————————, **1996**

[This page marks the start of your "after" tape. Fill in the date of this taping. Hold this shot for five seconds. Follow with two to three minutes of your improved workplace.]

4

Tune in Next Time!

[This is the last shot. Hold about six seconds.]

5

---

an exact location and returning to that spot, you can develop a photographic record of the improvements that are made in your area, frame by frame. In this way, you will be able to notice and share all the changes, large and small—an excellent learning and teaching tool.

4. *Have teams transfer new learning directly.* There is wisdom in the saying *We learn what we teach.* Teaching area associates is done best by those who attended the formal training. They do the transfer. The lessons are simple and the transfer of them is a part of the action assignment that follows each classroom learning module.

Keep Up the Pace—But Leave Space

Learning 5S + 1 principles, values, and tools is straightforward. One comes after another, in logical order. Keep up this learning. And make sure to factor in adequate time for teams to apply each step. The time needed for each can vary. As a rule of thumb, do not teach more than one module per week, and try not to allow more than three weeks to elapse between modules.

But be warned: Keep true to your training schedule and the pacing of action assignments between the formal sessions. You are likely to get heart-wrenching pleas for just one more day for completing an action assignment—or one more week or one more month. Give it if you feel so moved and know that if you make a habit of it, you take the chance of eroding the very improvement momentum you are trying to power. You may find yourself left with a pretty but limp balloon that never did get enough air. In other words, set a schedule and keep to it.

Exhibit 15-2 details the pace I suggest when working as an outside trainer/consultant. Notice the longer lag time between the third and the fourth learning session and between the fourth and the fifth. This is to provide time for the learning to deepen and spread.

Who Should Be Trained?

The people who go to the formal team training are drawn from the start-up areas, finalized on your laminated map. Associates from each of these areas attend the training as a team (with the same associates attending all the training sessions). The rule of thumb is: not less than three individuals per area and not more than five (in the case of starting very small, two associates from one to three areas is acceptable). And bear in mind that the folks who go through the first implementation cycle will need *your* support. They are the pathfinders for the company and are likely to have to apply themselves more strongly than teams that are trained later.

Who gets to go to the training? The best way to answer that question is to let people self-select. This is accomplished simply by posting a sign-up sheet in each area, with enough spaces for the size team needed. Let people know that sign-up is on a first-come/first-served basis. Still, leave room for other names. If things don't work out (for example, in case of illness or unforeseen unavailability), you will already have a source for backups.

Exhibit 15-2. Sample Action Learning Schedule.

Time Frame	Session Content—Module by Module*	Action Assignment
Week One	• Through exercises and slides, teams learn about visual systems basics, the *Blueprint for a Visual Workplace,* and 5S + 1 (principles of visual order). • Teams learn and apply *S1/Sort Through and Sort Out* (3-Tagging).	Each team makes a short videotape of *before* conditions, transfers learnings to area associates, applies S1, and then makes a short video of results.
Week Two	• Session begins with each team showing its video report card, followed by relevant feedback, support, troubleshooting, and reinforcement training. • 5S learning continues. Focus is on *S2/Scrub the Workplace,* and *S3/Secure Safety*. Teams learn about clean scales.	Each team transfers learnings to area associates, applies S2 and S3, and then makes a short video of results. The steering team is formed.
Week Three	• Session begins with video report cards, followed by relevant feedback, support, troubleshooting, and reinforcement training. • 5S learning continues. Focus is on *S4/Select Locations* and *S5/Set Locations*. Teams learn and apply floor plan mapping and location/address campaign techniques.	Each team transfers learnings to area associates, applies S4 and S5, and makes a short video of results.
Week Five	• Session begins with video report cards, followed by relevant feedback, support, troubleshooting, and reinforcement training. • 5S continues. Teams learn about + 1/*Sustain the 5S Habit* and its key tools, including 5S corner, 5S checklists, 5S patrol, Visual Workplace steering team, and management watch. Each team develops a 5S checklist for its own area.	Each team transfers learnings to area associates, applies + 1 (5S corner, checklists, patrol), and makes a short video of results (showing patrol in action). The management watch is launched.

Time Frame	Session Content— Module by Module*	Action Assignment
Week Seven	• Session begins with video report cards, followed by relevant feedback, support, troubleshooting, and reinforcement training. • Together, instructor and teams assess implementation progress, work with steering team, and identify needs for additional feedback, troubleshooting, and re-inforcement training. Management may sit in and may participate.	Teams continue transferring, implementing, coaching, and documenting progress on video. Steering team and watch continue.
Week Ten	• Session begins with video report cards, followed by relevant feedback, support, troubleshooting, and reinforcement training. • Teams plan next steps and graduate. Management is invited graduation ceremonies.	Implementation continues. Company plans for next cycle.

* Awareness Session(s) get scheduled before the first learning module or, at the latest, between the first and the second.

And once again: If you choose to follow the building-block learning approach recommended above, make sure people know at the beginning that they must attend all sessions: no skipping, no substitutions, and no exceptions.

A second way to self-select is to simply let associates from a given work area discuss the matter themselves and come up with a team.

While we are on the topic of selecting teams, understand that it is generally not advisable to select the steering team prior to the training. Selection of this team seems to work out best when it happens after the second or third training session. With two or three sessions under their belt, people will know if they are genuinely interested in serving. Let fires ignite in the belly and stars blaze in the eyes—and make sure that people have the correct and realistic set of expectations before they sign on. And remember: one steering team representative per work area.

One other word of caution: If there is a preexisting team already involved in workplace order, industrial housekeeping, or safety issues, you need to finesse the creation of a 5S + 1 team. Appreciate and utilize the experience of the veterans, but also do not close out fresh faces.

You now have all the tools and information you need to bring the visual order revolution into your company. All that is left to do is to commit yourself to it.

One: The Big Picture		
1. Toward a Visual Workplace	2. Visual Systems in Context	3. The Five Start-Up Requirements
Two: 5S Method		
4. S1/Sort Through and Sort Out	5. S2–S4/ Scrub, Secure Safety, and Select Locations	6. S5/Set Locations: Borders
7. S5/Set Locations: Addresses	8. 5S Stories From the Shop Floor	9. 5S+1 and White-Collar Applications
Three: +1 Method		
10. People: What to Expect	11. +1: Building and Sustaining the 5S Habit	12. +1: Leading by Example	13. +1: Leading Through Standards
Four: Go!		
14. Showcase, Scope, and the System	15. Training and Education	16. The Hundredth Monkey

Chapter 16

The Hundredth Monkey

If you have read this far, you are a true seeker of improvement for your company. You know that all competition today is world-class. Not only is the playing field no longer level, it is not even the same acreage. No company today can apply the same old "cost plus profit" formula in offering its products. That means that no company can afford to overlook any opportunity to get leaner—to reduce waste and quicken the flow.

Dare to Commit

There are many excellent improvement strategies out there for you to use—and you will gravitate to those that support your aims. But every single strategy will be strengthened and its goals accelerated through an application of 5S+1. Every single one of them.

The methodology described in this book is rooted in the actual experience of American companies and the American workforce. The tools described in these pages are exceptional in their ability to create a new environment for work—one that is clear, clean, safe, and orderly and where motion is at an absolute minimum. These tools are also exceptional in their ability to ignite a new spirit in the workplace, one that is fueled by the power in each of us to see the vision of our future and know we can get there.

The methodology presented here is revolutionary for the vast majority of companies, revolutionary because these companies have avoided visual order for decades. In this sense, 5S+1 is dangerous—dangerous if it is not implemented, dangerous if you are afraid to improve, afraid to dare, afraid to have your beliefs changed forever. If you hesitate to step forward into visual order, the future of your organization may be at risk. Your competitors are looking for ways to gain an edge, and this book is available to them as well.

If you choose to proceed, implementing visual order in your company is an exciting challenge. You have all you need to succeed within the pages of this book: a proven, complete, and systematic method, the truth about people, and tools for optimizing that truth. As you proceed, let us hear from you. Let us hear about the successes and challenges of the 5S+1 process as it unfolds in your organization.

Dare to commit and you are on your way. Do it now. As the following story will attest, the time to get started was yesterday!

The Hundredth Monkey Principle

The remote island of Koshima in the Pacific is home to the macaque monkey (*macaca fuscata*). A troop of these monkeys lives in the wild on that island and has been the subject of intense research for decades. In 1952, something happened to the monkeys on Koshima that has very much to do with your implementation of visual order and your march toward achieving a visual workplace. Hear me out.

Like most wild creatures, the macaques spend much of their time gathering food. Their diet consists of an elaborate mix of fruits, buds, leaves, shoots, and bark—all of which require a range of collecting and feeding behaviors from the monkeys that are passed on *by example* from mother to young.

In 1952, a group of scientists were researching macaque feeding behaviors and, as part of their experiment, set stacks of raw sweet potatoes in selected spots on the beaches of Koshima. Quite naturally, the potatoes were quickly covered with sand, presenting the monkeys with a dilemma: every time they took a bite of these delicious new treats, they also got a bite of sand and grit.

One day an eighteen-month-old female monkey named Imo carried a sand-covered sweet potato to a stream and solved the problem by washing it off before putting it into her mouth. She then taught this new procedure to her mother (a role reversal) and to her playmates. The behavior began to spread. Slowly over the next six years—in full view of the team of scientists who set up the experiment (and without their interference)—monkeys on Koshima learned the procedure and taught it to others in the troop: Wash the sand off food before eating it.

When reports of this occurrence reached the outside world, it created quite a stir in scientific circles. Here was Imo, a wild monkey, changing her relationship with her physical reality through a new behavior that she had discovered on her own. A new need, a new thought, a new behavior. Then she had shared it with others of her kind who, in turn, learned it and shared it with yet others. As scientist Lyall Watson writes in *Lifetide*, his remarkable book on behavior and consciousness: "In monkey terms this [was] a cultural revolution comparable almost to the invention of the wheel [in our terms]."[1]

But things were just heating up. Something *really* extraordinary was about to happen, something that no one had ever before observed. Though the exact details remain sketchy because, according to Watson, the scientific constructs of the time were not designed to describe them, the following was observed to have happened. By the fall of 1958, many of monkeys on Koshima had already adopted the new washing behavior. An exact number is not specified so let's take our cue from Watson and set that number at ninety-nine. Ninety-nine monkeys were now washing the sand off food before eating it. Then one more monkey began to do it—the hundredth monkey. And the inexplicable happened—the behavior jumped. Suddenly and mysteriously, macaque monkeys on a nearby island began to wash the sand off food before eating it. The behavior kept jumping. It jumped to the islands surrounding Koshima, and then it jumped to mainland Japan, hundreds of miles away. The macaque monkeys there began to do the same thing—to wash the sand off food before eating it.

Remember, we are talking monkeys here. It is not as if Imo picked up the phone and called her relatives and other members of her species to share the news. The thought form called "washing the sand off food before eating it" jumped from one physically removed group to another. A critical mass was reached, says Watson, and when the hundredth monkey learned the behavior, the understanding jumped *on its own*. It transferred. It went into the knowledge grid of the species. That meant any member of that species could access the new behavior because that behavior was now part of the realized body of understandings they shared, part of macaque consciousness.

More than forty years have passed since that event was recorded in the area on and surrounding Koshima. A great deal of research has been done on the how and the why of this type of transfer, a jump in consciousness. The phenomenon, which is now actually called the Hundredth Monkey Principle, provides an explanation of how discoveries of all kinds seem to happen nearly simultaneously in distant and unconnected parts of the world. Ask Nobel Prize winners and their also-rans. Scientists and inventors are often accused of stealing the ideas of others. But that is rarely the case. It is instead the grid of thought that connects them and us intimately with each other—all the time, anytime. Critical mass was reached and the new knowledge became part of the collective.

If we accept the possibility of Watson's explanation (and there is much in the new physics and modern science to suggest it is valid), then the Hundredth Monkey phenomenon can tell us a great deal.

For one, it tells us that change is inevitable. It tells us that it is the nature of improvement to jump. It cannot be stopped because it is its nature to spread. For another, it

---

1. Lyall Watson, *Lifetide: The Biology of the Unconscious* (New York: Simon and Schuster, 1979). For additional discussions of consciousness grids, read Rupert Sheldrake.

recasts the whole notion of competition. Competitiveness becomes a time-bound event and not dependent on a superior set of skills or secret or proprietary information. In a world of knowledge grids, nothing is proprietary for very long.

Said another way, new ideas stay new only briefly. They have a short shelf life. What is innovative today can quickly become commonplace and routine tomorrow. This is as true in the realm of human behavior as it is in technology. How many people can you recollect having seen run up and down the streets twenty years ago—summer and winter? How many months—or even weeks—after you bought that new computer did you realize it was about to become obsolete? The edges of all the envelopes just keep getting pushed farther and farther out.

Superior performance no longer depends solely on who gets there first. It depends on our ability to hold steady to a state of learning, which in its turn depends on our valuing freedom. And that all ties up to life itself.

Visual order is a best practice of lean production. It is in the knowledge grid now, ready and available to be harnessed. It can be accessed today in a much more powerful form than the words of this book might imply because it is already powered by all the thought forms that preceded this manuscript. The pool of understanding is widening even as you read these words. You are adding to the knowledge net of visual order at this very moment simply by considering the approach.

In the world of manufacturing improvement, the breakthrough methodology you and your company adopted to win the race yesterday barely qualifies you to be on the playing field tomorrow.

Visual order is a crucial component of JIT and lean manufacturing and perhaps even more so for traditional manufacturing. I know you realize that. Yet at the writing of this book, few companies have implemented visual order, let alone a visual workplace. In five years, all that will have changed. In ten years, people will chuckle at the backwardness of these times. The behavior we call *visual order* is a powerful thought form that is gaining in use. In ten years, that behavior will have jumped—and the visual workplace will not give a competitive edge to any company. Instead, it will be considered fundamental and required, just as waste reduction and flow manufacturing are today. Visual order is not the wave of the future. It is the wave of the now.

There is another lesson to be learned from Imo and her species. Imo demonstrated to us the power of directing our attention, the power of thought to shape, move, and transform. She figured something out. She made a connection. Her own consciousness reached for a new solution. I see this happen over and over again in organizations. Please don't let the monkey connection offend you. That is not what I intend. Just look for parallels. An engineer is tired of hearing complaints that her designs are not manufacturable and decides to find new ways to structure the product architecture—and succeeds beyond anyone's wildest dreams. A shopfloor associate is tired of the bother of searching and waiting and decides to invent a visual solution to those senseless activities. He cracks the code, develops a visual minisystem, and the idea spreads.

This is precisely what we saw happen with Bill Antunes and John Pacheco. They cracked the code for their organization, and the level of 5S + 1 awareness throughout the enterprise jumped. It jumped, and those who next got on board began their work on a higher level than the one on which Bill and John began. Those who came later stood on the shoulders of these two energetic and resourceful men.

One of the main points about the methodology in this book is that it gives you a framework of values, ideas, and behaviors that has already been developed, proofed, and established. Use that as your own jumping-off place and find a new way of working, thinking, *and* being. Let that get structured into the consciousness of your company.

Changing the consciousness of your company can never happen through sheer dint of efforts—as legions of exhausted and disappointed change agents can attest. It happens when we tie into the deep force within us that is the source of all positive change. In combination with us, this force works to inspire, transfer, and translate the new thought. The kind of changes that take place as you implement the principles of visual order through 5S + 1 change the way that work gets done in your company—and change you in the process. This is what you want to happen. This is what is meant to happen.

When you do your own work with full spirit, you layer new thought forms into the knowledge grid that surrounds you and your company. You hook up to new dimensions of change that can ease you and your company through the challenging times ahead. You hook into a new notion of flow, precision, and spirit. Do these translate into significant measurable benefits? You bet your bottom line they do: reduced lead times, higher quality levels, increased employee participation and morale, greater service to the community, and greater profitability.

We are all connected. You know that. You have known that for a very long time. Now it is time to harness the power of that knowledge and let its benefits spread. Now it is time to harness the power of the visual workplace. Begin by implementing visual order. Begin simply. Begin with the first of the principles. Clear out the clutter. Then clean up what's left and make it safe. Then put things in order based on the logic of the flow, not the logic of the past. And make sure that flow can find its own way by anchoring the elements of that flow through borders, home addresses, and ID labels.

Support this swift and accelerating flow by strengthening the values that drive it—the code of conduct you learned about way back when. Stabilize and strengthen that flow by having the right supplies on hand (5S corner), through 5S checklists and 5S patrols, by promoting visual minisystems, and by fostering the strengths of the steering team, coordinator, champion, and watch. Watch smart placement take hold and see how work takes on new meaning. Develop a complete approach, a system of everwidening improvement that is sustainable. And let it surprise you.

And watch the consciousness of this change jump. Watch it jump into nearby work areas, jump into nearby companies, jump into the organizations in your supplier chain. And you know what comes next. Watch the same systematic, spirited approach we call 5S + 1 jump into the enterprise of your competitors. It's going to happen anyway.

You can't stop it, anymore than a scientist working on subatomic particle research in Germany can keep new thought forms from jumping into the consciousness of a scientist in New Zealand, another in Zimbabwe, another in Brazil, and another in Dayton, Ohio. Since you can't stop it, why not join it?

Somewhere out there a monkey is washing off a sandy sweet potato, and it is about to change your life.

Appendixes

Appendix A

Improvement Time: Policy and Materials

Improvement Time vs. Production Time: Procedure for Developing This Policy

The following is a step-by-step procedure for developing an improvement time policy.

Step 1. Management States Its Rationale

Top management announces the reason an improvement time policy is needed. Here's an example from XYZ Company:

> The management of XYZ Company has asked you and the rest of the production workforce to participate in a process of continuous systematic improvement called visual order in order to improve the functioning of our production system and reduce lead times. There is reason to believe that our competitors are engaged (or about to engage) in a similar process of continuous improvement.
>
> As things now stand, you and your associates are occupied in running production full-time across three shifts. There appears to be little designated

time for you to get involved in implementing visual order. The company needs an improvement time policy.

Step 2. Management States Its Goal

Top management explains the benefits of such a policy. For example:

Once an improvement time policy is in place, we anticipate that not only will operations improve but we will find more time for production. That is, our capacity will expand. Just as important, everyone at XYZ Company will recognize that improvement is an organizational priority.

Step 3. Management Drafts a Policy

Top managers put a policy in writing (see the following worksheet for help in defining the issues surrounding an improvement time policy).

Step 4. Management Pilots the Policy

Once a policy is drafted, top management pilots or tests it in order to get the bugs out, make adjustments, and make it viable. Invite the input of others with such words as:

While management is responsible for all policy making and policy administration, all associates are welcome to ask questions, raise issues, and/or make suggestions.

Step 5. Management Finalizes and Monitors the Policy

Once the policy has been tested, management makes any final changes and then announces the new policy. Managers also identify ways to monitor adherence to the new policy. Exhibit A-1 (at the end of this appendix) shows you one such tracking mechanism.

Improvement Time Policy: A Worksheet for Managers and Associates

Consider the following questions and choices when developing an improvement time policy. Go through them and check off what makes sense to you and your team—or come up with ideas of your own.

1. Employees need time to develop or implement their improvement ideas. How often should this take place?

   a. _____ Daily

   b. _____ Weekly

   c. _____ Other (specify)

---

2. How much time should be set aside for this?

   a. _____ 0.5 hour daily

   b. _____ 0.25 hour daily

   c. _____ Other (specify)

---

3. When should that period of time take place?

   a. _____ After hours/daily

   b. _____ Before hours/daily

   c. _____ Half at the start and half at the end of each shift

   d. _____ One specific day a week

   e. _____ Other (specify)

---

4. How should that time be clocked or treated?

   a. _____ As paid overtime

   b. _____ As voluntary overtime

   c. _____ As a 50/50 split between company and associate

   d. _____ Other (specify)

---

5. How long should the draft policy get piloted to give it a fair test?

   a. _____ One month

   b. _____ One week

   c. _____ Three months

   d. _____ Other (specify)

6. Which groups of associates should participate in the pilot process?

   a. _____ Only areas to which a steering team member is assigned

   b. _____ Only the following selected areas:

   _____

   _____

   c. _____ Production areas only

   d. _____ The entire plant—production and nonproduction areas

   e. _____ Other (specify)

7. How should associates be informed about this effort in order to gain their full cooperation and support—even when they are not participating in the pilot?

   a. _____ The plant manager announces it at a special meeting for the entire workforce.

   b. _____ Management advises supervisors who then make an announcement to work groups.

   c. _____ Other (specify)

8. Other questions that need to be answered:

   a. _____

   b. _____

   c. _____

   d. _____

Exhibit A-1. Improvement Time-Tracking Chart.

Use this page to keep track of the hours spent on improvement activity.

- **Time is tracked by the hour, in 15-minute increments (see cells below).**
- **Write in the names of each participating person (including managers).**
- **Use the boxes to darken in the exact time each person contributes by quarters.**
- **The space on the bottom is for your daily comments.**

Name		M	T	W	Th	F	S	S	Total
	1								
	2								
	3								
	4								
	5								
	6								
	7								
	8								
	9								
Daily Hour Totals									

Comments 1

Comments 2

Comments 3

Appendix B

Consensus and Team Decision Making

1. Most decisions that a team needs to make can be made simply and smoothly because the needs of the project are easy to spot: It is clear what needs to be done. At other times, when matters are more complex, there is often more than one clear action path. In these cases, a fuller understanding of the issues is important, and you and your team can use a **consensus approach** as a tool.

2. The concept of consensus is often misunderstood. Many people think they are applying consensus when they say, "Come on, let's not argue. Let's hurry and agree so that we can get on with our work." Consensus used like this is at best another form of voting—and at worst, coercion. When "voting" occurs, people feel pressured to conform with the "greater good." As a result, they may cave in and go along with the group, and keep their true feelings and opinions to themselves.

3. While voting has its place, it is often overused—or used too early in the life of the group. Voting tends to polarize a group, forcing members to take sides on an issue. In many cases, it is used in place of exploration, discussion, and discovery. Sad to say, some people will call for a vote because they believe the vote will go in their favor.

4. The correct definition of *consensus* is as follows:

    > **Consensus** is the active search for disagreement—until enough agreement is reached for the group to move forward together.

5. Consensus requires a willingness on the part of people to share their true opinions and feelings and to listen to and consider those of others. Building a consensus within a team can seem like a slow process. And it certainly takes more time than voting. But done too early or too often, voting can actually slow the group down in the long run because it emphasizes action over people, and task over process. In fact, both action and people are important. The challenge is to balance the two.

6. Consensus building is especially important for a group that is just getting started. The consensus process can build the relationship between team members by increasing listening skills, establishing respect, and developing trust. Once these become a normal part of the group's approach, the need for consensus decreases. The work of the team moves forward more smoothly because the groundwork is in place.

7. If the discussion really heats up, borrow a tool used by Native Americans: the talking stick. Simply bring a small tree branch into the meeting and put it in the center of the meeting table, within reach of everyone. The one simple rule is: Whoever holds the stick gets to talk—and keep on talking until done. The talking stick is a great way to help people speak *and* listen. Sometimes a person will pick up the stick and hold it in complete silence—just to calm the room, or themselves, down. If you have ever had this experience, you know that it is like letting the silence speak.

8. From time to time, team members may decide to vote as a way to settle a matter. There is no problem in that as long as everyone realizes that voting can bring discussion to an end.

9. When and if the team gets stalled and *cannot* make up its mind, the team leader can elect to decide the matter on his or her own so that the process can move forward. This is the right thing to do when the matter is simple and straightforward, but when the discussion is heating up, a team leader would be wise to move the group to greater clarity through a consensus approach.

Appendix C

Team-Meeting Norms

About Team Meeting Norms

The term *norm* is short for "normative behavior" and refers to how a team has decided to go about the purpose for which it was formed. Norms spell out what team members expect of each other. Once established, norms represent the team's code of conduct. Research has shown that without norms in place, a team can stall before ever getting started.

Your team's first order of business is to set its meeting norms. And this packet is designed to help you. Three kinds of meeting norms are covered in this packet: logistic norms, task norms, and process norms.

1. *Logistic norms.* These norms deal with the where, when, how many, and how long side of team meetings.
2. *Task norms.* These norms deal with the way the team will divvy up and accomplish its duties or tasks during and between meetings; they encompass team roles and team tools. Task norms deal with the action or content side of team sessions.
3. *Process norms.* These norms address how team members agree to treat each other during and between meetings, how discussions will be conducted and decisions

made, and how the business of the team will get done; process norms deal with the people or values side of team sessions.

Procedure for Setting Norms

This packet contains twenty-four items designed to guide you and your team through the norm-setting process. Most items are in the form of a question, followed by several preset answers from which you may choose. One or a combination of these may suit you perfectly. If not, develop a choice of your own (see "other" below). The asterisk (*) indicates the choice or choices that are often selected by teams in other companies.

Ideally, each team member gets this packet of materials a few days before the first team meeting. In that way, everyone has time to review the document in advance and sort through his or her own preferences. Coming to a common or joint agreement on these norms becomes the first order of business at the team's first meeting.

Keep a sense of urgency about this process—and expect it to take from one to three sessions to complete. By the time your norms are set, you and your associates will have a much clearer sense of each other and how to proceed with the business of steering an effective implementation of a visual workplace in your company.

Logistics Norms

1. *Meeting frequency.* How often will we meet?

   _____ a. Twice a week
   _____ b. Once a week*
   _____ c. Twice a month
   _____ d. _____

2. *Meeting length.* How long will we meet?

   _____ a. 15 to 30 minutes
   _____ b. 30 to 45 minutes
   _____ c. 45 to 60 minutes*
   _____ d. 60 to 90 minutes
   _____ e. _____

3. *Meeting time.* Exactly what time will we meet?

   _____ a. Lunch hour (specify time _____)
   _____ b. 30 minutes before lunch + lunch (specify time _____)
   _____ c. Lunch + 30 minutes after lunch (specify time _____)
   _____ d. First thing in the morning (specify time _____)
   _____ e. _____

4. *Meeting day.* On what regular day of the week will we meet?

     _____   a. Monday
     _____   b. Tuesday*
     _____   c. Wednesday*
     _____   d. Thursday*
     _____   e. Friday

5. *Location of meeting.* Where will we meet?

This should be a place that is quiet, well ventilated, and allows for open (confidential) discussion. A space that is centrally located is preferred. Write down your options here. Then choose one and one backup.

a. _____
b. _____
c. _____
d. _____

6. *Majority.* Exactly what does the term *majority* mean for us?

Based on the number of your total group (excluding management representative), give the exact number of people that represents the majority on your team: _____

7. *Timeliness.* When will our meetings start?

     _____   a. Begin the meeting exactly on time.
     _____   b. Wait until everyone arrives.
     _____   c. Wait until three people arrive or seven minutes have passed since the time the meeting should have begun—whichever comes first.*
     _____   d. Wait until half the team arrives (specify the exact number _____).
     _____   e. Wait until a majority is present (specify the exact number _____).
     _____   f. Other _____

Task Norms: Roles

8. *Leadership roles.* What leadership roles are essential to running an effective meeting?

     _____   a. The *leader* will be responsible for organizing and facilitating sessions.*
     _____   b. The *leader* will be responsible for moving the group forward and making controversial decisions when the group is stuck or polarized.*
     _____   c. The *timer* will be responsible for keeping agenda items on time and on track.*
     _____   d. The *recorder* will be responsible for making note of what occurs in sessions: decisions and action items.*

_____ e. The *gatekeeper* will be responsible for making sure that everyone has the chance to contribute his or her ideas.*

_____ f. Other _____

9. *Type of gatekeeping.* Exactly how will we ensure that all members get a chance to contribute on agenda items? How will the gate of our discussion be opened or shut?

_____ a. The *leader* will be responsible for gatekeeping our sessions.

_____ b. A *gatekeeper* will serve in this role.*

_____ c. No separate gatekeeper is needed. We will gate-keep for each other.

_____ d. Other _____

10. *Timeliness.* How do we keep our session on track and keep to our timeline?

_____ a. A *timer* will keep the meeting on track.*

_____ b. The team will acquire a *countdown timer* to help it stay on track.*

_____ c. The *leader* will be responsible for keeping it timely and on track.

_____ d. *No separate timer* is needed. We will keep time for each other.

_____ e. Other _____

11. *Team role rotation*

_____ a. Roles will be rotated across all team members in alphabetical order by first or last name.*

_____ b. Roles will be rotated across all team members on a volunteer basis.

_____ c. Roles will be rotated on a monthly basis.

_____ d. The role of leader will be rotated every three months.*

_____ e. The role of leader will be rotated every six months.

_____ f. Other _____

12. *Participation:* What is our expectation about how often team members must show up for team meetings? And what shall we do if a member does not (or is not able) to meet this expectation?

_____ a. We expect each team member to attend each team session.*

_____ b. If a team member misses two sessions in a row (except for the reason of illness), he or she will be asked to leave the team.

_____ c. If a team member misses two sessions in a row for any reason, he or she will be asked to leave the team.

_____ d. If a team member misses two sessions during a three-month period, he or she will be asked to leave the team.*

_____ e. If a team member misses four sessions during a three-month period, he or she will be asked to leave the team.

_____ f. Other _____

13. *Leaving the team/expanding the team:* What is our procedure for members leaving or being added to the team?

       _____ a. A member who wants to leave the team must give a two-meeting notice (that is, notify the team two meetings before leaving).*

       _____ b. A member who wants to leave the team will first find a willing associate from his area to take his place on the team.*

       _____ c. A member leaving the team will spend at least thirty minutes briefing her replacement on how the team works.*

       _____ d. A member leaving the team will accompany his/her replacement to his first team session and debrief with him/her for at least thirty minutes after the session.*

       _____ e. Other _____

14. *Outside participants:* How do we feel about nonteam members sitting in on team sessions?

       _____ a. Anyone who wants to can attend any of our sessions without notifying us first; they can just walk in.

       _____ b. Anyone who wants to can attend any of our sessions as long as he or she notifies us at least twenty-four hours in advance.

       _____ c. We will set aside an empty chair in our meeting room for outside participation, and we will actively solicit a new associate each week to attend the session so that everyone gets a chance to experience what goes on in our meetings.*

       _____ d. We will put up a sheet so people can sign up for the empty chair in advance.*

       _____ e. We will welcome nonteam members to observe our sessions except when the team needs its own process time to sort out differences within the team itself.*

       _____ f. Nonteam members are invited as observers; we welcome their opinions, but they will not have decision-making privileges.*

       _____ g. Other _____

Task Norms: Task Tools

15. *Meeting agenda:* What tool will we use to make sure we know what tasks need our attention?

       _____ a. We will use the Meeting Worksheet provided in the Visual Systems Participant Workbook (Appendix D).

       _____ b. We will use a form already in use in our company. Please specify: _____.

       _____ c. We will not use any form because we will all be able to remember, without using a form, what we said and what we need to do.

       _____ d. Other _____.

16. *Agendas:* How will our meeting agendas get prepared?

       _____ a. The leader and recorder will finalize the agenda and distribute it to all members in advance of each meeting.* (If you choose this, define "in advance''; does it mean twenty-four hours in advance?* two days in advance? anytime on the day before the session? Put your answer here: _____.)

_____ b. The leader and recorder will prepare the agenda together and present it at the beginning of each meeting.*

_____ c. A core agenda for the next session will be prepared by team members at the end of each session.*

_____ d. Additional agenda items may be submitted to the leader at the start of each meeting and get addressed if time permits.*

_____ e. Other _____.

17. *Tasks/action items:* How will we know what tasks or action items need to be done for the next meeting and who will do them?

_____ a. As the need for action items surface, volunteers will take responsibility.*

_____ b. The leader will assign action items in the absence of volunteers.*

_____ c. At the end of each meeting, the leader will summarize action items and remind members of their tasks.*

_____ d. Other _____.

18. *Statement of purpose.* Will we develop a statement that puts into the written word why this team was formed, what we are trying to accomplish, how we will conduct ourselves, and how the work of this team will help the organization meet its business and people goals?

_____ a. Yes, we need a written statement of purpose.*

_____ b. No, we do not need a written statement of purpose; we know what we are about without having to put it into writing, and we do not need to worry about what other people think about our efforts.

_____ c. Other _____

Process Norms: Discussion

19. *Discussions:* How will we approach discussions during our meetings?

_____ a. Only one person may speak at a time, with no interruptions or side conversations.*

_____ b. A member may interrupt the speaker to ask a clarifying question.*

_____ c. A member must be recognized by the team leader before speaking (raised hand).

_____ d. Members may enter discussion freely—being careful to give any speaker a chance to complete his/her thought.*

_____ e. Other _____.

Process Norms: Decision Making

20. *Decisions:* How will we make decisions?

    _____ a. We will make decisions by consensus *only*. (*Consensus means the active search for disagreement until enough agreement is achieved to move forward.*)
    _____ b. We will decide by majority voting *only*.
    _____ c. Some decisions will be consensual, others by voting; we will decide on a case-by-case basis.*
    _____ d. The leader makes all decisions.
    _____ e. Other _____.

21. *Decision-making percentage:* What percentage of members must be in attendance in order for a decision to be passed.

    _____ a. All team members must be in attendance.
    _____ b. A majority of the team must be present. (Define *majority* here _____).*
    _____ c. At least half of the members must be present.
    _____ d. Other _____.

22. *Changing decisions:* How will decisions that were made be changed?

    _____ a. We will never change a decision that has already been passed.
    _____ b. The leader will have the only authority to make these changes.
    _____ c. The team will vote on such changes; majority rules.
    _____ d. If a team member thinks that an agreed-upon decision needs to be changed, it will get submitted as a regular agenda item and not changed until it is discussed and resolved by the team. Change-by-consensus will be practiced as much as possible.*
    _____ e. Other _____.

23. *Affirming direction:* How often will we review all our norms for relevance?

    _____ a. We will review our norms every month and adjust as needed.
    _____ b. We will review our norms every three months and adjust as needed.*
    _____ c. We will review our norms every six months and adjust as needed.
    _____ d. We will not review our norms; they are perfect now.
    _____ e. Other _____.

24. *Confidentiality:* To what extent will each one of us commit to confidentiality on and about the information and feelings shared and discussed during our sessions *and on and about how* these are shared and discussed with others?

    _____ a. Each one of us agrees to strict confidentiality so that we can feel comfortable about freely sharing personal feelings and sensitive information. That

Appendix C

means we agree not to share personal feelings and sensitive information except if we specifically decide to do so.*

_____ b. Each one of us agrees that confidentiality shall be according to each person's sense of discretion and personal judgment.

_____ c. We do not need a norm on confidentiality. Each one of us agrees that none of us is obliged to keep anything confidential. Team members may share freely.

_____ d. Our agreement on the matter of confidentiality (whatever it turns out to be) will apply to us alone.

_____ e. Our agreement on the matter of confidentiality (whatever it turns out to be) will apply to us, the visual systems coordinator, other implementation facilitators, and the management champion.

_____ f. If our agreement on confidentiality is breached (whatever that breach turns out to be), we will post it as an agenda item and discuss it openly within a regular session as soon as possible in an effort to resolve the breach.

_____ g. Other _____.

_____ e. Other _____.

25. *Other:* What other norms do we need to adopt to ensure the success of our efforts?

a. _____.

b. _____.

c. _____.

d. _____.

Appendix D

Meeting Worksheet

The following Meeting Worksheet is a single sheet of paper designed to hold the information needed and generated at a team meeting.

Face. On the face is all the attendance information you need to keep track of who did and did not participate, plus the day's objectives and agenda. There is also a space for "Catch-Ups," the people who will brief those who cannot attend and late comers. A space for the next meeting's agenda is also provided.

Reverse. On the reverse of the worksheet are spaces to clearly indicate the decisions that came out of the day's session and spaces for questions that need answers. Most of the space on this side of the Meeting Sheet is reserved for the all-important action items, complete with who will take responsibility for seeing that a given item is completed ("By Whom?") and when it will be completed ("Due-By?). Both sides of this meeting sheet are completed *during* the meeting itself. That means it can then be photocopied at the end of the session and everyone can walk away with completed minutes, their respective action items, and a tentative agenda for the next session.

Visual Workplace Steering Team ~ Meeting Work Sheet

Day of Week:_____ ◻ **Time:**_____ ◻ **Place:**_____

Team Leader _____   **Today's Date** _____

Recorder _____

Gatekeeper _____   **Timer** _____

Area Representatives _____ Mgmt Rep _____
(circle those **not** attending)

Visitors _____   **Catch-Ups** _____

Goal	*Focus, strengthen, and sustain visual workplace activity, starting with 5S+1.*
Objectives	*1. Keep implementation focused and on track*
	2. Coordinate and facilitate improvement activity, especially minisystems
	3. Make recommendations for upgrading and improving the approach and results
	4. Stay available and open to the input and feedback of others
	5. Report needs and concerns to visual workplace coordinator and/or management champion
	6. Model the values and behaviors of the visual workplace code of conduct

Objectives for Today's Meeting (try to limit these to two objectives please)

1. _____

2 _____

	Agenda Items for This Meeting*	Time Allocated (mins)	Who Leads Item?
	1.		
	2.		
	3.		
	4.		
	5.		
	6.		
	7.		
	8.		
	9.		

New Items for our Next Meeting Agenda	Time Allocated (mins)	Who Leads Item?
1.		
2.		
3.		
4.		
5.		
6.		

* If an agenda item needs to be *tabled,* mark a *T* beside it (left-hand margin) and the date of its next agenda -- for example, *T-9/15*.

Decisions We Made During Today's Meeting	Today's Date

1. Today we decided that _____

_____

2. Today we decided that _____

_____

3. Today we decided that _____

_____

4. Today we decided that _____

_____

Questions That Need Answers

1. _____ ?

2. _____ ?

3. _____ ?

Action Items* (print small)	Due-By?	By Whom?	Completed?
1.			
2.			
3.			
4.			
5.			
6.			
7.			
8.			
9.			
10.			

* Action Items are small, well-defined tasks which, taken in their sum, keep the team moving forward. The success of your team is most closely linked to using Action Items effectively. They are the way the team gets things done. When group discussion gets bogged down, over-heated or confused, clarify the discussion into one or more action items and move on.

Appendix E

The Seven Deadly Wastes

The short definition of the term *waste* is, "anything for which the customer is not willing to pay." The longer definition is, "any activity that adds cost and not value to the products and services that the company offers to its customers."

Waste in the workplace comes in seven broad varieties, collectively known as The Seven Deadly Wastes. They are defined as follows:

1. Motion. Moving without working; walking between machines; searching for tools, people, parts, etc.; reaching, bending, sidestepping, asking, storing, retrieving, putting down/picking up, counting.

2. Delays. Waiting for work, information, and/or approvals; waiting for parts, materials, tools, equipment availability, etc.

3. Transporting/Material Handling. Moving work over short and long distances.

4. Making Defects. Not doing it right the first time; causing rework or scrap.

5. Overprocessing. Drilling a hole where no hole is needed; inspecting—checking your own work or that of another; handling parts, products, tools, and/or paperwork more than once.

6. Overproducing. Producing more units than ordered—just in case; creating inventory.

7. Storing Inventory. Storing units, however briefly, that are not yet ordered or cannot yet be delivered.

To these the wastes, add the waste of lost opportunities: the loss of resources that could have been used for growth and expansion but are tied up in non-value-adding activity instead. This is the loss of the time and money the company spends on re-work, scrap, material handling, and making and storing inventory that might otherwise be used to invest in new markets, designing new products, providing more and better training for the workforce, and so on and so forth.

Exhibit E-1 shows you the relationship between these Wastes and the 95:5 ratio on the outer edge of the wheel.

Exhibit E-1.

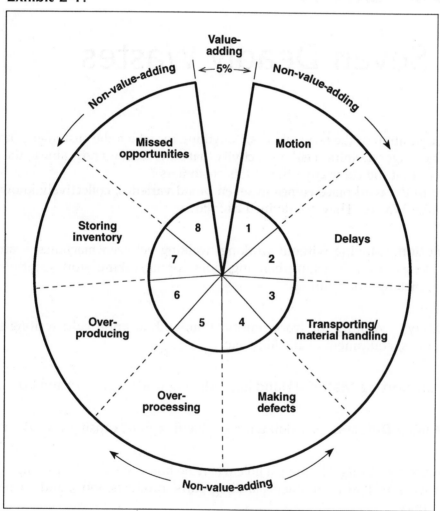

Glossary

abnormality Any gap between what is *supposed* to happen and what *does* happen—that is, between standard performance and actual performance.

associate A term of respect used in many companies (and in this book) to refer to those people who do the value-adding work of the enterprise, the employees who work directly on the line or shop floor (formerly known as workers, hourly employees, line employees, and operators).

baseline metrics (5S + 1) A set of measures tracked before the start of a 5S + 1 implementation as a yardstick against which to measure your 5S + 1 improvement. Sturdy 5S + 1 metrics include: (1) manufacturing lead time, (2) lead time vs. conversion time (NVA versus VA), (3) flow/travel distance, (4) floor space utilization, (5) number of forklifts, tow motors, and material handlers, and (6) equipment changeover times.

Blueprint for a Visual Workplace The eight-level framework that shows teams where to begin their journey to a visual workplace—5S + 1—and each subsequent step. The Blueprint is the road map for building adherence to standards in the workplace so that what is *supposed* to happen *does* happen. (*See* visual workplace.)

cell design A system of shopfloor layout that groups different machines that perform different functions in the same location or cell. This makes it possible to complete many operations with minimum movement of materials, people, and tooling. Cell design links machines and value-adding operations in a single production sequence so that the end of the sequence is as easy to access as the start. The goal is one-piece flow. (*See* cycle time; standard work; *takt* time.)

clipboard checklist A self-report and self-diagnosis checklist used to drive higher and higher levels of visual order. Conducted by the 5S patrol, the clipboard checklist is a sheet of paper with ten to twelve specific items that change frequently. This checklist also includes some type of scoring scale and enough space for written comments and feedback.

consensus (true) The active search for disagreement until enough agreement is reached to enable people to move forward together.

cycle time The total time required for a sequence of operations to complete in the process of working on a part, product, or service. Includes the time required for walking, loading/unloading, inspection, etc. (*See* cell design; standard work, *takt* time.)

delays The need to wait for work, information, approvals, parts, material, tools, equipment availability, etc. Delays is one of the seven classic wastes or non-value-adding activities.

economic order quantity (EOQ) Fixing the run or lot size based on the least amount of items that need to be produced (and then sold) in order to justify or absorb acquisition and carrying costs. (*See* quick changeover.)

5S checklist A list of specific tasks that area associates have agreed need to be done on a regular basis so that visual order in the area is maintained and improved. The 5S checklist is the fifth of the nine +1 tools. 5S checklists come in two varieties: wall chart checklist and clipboard checklist. (*See* clipboard checklist; wall chart checklist.)

5S corner The supplies that individuals and teams need to have handy in order to rapidly create and implement their own visual solutions. The 5S corner is one of the nine +1 tools.

5S patrol A small, rotating team of area associates charged with applying 5S checklists in their area and sharing the results. The 5S patrol is one of the nine +1 tools.

5-whys   A simple, powerful improvement tool used by teams or individuals to help them discover the real or root cause of a problem. When a problem occurs (defect, unscheduled downtime, accident, late delivery), ask *why* five times for each reason you come up with as a cause. Keep going until you have dug five levels deep into the causal chain.

Grumblers   Those people who usually broadcast that they have no interest in ever getting involved in any improvement process. Grumblers can be vocal, even dramatic, in their lack of support. They are at the opposite end of the spectrum from Rowers. Sometimes, but not often, Grumblers will have a miniconversion experience (see the light) and begin to row—but they do so only when and if they choose to. (*See* inertia; resistance; Rowers; Watchers.)

inertia   In physics, the tendency of matter to remain at rest, if at rest—and, if moving, to keep moving in the same direction unless affected by some outside force. In people terms, inertia applies to the tendency of people to not feel motivated to join in or participate. Usually, these folks just don't want to be bothered, not right now, anyway. They are busy maintaining their current state, continuing to move in the direction in which they have been moving—or staying at rest. (*See* resistance.)

information deficits   Work slowing down or stopping because certain key information (location and/or specification information) is missing or not easily available from the workplace—not available at a glance. (*See* location information; specification information.)

information users (users)   Person(s) to whom a visual device is directed. Users can choose (or not choose) to respond to the information a visual device shares.

item recoil   The capacity of an item to find its way back to its designated location (home address) based solely on the location information of the item's border, home address, and ID tag.

just-in-time (JIT)   A production approach where downstream operations pull required parts from upstream operations in the exact quantity downstream needs to meet an actual customer demand. At its ultimate, the production floor runs lean, no extras, no buffer stock, no just-in-case. The opposite of traditional manufacturing that builds inventory and satisfies the demands of the customer by selling them units from a finished goods warehouse. (*See* lean production.)

kanban   A visual pull system for parts usage, used to create and ensure minimum levels of WIP and inventory. It is a methodology that supports or enables JIT, cells, lean production, or any type of pull system. A kanban means a card or container that signals what product needs to be made and in what quantity. Downstream processes produce only in response to a kanban signal from upstream. Without a kanban, no work can be done.

lean production   A production approach whereby downstream operations pull required parts from upstream operations in the exact quantity downstream needs to meet an actual customer demand. At its ultimate, the production floor runs lean, no extras, no buffer stock, no just-in-case. It is the opposite of traditional manufacturing that builds inventory and satisfies customers demands by selling them units from a finished goods warehouse. (*See* just-in-time.)

location information   The most basic form of workplace information, the kind that tells where things are. When it is absent, people spend a lot of time in motion—searching, waiting, wondering, asking, and interrupting. Location information answers the *where* question.

making defects   The result of not doing it right the first time, a major cause of rework and scrap. Making defects is one of the seven classic wastes or non-value-adding activities.

Malcolm Baldrige National Quality Award   Named after the late Senator Malcolm Baldrige, a national award that recognizes companies with an overall and well-integrated approach to business excellence. The Baldrige Award is awarded by the U.S. government. For an application and the guidelines, phone 800-248-1946, or fax 414-272-1734.

management watch   The regularly scheduled time slot when the management champion tours the work areas under 5S+1 improvement in order to visibly and concretely recognize and influence the effort through the use of watch cards. The watch is one of the nine +1 tools. Has been termed the *leadership watch* when the union was involved as a partner.

management champion   The manager/executive with high credibility, responsible for visibly supporting the 5S + 1 process, providing it with regular top-management feedback, and going to bat for it if needed. Conducts the management watch. The management champion is one of the nine + 1 tools.

missed opportunities   (1) The loss of opportunities to grow and expand because company resources are tied up in non-value-adding activity; (2) the failure to solicit and invest in employees' ideas or involve employees in waste-reduction activity. We add missed opportunities to the seven classic wastes or non-value-adding activities because it is so closely tied to them.

motion   The need to move but without doing work—that is, without adding value. Common examples include walking between machines; searching for tools, people, and parts; reaching, bending, sidestepping, asking, storing, retrieving, putting down/picking up, and counting. Motion is one of the seven classic wastes or non-value-adding activities. In this book, motion is the umbrella under which all other wastes are grouped.

non-value-adding activity (NVA)   An activity that adds cost but no value. Also known as waste. NVA is usually divided into seven categories (seven deadly wastes): (1) motion, (2) delays, (3) transporting/material handling, (4) making defects, (5) overprocessing, (6) overproducing, and (7) storing inventory. It can include opportunity loss. (*See* missed opportunities.)

normal   A predictable outcome resulting from the performance of a specific standardized procedure. Normal is "what is supposed to happen."

overprocessing   Unneeded activity. It includes such activities as drilling a hole where no hole is needed; inspecting or checking your own work or that of another; and the handling and multiple handling of parts, products, tools, and/or paperwork. Overprocessing is one of the seven classic wastes or non-value-adding activities.

overproducing   Producing more units than are ordered, just in case; creating inventory. Overproducing is one of the seven classic wastes or non-value-adding activities.

paper doll layout   A technique used in designing the layout of a cell before anything is actually moved. It is used to identify and reduce motion and to correct conceptual errors prior to the actual change.

***poka-yoke* device**   A visual guarantee—a device that tells us when a defect has just happened or is about to happen. At its ultimate, the device can prevent the error that leads to the defect. It is also known as error proofing, failsafe systems, and mistake proofing. (*See* visual guarantee; zero quality control.)

process   A sequence of tasks, steps, or operations that are performed in order to produce a specific production or nonproduction outcome.

product   A group of elements or parts that, when fabricated or assembled, becomes a unit of function that fulfills preplanned customer requirements.

pull system   The production of items only when there is an actual demand for them from a customer. The demand of that customer pulls them into the production process. The visual workplace is based on the pull system principle because the demand of the customer for information causes that information to be put into the physical workplace. Then it is there at point of use, exactly when the customer needs it. That customer is *you*. A pull system is the opposite of a push system (see below). (*See* just-in-time; kanban; lean production.)

push system   The production of items based on a predetermined schedule or forecast. The result is inventory—manufactured items for which there is not yet a customer. A push system is the exact opposite of a pull system. When information is shared based on the push system principle, it is often the wrong information and/or in a form that few find useful. This is information that has no authentic customer. (Also known as traditional or large-lot/high-volume production). (*See* just-in-time; kanban; lean production.)

quick changeover (QCO)   The process by which machine dies and tooling for making one product are removed at the end of a production run and replaced with the dies and tooling for a new product. Changing over a machine as quickly as possible allows companies to produce in smaller batches than required by an EOQ approach (*see* economic order quantity). The goal is nine minutes or less. This process is also known as single-minute exchange of dies (SMED).

reliable method   A procedure that is made up of only those elements that, when not followed, result in a predictable defect or waste (by permission of Dr. R. Fukuda). (*See* standards.)

resistance   In medicine, the ability of an organism to ward off disease. In people terms, resistance is the decision to actively oppose or hinder something. (*See* Grumblers; inertia; Rowers; Watchers.)

Rowers   Those people involved in improvement activity who, from the outset of the process, display a high level of enthusiasm, excitement, and willingness to do. Rowers make "it" happen. (*See* Grumblers; inertia; resistance; Watchers.)

S1/Sort Through and Sort Out   The first step in achieving visual order. It means clear out the clutter, remove all nonrequired items, keep only what's needed, and get rid of the junk.

S2/Scrub the Workplace   The second step of visual order. It means remove grit, grime, and grease from all items; paint as needed; promote dirt prevention; and come to know cleaning as inspection and cleaning as ownership.

S3/Secure Safety   The third step of visual order. It means make all items in the area and the area itself safer through visual order and promote greater safety awareness.

S4/Select Locations   The fourth step of visual order. It means locate each remaining item in a spot that supports an accelerated flow of work and information and get rid of the waste of motion.

S5/Set Locations   The fifth step of visual order. It means designate a fixed location or home for each item in the work area by using a border, home address, and item ID. The goal is item recoil and a place for everything and everything in its place. (*See* item recoil.)

scoreboarding   A comprehensive, team-based, results-oriented method for (1) putting measures in place that drive (not merely monitor) daily improvement, (2) upgrading weak process and technical standards, and (3) stabilizing performance outcomes by strengthening adherence measures. Scoreboarding is an interactive, cross-functional approach that gets people directly involved in finding the facts, identifying true cause, and developing solutions that last. It is part of the second phase found in the *Blueprint for a Visual Workplace.*

Shingo Prize   The Shingo Prize for Excellence in Manufacturing named after Dr. Shigeo Shingo, one of the chief architects of the Toyota Production System. It recognizes companies that have demonstrated outstanding achievements in manufacturing processing, quality enhancement, productivity improvement, and customer satisfaction. For an application and guidelines, contact Utah State University. Phone 801-797-2279, or fax 801-797-3440.

specification information (spec information)   The details that describe products or services and how to make them, such as product requirements that relate to technical standards (tolerances, dimensions) and to procedural standards (operating procedures and methods). Spec information answers the *what, who, when, how,* and *how much/how many* questions related to work. When spec information is missing, employees do not know what is required of them. (*See* information deficits; location information.)

standards   The detailed information required to get the right work done, of the right quality, in the right quantity, by the right person (or machine), at the right time, for the right cost—safely. There are two types of standards: technical and procedural. A *technical* standard relates to tolerances, dimensions, etc.; a *procedural* standard relates to operating procedures and methods (also known as an SOP: standard operating procedure). (*See* reliable method.)

standard work (SW)   A definition for *and* standardization of the interaction between man and machine in producing a unit. It separates what the machine can do from what the person can do. The focus is on improving that process so that as much variability, waste, and chance for error can be eliminated from it. SW takes the motion out of the process.

SW represents the precise motions of an operation, defining cycle time by standardizing literally every second of an operating procedure. SW is indispensable for cellular manufacturing, but it is never written in stone; instead it is constantly being revised to remove more and more waste. (*See* cell design; cycle time; *takt* time.)

statistical process control (SPC)   A method for gauging the likelihood that the output of a process will fall within acceptable limits. Well-known SPC tools include check sheet, cause-and-effect diagram, bar graphs, scatter diagram, and other assorted graphing techniques.

storing inventory   Storing units, however briefly, that are not yet ordered or cannot yet be delivered. Storing inventory is one of the seven classic wastes or non-value-adding activities.

takt **time** (from the German meaning "drumbeat")   The rhythm or pace of production that is set by customer demand and which is the governing beat of cellular production. *Takt* time works hand in hand with standard work to set up a framework that defines cycle time by standardizing literally every second of an operating procedure. (*See* cell design; cycle time; standard work.)

total productive maintenance (TPM)   A set of activities for restoring equipment to its optimal condition and changing the work environment to maintain that condition. TPM succeeds when maintenance personnel, operators, and managers are in day-to-day partnership.

total quality control (TQC)   A quality system that attempts to ensure that no defective products are shipped—or even produced. TQC depends heavily on statistical process control and is therefore a reactive technology. Compare it with zero quality control (ZQC), which eliminates the need for SPC and other quality containment techniques by eliminating the source of errors that lead to defects through *poka-yoke* devices, or visual guarantees. ZQC was developed by Dr. Shigeo Shingo, a major pillar of the Toyota Production System. (*See poka-yoke* device; visual guarantee; zero quality control.)

transporting/material handling   The need to move work over long distances. Transporting/material handling is one of the seven classic wastes or non-value-adding activities.

value-adding activity (VA) (or conversion activity)   Workplace activity that changes or transforms material so that it more closely conforms to customer requirements. It is an activity for which the customer is willing to pay.

visual competence   The ability of an organization or work area to share workplace information, including information that changes rapidly and without warning, quickly, accurately, and completely through visual devices.

visual control   A visual device that shares workplace information but physically regulates or limits our response. It narrows the way we can respond, giving us less of a choice about whether we will respond to or ignore the message (or information) conveyed by the control. Because it impacts us directly, a visual control is considered *aggressive* in its approach to adherence.

visual device   A mechanism, gadget, or apparatus that is intentionally designed to make workplace information vital to the task at hand available at a glance—without speaking a word. Its purpose is to influence, direct, limit, guarantee, or otherwise impact human behavior relative to a specific performance process or outcome.

visual guarantee (or fail-safe solution)   A physical device (mechanical or electronic) used to 100 percent inspect a part or product at, or near, the source of its fabrication and/or assembly in order to minimize the possibility of a defect—or even the error leading to a defect. It ensures a predetermined outcome by narrowing all possible responses to a single correct one. A visual guarantee can solve problems irreversibly and is therefore described as a *proactive adherence approach*. (Also known as error-proofing, mistake-proofing, wise-proofing, fail-safing, or *poka-yoke* systems.) (*See poka-yoke* device; zero quality control.)

visual indicator   A device that shares workplace information by telling, showing, or displaying (indicating) that information. It relies on the written or shown word (or number). Because it tells only, a visual indicator is a passive approach to adherence.

visual minisystems   A cluster of visual devices that work together to promote a single performance outcome and provide individuals with a concrete way to get involved. Minisystems are one of the nine +1 tools.

visual order   Another term for 5S + 1. It is also sometimes referred to as workplace order, workplace organization, and/or industrial housekeeping.

visual signal   A visual device that "changes," sharing workplace information by grabbing our senses (sight/smell/touch/hearing/taste). When the visual signal changes, it catches our attention and then delivers its message. Because a visual signal reaches out to us in this way, we say it is a more active or assertive approach to adherence.

visual system (or visual minisystem)   A group or cluster of visual devices that work together to promote normal outcomes and reduce abnormal ones in support of a single performance outcome. Minisystems provide individuals with a concrete way to get involved in increasing the possibility that what is *supposed* to happen *does* happen.

visual workplace   A work area or an entire company that is self-explaining, self-ordering, self-regulating, and self-improving—where what is *supposed* to happen *does* happen, on time, every time, day or night. (*See Blueprint for a Visual Workplace.*)

visual workplace coordinator   The person responsible for providing administrative and logistical support to the implementation and who coordinates its various activities. This coordinator is one of the nine +1 tools.

visual workplace steering team   A group of area volunteers, charged with coordinating, monitoring, and leading the implementation. This steering team is one of the nine +1 tools.

visual workplace code of conduct   The standards of conduct that spell out the values and behaviors needed, from the outset, to create an environment favorable to achieving a visual workplace. This code of ethics is one of nine +1 tools.

wall chart checklist   A large laminated chart that lists five to ten action items that area associates agree to do on a regular basis. This checklist gets posted prominently in the area. The wall chart checklist is one of the nine +1 tools.

Watchers   Those people who do not get involved in an improvement process at its outset. They wait, watch, and may get involved slowly and gradually or not at all—depending on what the Rowers do. (*See* Grumblers; inertia; resistance; Rowers.)

work-in-process (WIP)   All the materials, parts, and subassemblies on the plant floor that exist between the release of raw material and finished-goods inventory.

zero quality control (ZQC)   A quality system designed to inspect each unit 100 percent at the source and eliminate the possibility of defects at the source by eliminating errors that lead to defects. ZQC eliminates the need for SPC (except in the planning process) and therefore makes TQC obsolete. ZQC was developed by Dr. Shigeo Shingo, a major pillar of the Toyota Production System. (*See poka-yoke* device; total quality control; visual guarantee.)

Suggested Readings

Lean Production Essentials

Brassard, Michael. *The Memory Jogger Plus + : Seven Management and Planning Tools* (Methuen, Mass.: Goal/QPC, 1989).

Coonradt, Charles A., with Lee Nelson. *The Game of Work: How to Enjoy Work as Much as Play* (Salt Lake City, 1985).

Costanza, John R. *Quantum Leap: In Speed to Market* (Denver: JIT Institute of Technology, 1989).

Galsworth, G. D. *Smart Simple Design: Using Variety Effectiveness to Reduce Total Cost and Maximize Customer Selection* (New York: Wiley, 1994).

Goldratt, Eliyahu M., and Jeff Cox. *The Goal: Excellence in Manufacturing* (Croton-on-Hudson, N.Y.: North River Press, 1984).

Hirano, Hiroyuki, ed. *JIT Factory Revolution: A Pictorial Guide to Factory Design of the Future* (Portland Ore.: Productivity Press, 1988).

Japan Management Association Kanban, ed. *Just-in-Time at Toyota: Management Begins at the Workplace* (Portland Ore.: Productivity Press, 1986).

Kobayashi, Iwao. *Twenty Keys to Workplace Improvement* (Portland Ore.: Productivity Press, 1990).

Maskell, Brian H. *Performance Measurement for World Class Manufacturing: A Model for American Companies* (Portland Ore.: Productivity Press, 1991).

Nakajima, Seiichi. *TPM Development Program: Implementing Total Productive Maintenance* (Portland Ore.: Productivity Press, 1989).

____. *TPM: Introduction to Total Productive Maintenance* (Portland Ore.: Productivity Press, 1989).

Nakamura, Shigehiro. *New Standardization: Keystone of Continuous Improvement in Manufacturing* (Portland Ore.: Productivity Press, 1993).

Sekine, Kenichi. *One-Piece Flow: Cell Design for Transforming the Production Process* (Portland Ore.: Productivity Press, 1992).

Shingo, Shigeo. *A Study of the Toyota Production System: From an Industrial Engineering Viewpoint* (Portland Ore.: Productivity Press, 1989).

____. *Poka Yoke: Improving Product Quality by Preventing Defects* (Portland Ore.: Productivity Press, 1988).

____. *Zero Quality Control: Source Inspection and the Poka-Yoke System* (Portland Ore.: Productivity Press, 1986).

____. *Revolution in Manufacturing: The SMED System* (Portland Ore.: Productivity Press, 1985).

Stack, Jack, with Bo Burlingham. *The Great Game of Business: Unlocking the Power and Profitability of Open-Book Management* (New York: Doubleday, 1992).

Wantuck, Kenneth A. *Just-in-Time for America: A Common Sense Production Strategy* (Southfield, Mich.: KWA Media, 1989).

Visual Workplace

Aslett, Don. *Clutter's Last Stand: It's Time to De-Junk Your Life* (Cincinnati: F&W Publications, 1984).

A Disciplined Approach to Continuous Improvement: A Plant Manager's Personal Account of Instituting Japanese Methods in a Mexican Factory of a United States Company (Warren, Ohio: Packard Electric, a division of General Motors, Inc., 1988).

Greif, Michel. *The Visual Factory: Building Participation Through Shared Information* (Portland Ore.: Productivity Press, 1991).

Hirano, Hiroyuki. *The Five Pillars of the Visual Workplace* (Portland Ore.: Productivity Press, 1995).

Norman, Donald. *The Design of Everyday Things* (New York: Doubleday, 1988).

Osada, Takashi. *The 5S's: Five Keys to a Total Quality Environment* (New York: Asian Productivity Organization, 1991).

Rossbach, Sarah. *Feng Shui: The Chinese Art of Placement* (Arcana, 1983).

Shimbun, Nikkan Kogyo, ed. *Visual Control Systems* (Portland Ore.: Productivity Press, 1995).

Young, Pam, and Peggy Jones. *Sidetracked Home Executives: From Pigpen to Paradise* (New York: Warner, 1981).

Resources

About the Author

Gwendolyn D. Galsworth, Ph.D., is founder and president of **Quality Methods International Inc.** (QMI), a consulting, training, and development firm. Founded in the early 1990s, QMI specializes in systematic methods that help companies (1) increase standardization and adherence through 5S + 1, scoreboarding, mistake-proofing, and other visual workplace technologies; (2) reduce parts inventories and decomplicate the organization through smart simple design; and (3) build employee/managerial alignment through strategic policy deployment (*hoshin kanri*).

With nearly two decades in the field of manufacturing, Dr. Galsworth has assisted companies, large and small, in accelerating their rate of improvement and becoming superior competitors. Clients include BHP/Australia, Crompton Greaves/India, Culinar Foods/Canada, Curtis Screw, Fleet Engineers, Gates Rubber, Greene Rubber, General Motors/Canada, Hamilton Standard, ITT/Aerospace, Kaiser Aluminum, Motorola, Marada Industries, Pratt & Whitney, Prince Corporation, Simpson Timber, TVS Sundaram Clayton/India, United Electric Controls Company, and Venmar Ventilation.

Prior to forming QMI, Dr. Galsworth was the head of consulting and training development at Productivity Inc. and principal developer of such core Japanese-based methods as the Visual Factory, 5S, zero defects through *poka-yoke*/failsafe systems, and CEDAC® (cause and effect diagram with addition of cards); she was also instrumental in adapting TPM (Total Productivity Maintenance), SMED (single minute exchange of dies), and TEIAN (Japanese suggestion approach) for Western audiences.

A two-term Baldrige examiner and international speaker on lean production, Dr. Galsworth is author of *Smart Simple Design: Using Variety Effectiveness to Reduce Total Cost and Maximize Customer Selection.* Dr. Galsworth has a Ph.D. in adult education and statistics. She is also a senior fellow at the University of Dayton's Center for Competitive Change.

QMI On-Site Training and Consulting

Dr. Galsworth offers a wide range of consulting, training, and licensing options to support 5S + 1, visual standardization, scoreboarding, error-proofing (*poka-yoke*) systems, and other visual workplace technologies. Learning events include senior management briefings, team implementation training workshops, on-site consulting, and 5S + 1 audits as well as stand-alone video training packages. For more information, contact:

Quality Methods International Inc.

Phone: 617-489-9909
Fax: 617-489-6276
E-mail: QMIQMI@aol.com
Internet: www.visual-workplace.com

Public Seminars

A number of nationally based organizations sponsor QMI public seminars and workshops by Dr. Galsworth. These include:

- The University of Dayton's Center for Competitive Change (937-229-4632)
- Association for Manufacturing Excellence/AME (847-520-3282)
- New England Suppliers Institute/NESI (617-727-8158)
- Delaware Valley Industrial Resource Center/DVIRC (215-464-8550)
- Various chapters of the American Production and Inventory Control Society/APICS, and the American Society of Quality/ASQ

You can check with them for dates or call QMI directly (see above).

The Visual Workplace Clearinghouse Network

Dr. Galsworth at QMI is in the process of creating The Visual Workplace Clearinghouse Network, a database of people and organizations in the process of implementing visual systems. We invite you to join us in this. Let us hear about your successes, challenges, and the specific visual solutions you and your workforce have developed. We are particularly interested in developing a broad-base inventory of case and situational studies and examples from the American experience so that they may be shared with others. Call QMI for more information and to tell us about your needs and preferences.

Team Resources

ID Product Catalogues

Industrial supply catalogues contain lots of good ideas related to 5S + 1 and visual systems. They are free, so get some for yourself and your teams to trigger improvements. One of my favorite suppliers is **Seton Name Plate Company**, which specializes in a range of identification products. For free catalogues, call or fax Seton directly:

Phone: 1-800-243-6624
Fax: 1-800-345-7819

In addition, Seton offers a free service called **Smart Trac** (technical regulatory assistance center) to answer questions on state and federal regulations related to health, safety, and the environment, as well as international and industry-specific standards. It is an excellent resource. For more information:

Phone: 1-800-420-7572

Seton offers its complete catalogue and other services (including Smart Trac) on the Internet:

Internet: http://www.seton.com

ID Labeling Systems

Many companies offer label and sign-making systems that help you produce one simple label or hundreds for your entire plant. They range from rack and pipe markers to equipment and inventory labeling.

For example, the **Labelizer Plus**, an industrial labeling machine made by Brady USA (Singmark Division) offers a wide range of features, including variable size and style of type, underline, vertical print, graphics and symbols, multiple lines of text and bar codes (in outdoor and indoor materials and colors and in one-half- to four-inch widths). For the name of a local dealer, call Brady USA at:

Phone: 1-800-635-7557

The **ProImage PosterPrinter** by Varitronics creates poster- or banner-size output from a hard-copy original or directly from your PC or Mac in minutes. Ideal for directional signs, production information posters and announcements, and training charts. For the name of a local dealer:

Phone: 1-800-637-5461

Brother offers the P-touch Excel 30 Label Maker, a less expensive machine with many fewer features than the Varitronics systems but reliable and serviceable nevertheless. Contact your local Brother dealer for more information:

Film, Photographs, Slides

Seattle Film Works (SFW), a mail-in film processing company in Seattle, Washington, sells some of the best all-purpose film available, especially for factory settings and taking shopfloor shots without a filter (no greenish overcast).

SFW also lets you order slides and photos at the same time from the same film roll.

You can also get your photos on disk. SFW will send you its software, PhotoWorks, with your first order (less than $15 at this printing). That allows you to create a 35mm slide show and a computer slide show from the same roll of film and still have photographs for your 5S + 1 bulletin board. For more information:

Phone: 1-800-445-3348

Index